THE GREENING OF A RED

By the same author

Crisis in Architecture, 1974
Future Landscapes, 1976 (ed.)
National Parks; Conservation or Cosmetics?, 1982 (with A.M.
  MacEwen)
*Greenprints for the Countryside? The story of Britain's National
  Parks*, 1987 (with A.M. MacEwen)
New Life for the Hills, 1983 (with Geoffrey Sinclair)
Countryside Conflicts, 1987 (with Lowe, Cox, O'Riordan and
  Winter)

THE GREENING OF A RED

Malcolm MacEwen

Preface by E.P. Thompson

PLUTO PRESS

London • Concord, Mass

First published 1991 by Pluto Press
345 Archway Road, London N6 5AA
and 141 Old Bedford Road,
Concord, MA 01742, USA

British Library Cataloguing in Publication Data
MacEwen, Malcolm, 1911–
    The greening of a red.
    1. Great Britain. Environmental movements – Biographies
    I. Title
    333. 72092

    ISBN 0-7453-0440-0 hb
    ISBN 0-7453-0441-9

Library of Congress Cataloging-in-Publication Data
MacEwen, Malcolm, 1911–
    The greening of a Red / Malcolm MacEwen.
        p.   cm.
    ISBN 0-7453-0440-0. – ISBN 0-7453-0441-9 (pbk.)
    1. MacEwen, Malcolm, 1911–. 2. Communists–Scotland–
–Biography. 3. Communist Party of Great Britain–History–20th
century. 4. Communism–Great Britain–History–20th century.
5. Green Party (Great Britain)–History–20th century. 6. Europe–
History–20th century. I. Title.
HX244.7.M25A3 1990
324.241'075'092–dc20
    [B]   90-6875
                                                           CIP

Typeset by Stanford Desktop Publishing, Milton Keynes
Printed in Great Britain by Billing and Sons Ltd, Worcester

Contents

Daily Worker cartoons 1936–56 by Gabriel appear between pages 190 and 191.

Abbreviations

AJ	*The Architects' Journal*
AR	*The Architectural Review*
the Bomb	the atomic bomb
CEGB	Central Electricity Generating Board
CLA	Country Landowners' Association
CND	Campaign for Nuclear Disarmament
CP	Communist Party
CPRE	Campaign for the Protection of Rural England
CPSU	Communist Party of the Soviet Union
EAM	the Greek National Liberation Front
EC	Executive Committee (Communist Party)
EEC	European Economic Community
ELAS	the Greek Army of National Liberation
ESA	Environmentally Sensitive Areas
FBR	Fast-Breeder Reactor
GNP	Gross National Product
ILP	Independent Labour Party
IUCN	International Union for the Conservation of Nature and Natural Resources
KKE	the Greek Communist Party
LCC	London County Council
LL/LF/LE	Long Life, Loose Fit, Low Energy
NCC	Nature Conservancy Council
NFU	National Farmers' Union
NLR	*The New Left Review*
NUWM	Nation Unemployed Workers' Union
POUM	Workers' Party of National Unity
PR	proportional representation
the *Reasoner*	*The New Reasoner*
RIBA	Royal Institute of British Architects
RTZ	Rio Tinto Zinc
SRC	Students' Representative Council
TUC	Trades Union Congress
UIA	International Union of Architects
ULR	*The Universities and Left Review*
UNEP	United Nations Environment Programme
UNRRA	United Nations Relief and Rehabilitation Agency
WCS	World Conservation Strategy
the *Worker*	*The Daily Worker*

Preface

E.P. THOMPSON

I do not know what I am doing writing a preface to Malcolm MacEwen's autobiography because I have always regarded him as my senior, and wiser (in some, if not in all respects) than I. When I was still a student, he was foreign editor of the *Daily Worker*, and author of those searching reports on the repression of the Greek Resistance which are a major theme of Chapter 12 of this book. When he joined the Editorial Board of the *New Reasoner* in 1957 he brought us not only his journalistic skills but also experience and ballast.

It was from 1957 to 1963, in the transition from ex-communists (with their familiar traumas and self-accusations) to founders of the first New Left, that I worked most closely with Malcolm. *The New Reasoner* had a curiously split geographical (and perhaps political) existence. It was initiated in Yorkshire by John Saville, Dorothy Thompson and myself. John and I were named as editors, and we were soon joined as co-editor by Peter Worsley, with an editorial board that included Ken Alexander (an exceedingly active and constructive editorial adviser, who was subsequently transmogrified into Sir Kenneth Alexander, Vice-chancellor of Stirling University), and Alfred Dressler, our seemingly omniscient editorial adviser on the Soviet Union and Eastern Europe (and sometimes courier between West and East). We very badly needed a London component and base, and Malcolm and Doris Lessing were the first to afford us this support. They were soon joined by Ralph Miliband and Mervyn Jones.

This meant that Malcolm was given all kinds of commission – there were calls not only upon his editorial advice and journa-listic skills, but he was asked to liaise with readers and contributors, to meet foreign visitors passing through London, and so on. Editorial boards were normally held in London (since it is hopeless to try to get Londoners to come to meetings in the provinces), and we met either in Doris Lessing's flat or at Malcolm's at 31 Tanza Road.

Reminiscences can be strangely untrustworthy sources. Several years ago I fell out of my chair while watching TV: Doris Lessing was being interviewed, and she seemed to be saying that while she had been a communist in Rhodesia, she gave up all that when she came to England. I may have misunderstood her, or she may have misunderstood the question. Or she might, on some technicality, not have held a British Communist Party (CP) membership card. But Doris very certainly *was* part of the CP (and then the CP opposition, or *Reasoner*, ambience). I met her first at a meeting of the Communist Party Writers' Group. She was (in 1956) an unusually honest critic of the CP, refusing the usual apologetics that it was all the fault of the leadership and 'we didn't know' the truth about Stalin etc. As she insisted, we might not know lots of things, but we knew very well about the general character of Stalinism and we had condoned it. Doris was a helpful and stimulating member of the *New Reasoner* board, reaching out to new and younger ('angry') constituencies and refusing to become locked in intra-communist or Trotskyist recriminations. Even if she prefers to forget it now, she was a founder of the New Left.

So was Malcolm, who had no more time than she for retrospective recriminations. His passage from ex-communist to post-communist was eased, as this book explains, by his immediate immersion in new projects, in architectural journalism and in urban planning. Although, as I now realise, he was of a youthful early middle-age, his role – when the *New Reasoner* and *Universities and Left Review* merged to form *New Left Review* – was sometimes that of an elder statesman: far more experienced than the enthusiasts of the Partisan Coffee House, and (when he served as Vice-chairman when I was Chairman of the *New Left Review* board) an avuncular paternalist restraining the 'polemical' excesses of E.P.T.: that is, as the opportunist blunting my high sense of principle. Well, however one reads it, Malcolm tended to smooth down ruffled feathers and find commonsense compromise solutions to intractable problems.

The tone of this book reveals this time and again. It is a very sane and measured book: the common sense of that very considerable part of the Left which was controlled by neither 'King

Street' (the CP) nor 'Transport House' (Labour Party officialdom). And, Malcolm's reminiscences are a trustworthy source, wherever I am able to check them. This is reinforced by the published record which he has been able to draw upon at every stage, in his own contributions to the communist, architectural and environmental press.

I do not on every occasion see the past as he does. He is somewhat bland about one or two issues which still raise my blood pressure. As befits the mellowing autobiographer he is more forgiving to the 'King Street' (British Communist) *apparatchiks* than I could be. He had to rub shoulders with them every week, in the *Daily Worker* offices, whereas from a greater distance I was outraged by their betrayal of their members' trust and their considerable repertoire of very dirty tricks. I do not think it has any political relevance if they could be charming and were kind to pussy-cats.

However, I am chiefly struck by how often my recollection of the past confirms the account which Malcolm MacEwen gives us. I mean the 'reasons' of the past. Obviously, as we lived through that past we did not know the full truth about it – the secret agendas of the politicians, the tangled motives which historians turn up and will continue to turn up. But there are other 'reasons': that is, the evidence then publicly available, the way political events were experienced by us at that time.

Again and again Malcolm recovers these reasons with authenticity. Ever since I have known him he has always puzzled over the reasons of things and tried to work out a coherent political world view. Very much of this book is concerned with a reworking of coherent understanding, whether it concerns the international communist movement, or urban planning and motor traffic, or strategies to defend Exmoor: Malcolm does not so much wish to tell us about his personal part in things (although he tells us something) as to explain what the issues were, what was the pattern of things.

This book does not pretend to give us the final word on Stalinism or on working-class housing, but it does tell us how the Molotov–Ribbentrop Pact was perceived by alert members of the Left at the time, how the enthusiasm of youthful post-war Yugoslavia found expression (I can certainly confirm this from my own experience), or how and why Ronan Point was a turning-point in attitudes to urban architecture. It is important now to recover these experiences and these 'reasons', when the mists of mythology are obscuring that past. There is a Tory myth, in which the Tories were ardent anti-Nazis in the 1930s and all of the Left were defeatist wimps (Malcolm's chapter on Chamberlain and Munich is a salutary dispersal of those myths). But there is also a Labour myth, in which both post-war Labour governments are seen as heroic ages of uncomplicated reformist endeavour, perhaps trammelled by the hostility of the United States' capitalism, and in which the obsessional anti-communism of Ernest Bevin and of many others around Transport House is forgotten, as well as the capitulationist propensity of Labour in the ensuing years, its willingness to avoid any serious engagements with privilege and with the prerogatives of money. Since these remain the characteristics of today's Labour leadership, it is important to recall their precedents.

There are two other books known to me which tell us about the reasons and experience of this Left, which was neither controlled by Transport House nor by King Street. Both are also good books and, strangely, neither they nor *The Greening of a Red* duplicate each other. I am thinking of Basil Davidson's *Special Operations, Europe* (more accurately described by its sub-title *Scenes from the Anti-Nazi War*) and Mervyn Jones's *Chances*. I hope that there will be other books to enlarge the testimony, because one thing which comes through from all of them – and strongly from Malcolm's book – is how very large has been the Left presence in Britain in the past 50 years, yet a presence which is not to be identified with official party-political expressions. It has been there, in the Left Book Club, in Aid for Spain, in the Common Wealth Party, in the New Left, in CND, in movements of social reform and in cultural expressions, all of them more vigorous and (perhaps) more effective than anything the politicians could offer.

This continues to be true. In the past decade or more, the emphasis of these informal and cultural pressures has shifted from red to green, for reasons which Malcolm fully explores and for reasons which I endorse. Since this is a world-wide shift – now finding vigorous expression on what used to be 'the other side' of the Cold War, but which it is increasingly obvious is the same side as our own – this book is not pessimistic but encouraging. One lays it down with renewed confidence that the world will go on.

E.P. Thompson, 1991

Introduction

The reader may wonder why, as I am neither famous nor noto-riously infamous, I wrote my political autobiography. It is a fair question to which the book itself provides the answer. I was attracted to communism as a student in 1935, and I was a dedicated professional communist (mainly as a journalist on the *Daily Worker*) from 1940 to 1956. I left the *Daily Worker* in 1956 in protest against its suppression of our reporter's despatches from Hungary, and was expelled from the Communist Party for helping to launch the *New Reasoner*, an independent Marxist journal edited by Edward Thompson and John Saville, which became *The New Left Review* in 1959.

However, I would not have written my story if my purpose had merely been to add to the number of confessions by former communists. The world has been drenched with stories, true and false, honest and mischievous, about the crimes, mistakes and inefficiency of communism, but there is a dearth of information about the real life of the Communist Party, and about the con-tribution that communists have made to the progress and the liberation of humanity – not least by paying the highest price for resisting Franco in Spain, defeating Hitler, frustrating American imperialism in Asia and opposing military dictatorships – and, I might add, contributing in all likelihood the largest number of victims to Stalin's purges. The release of Nelson Mandela and the legalisation of the Communist Party of South Africa on his insistence remind me that three South Africans (one of them a member of the Central Committee of the CP) found refuge with their families in our house when they were forced to flee the country. The South African CP and 'communism' itself were banned and persecuted for decades because the Party, from the first, opened its membership to all races and played a major role in organising the struggle against apartheid.

We have much to be proud of. Nor are we alone in needing to come clean about the shameful episodes in our past history. The Western politicians and the media have not begun to recognise the truth of their own history. I write these words from personal experience, for I was on the editorial committee of the *Daily Worker* in the early 1950s when we were threatened with prosecution for treason, for which the only penalty is death, because Alan Winnington, our reporter in Korea, told the truth about the genocidal war being waged by the US (and Britain).

After my break with the Communist Party in 1957 I gradually saw the need to add an ecological dimension to politics, and to make the conservation of natural resources an integral part of socialist thinking. 'Greening' is now in fashion, but so far the politicians do little more than pay lip service to the concept. It is not just a question of protecting threatened species or habitats or meeting the cost of cleaning up air and water. Quite apart from the constant threat of a nuclear holocaust, both capitalist and socialist systems have treated the biosphere as a cornucopia from which limitless wealth can be drawn forever. The conventional parties of right, left and centre have not yet begun to recognise that there are limits to everything, and (perhaps above all) limits to the extent to which the biosphere can be abused and mismanaged. The Green Party alone recognises these limits, but only a minority of Greens share my view that a socialist society based on co-operative principles and motivated by the betterment of the human condition offers a better chance of conserving the world's natural resources than a society driven by greed for profit and power.

I am grateful to the Nuffield Foundation, both for a substantial grant for research and for their tolerance and generosity in allowing me to suspend work for a year and a half while I and my wife, Anni, accepted an urgent commission to write our second book on the national park system – also with a Nuffield grant. As I was well over 70 they took a gamble on my survival which came off.

I am indebted to Professors Roderick Floud and Eric Hobsbawm for introducing me to Birkbeck College; to the college for electing me a Research Fellow and administering the grant, and to my research assistants Steve Parsons and Kathie Blair, both for their work and for their ideas. I would also like to thank all those who have helped me by reading parts of the book in draft: Peter Fryer, who was the immediate cause of my resignation from the *Daily Worker* by sending the despatches from Budapest in 1956 that the editor refused to publish; Colin Boyne, who took me onto the staff of *The Architects' Journal* when I parted company with the *Daily Worker* and taught me the abc of architectural journalism, and our dear friend Cedric Belfrage the editor of New York's *National Guardian* who was jailed and deported from the US at the height of the McCarthy witch-hunt. I owe a special debt to Marion Sarafis, the widow of Major General Stefanos Sarafis (the commander of ELAS, the Greek Army of National Liberation), for introducing me to many new studies of Greek politics during and after the war and for reading all my references to Greek events from 1943 to 1947 in draft. I am grateful to Jimmy Friel, otherwise 'Gabriel', the *Daily Worker* cartoonist from 1936 to 1956, for the cartoons which bring the pre-war and post-war *Daily Worker* to life, for the cover illustration and for spotting a howler in the text.

After I parted company with the Communist Party in 1956–7 Lewis Mumford did more than anybody else to open my eyes to the need for me to take account of ecological, technological and moral factors that we Marxists had ignored or underplayed. From Hiroshima onwards he denounced the immorality and destructiveness of nuclear weapons and mass extermination. His interpretations of history and his understanding of the consequences of misusing science, technology and economic and military power have been scandalously neglected. Humanity will not survive unless it takes his messages to heart, but if we have the sense to do so (as he believed we would) he will come to be seen as one of the most farsighted thinkers of the twentieth century. His death in January 1990, at the age of 94, prevents me from thanking him personally for the help and friendship he gave me and my wife Anni. I wish to acknowledge here the debt we owe both to Lewis and to Sophie, his wife and colleague.

Over the years I discussed many drafts with Anni, with whom my story is interlocked. We gave each other mutual support when we married as widow and widower, and our ideas and experience on the environment have been interacting for the past 40 years. Greening was a mutual process, and as the joint authors of two books on national parks we became professional colleagues as well as marriage partners. In addition to being a skilled professional planner, Anni is also one of nature's editors

– scrupulously accurate and painstaking, with an uncanny eye for logical arrangement and an ear for false notes. She bears no responsibility for the final text, but it is very much the better for her innumerable comments, her recollections and her ideas.

Malcolm MacEwen
Wootton Courtenay, 1991

Part 1
Before the Party

1

One Foot in the Grave

It would seem oddly perverse to begin this story by saying that
one of the best things that ever happened to me was to lose my
right leg in a motor bike crash when I was 21. I do not, in fact,
proclaim the slogan 'one leg good, two legs bad', in the manner
of Orwell's sheep. There are times, particularly in old age, when
it would be rather nice to have my own leg back again in good
working order, to replace the tin leg that I regard with some
affection and the phantom limb that gives me hell from time
to time, but the proposition that the crash was a blessing in disguise has a core of truth.

I set out from Inverness on my Norton motor bike on the
morning of 5 July 1933, to see the Tourist Trophy motor cycle
races in the Isle of Man. As I was rounding a left hand bend on
the bridge over the River Nairn, only five miles from my home
in Inverness, a car driven by a car hirer from Dufftown by the
name of MacWilliam came round the bend in the opposite
direction, on my side of the road. There was no way I could
avoid him, but MacWilliam saw me in the nick of time and
swerved to his left. Instead of being killed in a head-on collision I had my right leg crushed between the bike and the car. I
ended up on the grass verge, conscious but severely shocked,
unable to move and vaguely aware of acute pains. I have a
misty memory of an immense delay before an ambulance
came, and a very sharp recollection of the ambulance man
cutting off my trousers and revealing a pink thigh bone. On the
way to Inverness our GP, Dr Campbell, met the ambulance,
gave me morphia and told the driver, no doubt on my parents'
instructions, to take me, not to the Inverness Royal Infirmary
as he would normally have done, but to the private Viewhill
Nursing Home owned by a company of which my Dad was
chairman.

The 'Crash' Course

For five and a half months I was confined to a single room, with a view over the garden towards the forbiddingly high wall of Inverness Prison. There was nobody to talk to except the regular visitors (with whom I became increasingly bored), the overworked nurses and the doctors. There was no TV in 1933, but paradoxically it was precisely the solitary confinement with neither TV nor radio that forced me at the age of 21 into a crash reading course (averaging two books a day for a year). At the end of it the slump, unemployment, Hitler and the prospect of another Great War began to rate rather higher in my consciousness than motor bikes (which I could no longer ride) or golf, girls and Highland dancing.

Dr Campbell, who was a bit of a snob and a Tory, but a good GP and an intelligent man, argued me out of the built-in resistance to Dickens that I had inherited from my schooldays. To my amazement I found that Pickwick, far from boring me stiff, made me laugh so much that I was in some danger of shaking the bed to pieces, and with it the apparatus of weights and wires attached to my leg. Shakespeare, a name I'd associated with tedium and exams, turned out to be an extraordinarily penetrating observer of people and life. Dr Campbell suggested that I should try Bernard Shaw and start with the 'Prefaces', which I had never heard of, rather than the plays, which I *had* heard of but never read. I read them both, but it was the 'Prefaces' that proved to be the eye-opener both for their style and their content. They were written conversationally, in lively every-day language, and dealt polemically with people, life, politics and religion with such explosive vigour, common sense and wit that I was carried along as much by the fun as by the argument. I loved his iconoclastic attitude to religion, which I shared, and I acquired an admiration for his polemical, direct style that I have never lost. The 'Prefaces' led to the plays, and then (at whose suggestion I can't remember) to *The Intelligent Woman's Guide to Capitalism and Socialism*. Later on I found Shaw's attitude to the 'intelligent woman' insufferably patronising, and his approach to socialism (which he equated with absolute equality of income on the model of Edward Bellamy's American Utopia *Looking Backwards*) both unrealistic and unfair, but at the time his simple exposure of the inequity and wastefulness of the profit-driven capitalist system, and his outline of a socialist alternative of production for use based on the common ownership of the means of production, seemed to be no more than plain common sense.

This introduction to socialism hit me with special force while I was imprisoned in bed. I had begun to read the daily newspapers far more intensely than I had ever done before, and I began to see the events of 1933, which were daily shattering the foundations of the world in which I had grown up, in a new light. After reading Shaw I began to understand not only the sheer horror of the situation, but the necessity – and the possibility – of ending the human and material waste it involved. I had not paid much attention to what was happening earlier in 1933: in January Hitler's appointment as Chancellor of Germany by the President, Field Marshall von Hindenburg; in February the Oxford University Union resolution refusing to fight 'for King and Country' which underlined the strength of feeling among undergraduates about the uselessness of war and the dishonesty of jingoistic and 'patriotic' feeling, and in March the burning of the *Reichstag* (or parliament) which was the pretext for Hitler to seize power and unleash the Nazi terror. By September, when the trial began in Leipzig of George Dimitrov the Bulgarian communist (later Secretary of the Communist International) and of other communists who were accused by the Nazis of firing the *Reichstag*, my attitude had changed completely. I could not read too much about the trial, or about other developments such as Nazi Germany's withdrawal in October from the League of Nations and the Disarmament Conference, to free itself for the programme of rearmament and conquest that Hitler had outlined in *Mein Kampf*.

Family Origins

There was nothing in my ancestry or family circumstances, when I was born in Inverness on 24 December 1911, to suggest that I would be drawn towards communism. It is the family of my wife Ann that bears the political bar sinister on its genealogical tree (using the word 'sinister' in its literal Latin meaning of 'left'). For Ann's grandparents, the poets Dollie and Ernest

Radford, met in the British Museum reading room in 1880 through Dollie's friendship with Karl Marx's daughter Eleanor. They seem to have done much of their courting in Karl Marx's sitting room, where the younger circle of Marx's daughters' friends and admirers would get together for poetry, play reading and music. Ann's father, Dr Maitland Radford, was a lifelong socialist and Ann was not baptised. I, on the other hand, was brought up in a strongly Christian household, that was influenced very little if at all by socialist thinking, let alone by the works of Karl Marx, William Morris, Bernard Shaw, Graham Wallas and the other advanced thinkers who were known personally to the Radfords and were strong influences on their political and cultural development. I grew up in an entirely different political atmosphere, essentially Liberal and later Scottish Nationalist, which had little in common with socialist or free-thinking traditions. It did mean, however, that we were not imprisoned within the framework of conventional, Conservative thinking and were exposed to less orthodox political ideas.

The MacEwens were not untypical of the professional families in the Scottish Highlands, with impeccable middle-class ancestries on either side, who combined aspirations to materially greater prosperity and a share in political power with a strong sense of social service and responsibility. My father Alexander MacEwen, a solicitor, was born in India, the son of a judge in the British Indian Service. My mother, Beatrice Henderson, an artist, was born in what is now Pakistan, the daughter of a doctor in the Indian Medical Service. They married in 1906, when Dad was 31 and Mum 29, and had three sons and two daughters, of whom I was the fourth. After we had moved in 1915 to the select middle-class and professional 'hill' area of Inverness we lacked for nothing in the material sense, with a large house, a beautiful garden, a tennis court, six holes for pitch-and-putt golf, a car from 1914 (and two by the 1930s), servants, and at the height of our prosperity a chauffeur-gardener.

Although Dad was often away from home, he was more popular with his children than Mum. He told or read good stories and liked to play funny tricks, such as standing on a chair to pour syrup onto our bread and butter from an immense height. But he did not give us much of his time, for he was a man of extraordinary mental and physical energy who could get through more work in a day than anybody else I ever knew. He was senior partner in the family law firm of Stewart, Rule and Co. but he was also an entrepreneur who raised capital locally to float companies which operated tea estates in Ceylon (now Sri Lanka), two cinemas, a laundry, a nursing home, a sweet and lemonade factory and a bus network stretching from Inverness to the remotest parts of Sutherland. He even floated The Balkan Trading Company, in the hope of winning a contract to run buses in Bucharest, but he had not realised that nobody got contracts in Romania without paying bribes. As a local Liberal politician he was active in the causes of public housing and Highland reconstruction and a member of Inverness Town Council for 24 years (six of them as Provost or, in English terms, mayor) and of Inverness-shire County Council for ten years (during which he was Chairman of the Education Committee). He was knighted for his services to local government in 1932.

In his last decade, from 1931 to 1941, he was perhaps the best-known Scottish nationalist politician. He was one of the founders and leaders, first of a small, reformist Scottish Party, and then of a united Scottish National Party for which he fought elections in 1933 and 1935 at Kilmarnock and in the Western Isles. He was an enthusiast for the Gaelic culture and language (which he learned) and represented the Gaelic-speaking Hebridean island of Benbecula on the county council. He was a passionate Anglo-Catholic and an active member of the Scottish Episcopal Church, favouring such Roman practices as sung masses, midnight masses, incense, confession and processions with stations of the cross, but drawing the line at the Pope. He wrote a book on Scottish education and two books in which he synthesised his Scottish nationalist, Liberal and religious ideas into a moralistic political system that bore some resemblance to G.K. Chesterton's 'distributism'. The key to his thinking was his belief in small, decentralised nation states like Denmark, which he greatly admired, and which were, he thought, run much better than the big, imperial states with their aggressive and acquisitive policies, and repressive attitudes towards minority cultures. His European upbringing gave him a much broader cultural outlook than most Scottish politicians. He read widely in French, and spoke it, so far as I could judge, almost as well as a native.

I pushed Dad's belief in religious and political toleration to considerable lengths. I put up with the formalities of confirmation, and I was amused by the farce of having to confess my 'sins' from a printed list helpfully supplied by our priest, but I was utterly turned off by 15 chapel services a week at Rossall, the Church of England public school in Lancashire to which my brother David and I had been sent, and by my growing conviction that Christianity was a nonsense. The prospect of everlasting life going on *ad infinitum* had begun to take on the quality of a nightmare from which there was no escape, until I realised that there was no evidence whatever to support the theory. It must have been very painful for Dad when, at the age of 16, I finally revolted against Christianity and refused one Sunday morning to accompany the rest of the family on the usual church parade to morning service, but he offered no resistance or argument. Even when I joined the Young Communist League as a student he would not argue with me, although he argued the case against Marxism in his books, and he remained generous financially.

Mum's talents and interests were entirely different. She was a good painter, and exhibited before her marriage at the Paris Salon, but she never touched a brush after her marriage. Although she eventually found other outlets for her creative and artistic talents I feel sure that her decision to devote herself to creating a relaxed and comfortable home for Dad and to raising a family was a major source of frustration. The problem of bringing up her family was solved by the existence of a large staff and by packing all of us except my older sister Molly off to boarding schools, in my case immediately after my ninth birthday. It was not Mum but Lizzie Mackenzie, our nanny, who really brought us up, and for whom I felt the strongest affection, and Nanny, having committed herself as a young, Gaelic-speaking girl to the MacEwens, carried on as Mum's housekeeper after Dad's death in 1941.

For most of her married life music was Mum's supreme interest. She was a violinist whose enthusiasm for music was contagious. She founded the Inverness Amateur Musical Society, which for the first time brought front rank chamber music ensembles and soloists to Inverness. The comfort and warmth of her reception made Inverness a popular port of call for her favourites, but her efforts to have her children trained as musicians were an almost total failure and a major source of tension. I resented being pushed into violin lessons, and when these failed, into the flute. Mum also threw immense energies into securing a new deal for the district nurses, who had had to be content with getting around on foot or on bicycles until Mum's persistence got them motor cars.

'Bad' Families – and Philistine Schools

Why my parents sent four out of five of their children to boarding 'public' schools in *England* remains a mystery to me, although it is not difficult to guess some of the reasons. Mum's increasing involvement in activities outside the home, coupled with the social demands imposed on her as the wife of an active politician, go a long way to explain her need to banish us from the home for eight months in the year. I was sent to Inverness Academy initially, but was hastily removed when a gang of 'keelies' (Scots for hooligans) – big, nasty boys of six or seven from 'bad families' – punished me for my social airs and posh accent by spitting in my cap, clapping it back on my head and telling me to run for my life. I went next to the safety of a girls' school run by my godmother where (as one of my fellow schoolboys recently confirmed) I joined the Brownies. When I was nine I was sent to join my brother David at a prep school, St Salvator's School, St Andrews, which almost guaranteed that its pupils would win classical scholarships or bursaries to public schools, as we both did. I learned to adapt to the school's loveless and brutal environment after a traumatic initiation, but David never fully recovered from the cruel teasing of his schoolfellows, who called him 'sloppy face' after he had been facially disfigured by a mastoid operation. The only compensation I can think of is that it was probably the only school in the world where golf was compulsory, and where we were given time off to watch the championships.

Rossall, the 'public' school to which David and I both went at 13, was as narrow and philistine a school as could have been found. We were both on the 'classical' side and learned nothing whatever about art, music, nature, theatre, science, advanced mathematics, handicrafts or industrial processes. Rossall focused overwhelmingly on Latin and Greek, the Officers' Training Corps, and chapel, with cold baths every morning and endless (compulsory) games in a vain attempt to keep our minds off sex.

We left school with English accents and English attitudes, which may have helped all of us to move on the rebound towards Scottish nationalism. The main result of my exile to boarding school was to open up a gulf of mutual incomprehension between me and my mother. I think we all felt that her insensitivity to our needs reached its nadir when she got her secretary to distribute typed 'family letters' to keep us in touch with home when we were students – a device we all resented, although only David was bold enough to protest. Neither Mum nor Dad visited us at boarding school except in emergencies, as when I broke my arm in a fall from a high bar in the gym.

I had to wait until Dad's death in 1941 to appreciate Mum's real strength and creativity. His relatively early death was a shattering blow to her, not only because it destroyed the entire basis of her social and cultural life, but because he died almost bankrupt. The 'fortune' (I have no idea what it was worth) that Dad had inherited in Ceylon tea shares from his aunt in 1928 had disappeared almost overnight in the big stock market crash of 1931. At his death his insurance, his house and most of his shares had to be realised to pay his debts, and Mum was left at the age of 64 with no home and virtually no income. She rose to the occasion magnificently. She took a course with teenage girls at a school of domestic science and got a job running an Edinburgh University hostel for 'colonial' (that is, black) students with whom she got on very well. When she came back towards the end of the war I was able to give her the use of our cottage as I had left for London and the *Daily Worker*, and she created a new life for herself by taking up weaving and spinning at the age of 70. She rapidly established herself as one of the best weavers in the Highlands. She was a good designer too, and formed a village weaving co-operative. She enjoyed a vigorous, creative old age before she died at the age of 92. It was during Mum's heroic period in old age that I developed a great affection and respect for her, and she liked the way in which, as a communist, I was thumbing my nose at the Establishment.

Forestry Student

When I left Rossall in March 1929, soon after my seventeenth birthday, I had not the remotest idea what to do in life, apart from the fact that I was obsessed by motor bikes and had entered for the Scottish Schoolboy Motor Cycle Trials to be held in April. I raised no objections when Dad suggested that I should take a three-year science degree in forestry at Aberdeen University, and then go out to Ceylon, where I could eventually manage one of the tea estates owned by his company. This was an astonishing decision, for I had not done one hour of science at school, and did not even know that H_2O represented the chemical composition of water. The science course I embarked on in September 1929 was at first utterly beyond me, and even with some additional tutoring it took me two years to get through the first-year exams.

I cannot say that I applied my mind very hard to mastering elementary chemistry, physics, botany and zoology. I was an active cross-country runner, explored Deeside and Donside (on my motor bike, not on foot), and spent seemingly endless hours kissing my first girl friend passionately in the lovers' lane behind her parents' house, which was as far as most girls (or boys) would 'go' in those days. I joined a horse artillery brigade in the Territorial Army (TA) as a Second Lieutenant, primarily because the TA taught me to ride for nothing, but also because I thought that 'the Terriers' would be good fun, which they were in a classy sort of way. The officers bought polo ponies with the money allocated to the brigade to buy horses, and even the disgrace I suffered when my pony bolted the first time I turned up for polo could not dim my enthusiasm. The hatred for all things military engendered by Rossall's militarism, and by the all-pervading memories of the 'war to end war' with which I had grown up, subsided overnight. It never occurred to me that I was being trained to fight the Second World War, for it was government policy until 1933 that Britain would not fight a major war within the next ten years.

The main thing I got out of my two years at Aberdeen, apart from a useful grounding in the physical and natural sciences, was my first direct contact with working men when I worked on the Forestry Commission's Culloden Estate during the vacations. Sammy MacMillan, the foreman, who got about five shillings more than the basic 30 shillings (£1.50) a week for being in charge of the gang, was a fount of wisdom, who used to recount the story of his life and tell me how to prune trees in the soft, Inverness accent which, until that time, I'd despised as comically 'common'. It was the first time in my life that I had met men who lived in council houses, had to make do on less than the average wage, and eked out their wages by poaching rabbits and game. It humbled me a bit (although not enough) to find that they had far more to teach me than I, with all my 'education', could teach them. What the forestry course singularly failed to do, with its single-minded concentration on conifer production, was to interest me in nature or ecology, or the art of landscape.

The Magic of Neil Gunn

I took no interest whatever in politics at Aberdeen, but when I was at home in the 'vacs' I fell under the spell of Neil Gunn, the Caithness novelist, who was a leading figure in the Scottish literary renaissance of the 1930s. Neil was an exciseman and worked at the Glen Mhor distillery in Inverness. I often went to Neil's and Daisy's 'open house' at their bungalow 'Larachan' on Saturday nights, when a dozen or more people, ranging from a burly bus driver from Sutherland to lawyer friends of my oldest brother Robin, would cram into the Gunns' tiny sitting room to drink an exceptionally strong malt whisky that Neil smuggled out of the distillery and to talk into the small hours on every aspect of Scottish life and politics. My younger sister Margaret came so strongly under Neil's influence that, unknown to us, she became his lover for about 20 years. Neil's attitude to life was socialist, but he had become the centre of a Scottish nationalist circle, the 'grey eminence' who exercised enormous influence behind the scenes in promoting the unification of the two nationalist parties in 1933. The first result of this process was the decision of both parties to unite behind Dad's candidature in the Kilmarnock by-election of that year.

The Saturday nights at Neil's convinced me that Scotland could manage its own affairs very much better if it could recover the right to govern itself, but I enjoyed the evenings at Larachan as much for the warmth of the friendship and the stimulus of Neil's bantering wit, chuckling laugh and challenging questions as for the heady political optimism about Scotland's political and cultural future that they generated. It was Neil who gave me my first serious political jolt one day in October 1931, when I ran into him in the street and rashly expressed the opinion that it would be a disaster for the country if Labour were to win the general election. Echoing the words of a broadcast by Philip Snowden, the one-time Labour pioneer who was Chancellor of the Exchequer in Ramsay Macdonald's new so-called 'National' government, I told him that if Labour won there would be a run on the banks and the people would lose their savings. Neil deflated me by bursting into laughter. When he had recovered sufficiently he gave me a patient explanation of the swindle by which Macdonald and his Tory friends were bamboozling the people into voting for massive cuts in jobs, pay and social benefits in the mistaken belief that there was no other way out of the economic crisis. Had he attacked me for being a reactionary idiot, he wouldn't have made his point half as well. However, I could never be persuaded to join a nationalist party, although I supported them between 1931 and 1933.

I gave up the forestry course in 1931 after two years because the last thing I wanted to do by then was to plant tea, or for that matter trees. As I still had not the remotest idea what to do Dad suggested that as I had 'the gift of the gab' I should qualify both as an advocate (Scots barrister) and as a solicitor, by taking degrees in Arts and Law at Edinburgh University. It proved to be so easy to pass the ordinary MA course, which consisted wholly of compulsory lectures and set books (I had one tutorial in two years) that I was left with vast amounts of time to tear about on my new motor bike, to play golf on the seemingly infinite number of courses around Edinburgh and to indulge my passion for Highland dancing. Not even the appalling winter of 1931–2, which saw the massive demonstrations of protest against unemployment, cuts in benefit, and the means test, and the Invergordon naval mutiny against cuts in service pay, could stimulate my dormant interest in politics.

A Trip to Socialism

I often wonder how and when I would have got out of my social round had it not been for the motor bike trip I made in July 1933. As it turned out it was the experience of six months in bed with nothing to do but read followed by a prolonged convalescence after the amputation of my leg in December that jerked me out of an over-extended adolescence, pushed me out of the 'Terriers', turned me into an anti-fascist socialist, and

sent me racing down the path that led to communism and ultimately to what I now call 'reddish green'. Quite apart from the
fact that the newspapers (and soon *The New Statesman*) brought
me into daily contact with the Nazi menace, two other factors
encouraged me to think as a socialist. The first was the
Kilmarnock by-election in November, when Dad's performance
put Scottish nationalism firmly on the political map. I wanted
him to win, but the election helped to convince me that 'Home
Rule' was almost irrelevant both to Scotland's poverty and
massive unemployment (for which socialism seemed to offer
the only cure) and to the fascism that was beginning to transform the political map of Europe. The second was the bills I got
for private medical services. Out of the £2,000 I got in damages
£800 went in medical expenses (one surgeon getting £250) and
I had to buy two artifical legs, as amputees always need a spare.
They cost me £50 (£1,500 to £2,000 in today's money). My
nurses got only their miserable wages. The financial consequences left me a convinced supporter of the socialist concept
of a free public health service, though I have to admit that I
remained a bourgeois at heart. My priority was to spend £300
on a new sports car.

I am often asked nowadays how I coped with the trauma of
an amputation, but nobody had heard of trauma in those days.
Generally it seemed to be assumed that the only real problem
was the physical one of mastering the artificial limb, which is
in some ways the easiest part. Both physically and mentally it is
much easier to cope with an amputation when one is young,
and my heart goes out to the many elderly people I see at artificial limb centres nowadays trying to cope with amputations in
their seventies. In my case amputation brought relief, for as the
months went by and one operation followed another I began to
feel increasingly frustrated. When, towards the end of
November 1933, I was advised that the leg should be amputated below the knee I jumped at the idea, metaphorically
speaking. My leg was amputated by Scotland's leading ortho-
paedic surgeon, Walter Mercer, who made such a neat job that
my stump has been admired by surgeons for the past 50 years.

I went home the day before my twenty-second birthday,
Christmas Eve, and was soon walking and acquiring a speed
and agility with crutches which I have not quite lost in my late
seventies. In March I took delivery of two legs, and began to

walk again. I resigned my commission in the Territorial Army, although the War Office required me to present my stump for inspection at Edinburgh Castle before it would forgo repayment of the uniform allowance it had paid me. After a cruise in the Mediterranean with my father and my sister Margaret, and a holiday on the Basque coast of Spain with Neil Gunn and my brother Robin – who rendered an unforgettable service to Scottish literature and politics by saving Neil from drowning when he was being swept out to sea – I was able to walk the ten miles up the hill to the Culloden battlefield and back, albeit with a blistered stump at the end. By the autumn I was dancing reels as well with one leg as most young men could do with two, and was fit enough to return to Edinburgh to begin my law apprenticeship and my law degree course. However, I was a very different person from the motor bike-crazy Arts graduate who left Edinburgh 15 months before – and the change from two legs to one was the least of the changes I had experienced.

2

Fast Worker, Slow Learner

Going back to Edinburgh in October 1934 with one leg, a Triumph sports car, £800 in the building society and an increasingly radical slant on life proved to be an exhilarating experience. The Law degree course at the university (apart from Forensic Medicine's grisly fascination with corpses and with bizarre murders) proved to be as unimaginative as the Arts course, and served mainly to strengthen my growing conviction that the university itself stood badly in need of reform; but it took up very little of my time or energy beyond the compulsory lectures at 9am and 5pm, between which I worked in the office of Morton, Smart, Macdonald and Prosser, Writers to the Signet. In my spare time I plunged into student life, politics and journalism, first as a member of the Students' Representative Council (SRC) and then as editor, from 1936 to 1937, of its magazine, *The Student*. In my first term I joined the Socialist Society, and by 1935 I had found my way into the Young Communist League. My personal, political, legal and university lives were inextricably entangled with each other, and my lifestyle, although still indelibly stamped with my middle-class origins, underwent a rapid change.

I donned the neat blue suit, collar, tie and trilby hat required of law apprentices, and found myself apprenticed for three years to a firm whose clients included (to my astonishment) the King and other members of the Royal Family. The senior partner, Sir John Prosser, was the very soul of gravitas, respectability and incorruptible confidentiality. He had been awarded a knighthood and made a Companion of the Victorian Order for his services to royalty. When I was shown for the first time into Sir John's office I found him seated at his desk in a large room whose floor was covered by bundles of papers tied with red tape, while the walls were lined with books and battered black deed boxes bearing the names of his prestigious clients in gilt lettering. It was only when I spotted a box labelled 'HRH The Duke of Connaught' that I began to realise that here was something rather out of the ordinary. I looked again and saw that His Royal Highness nestled alongside other minor royalty and the big names of the Scottish brewing and cotton industries: the McEwans, the Youngers and the Coatses. Nothing leaked down to the likes of me about the affairs of the Royal Family, although it was rumoured at the time of the abdication of Edward VIII in December 1936 that the Balmoral Estate had been overlooked in the deal made with Edward in the hours before his abdication. We certainly believed the story that he had to be bought off with a very large additional sum of money.

Clipping the Brewers' Coupons

One of my first jobs was to complete the income tax returns of the McEwans, Youngers, Coatses and other Scottish millionaire families, under the stern direction of Mr Pirie, the Orcadian who ran the firm's income tax department. Although my father paid supertax on the excess of his income over £2,000 I had not realised how rich the *really* rich were until I sat, eyes boggling, with their dividend counterfoils in front of me. It was commonplace for individual members of these beer and cotton families to have incomes from dividends alone of £10–15,000 a year (multiply by 30 or more to get today's equivalent) – and this at a time of deep depression when the benefit for an unemployed married couple with two children under eight was only £78 a year. Mr Pirie told us with glee how Viscount Younger had been caught failing to disclose for supertax some dividends that brought in £10,000 a year, and was forced to pay a very large sum in tax and penalty. The Inland Revenue pounced just after he had given £100,000 to St Andrew's University to build The Younger Hall, and Mr Pirie had no doubt that if the Revenue had pounced a few weeks earlier St Andrew's would never have got its hall. I was not, of course, at liberty to broadcast my discoveries, my lips being sealed in return for an honorarium of £5 for my first year, £10 for the second and £15 for the third, but the more my eyes popped in amazement at the wealth of the ruling class, the more firmly a Marxist interpretation of the facts took hold of my mind.

My real boss was David Prosser, Sir John's son, who seemed to think that he had a duty to take a semi-parental interest in me. He was indulgent towards my increasing political activities, provided I did no political work in the office, and was greatly amused when the Earl of Suffolk and Berkshire turned up one day, threatening to horsewhip me on the office steps in revenge for a paragraph in *The Student's* gossip column. The Earl was a science student and had been elected a Fellow of the Royal Society of Edinburgh despite his repeated failures in the science exams. As we thought it unlikely that any other student duffer would be similarly honoured *The Student* observed that this showed the advantage of being two Earls at once, and asked the innocent question: 'What does one become if one passes physics first time?' I happened to be out when His Lordship arrived with his melodramatic invitation to be horsewhipped (he might as well have suggested a duel) and David talked him out of his silly idea.

I liked the idea of going to the Bar and becoming, if I had the skill and the luck, a Scottish Stafford Cripps or a Dennis Pritt, both socialist MPs and KCs (King's Counsel) whom I admired for combining strong left-wing political views and a readiness to plead political cases (often without fee) with the ability to extract huge fees from capitalists who needed their unique skills. But I found the Scottish Court of Session so profoundly conservative that I could see no possibility of making a career there as a left-wing socialist. Nor could I afford the high entrance fees to the Bar (then £500, or nearly all that was left of my damages) and the long years during which I could earn next to nothing. So I decided that when I had completed my apprenticeship I would try my luck in law and politics in the more familiar context of my father's office in Inverness.

Enter Barbara

Law classes and apprenticeship soon became peripheral to national and student politics. The University Socialist Society, which I joined soon after returning to Edinburgh in October 1934, was a small but lively group corresponding to what would now be called 'the Broad Left', opening its doors to socialists, communists, anarchists and anybody else who accepted the description 'socialist'. Its limitation was that its very breadth tended to make it little more than an interesting talking shop, at least until the Spanish Civil War broke out in July 1936. Far and away the most important thing the Socialist Society did for me was to introduce me to Marca Burns, the daughter of Emile Burns who was at that time head of the Communist Party's education department and a member of its Political Bureau – the Party's inner leadership. Marca was a slight, highly intelligent, good-humoured biology student with a passion for dogs, whose main interest lay in animal breeding and genetics. I now suspect that her eager commitment to the Communist Party and to Marxism owed more to her affection and sense of duty towards her parents – for her mother Elinor was also a leading communist in the co-operative movement – than to her own political instincts.

Marca unwittingly helped to transform my love life as well as my politics by bringing with her Barbara Stebbing, a geology student a year and a half older than I was and perhaps five years older than most of the students in her year. To say that Barbara was a daughter of a Sussex stockbroker and Master of Foxhounds would be true, but misleading. Although her family were wealthy by any standards, there was also a streak of unorthodoxy on her mother's side, and Barbara had grown up with her three sisters (she had no brothers) in a highly intellectual atmosphere. She had a lively political mind, but she was also better-read than anybody of my age I had ever met. She soaked up all the English novelists and poets who turned me off, or whom I had never tried. She illustrated her letters with wickedly funny sketches and wrote satirical verses and hilarious limericks and short stories in skilful imitation of other people's styles. She brought a rich blend of witty common sense and warmth of feeling to any meeting in which she took part. She got a first class degree in geology, and would have gone far had the geological world not been virtually closed to women, and had she not suffered seriously from diabetes and, as a consequence, from the ulcerative colitis that killed her in 1944. She knew that she had only a short time to live (something I could never really believe), and she was determined to savour every aspect of life.

Young Communist

As Gollancz had just published Emile Burns's, *Handbook of Marxism*, a compendium of basic texts ranging from the 'Communist Manifesto' to the latest speeches of Stalin, Marca arranged for Emile to come to Edinburgh to talk to students in the autumn term of 1935. He spoke with such persuasiveness that Marca, my friend John Beaton, Barbara and I and one or two others decided to form a student communist group and to join the Young Communist League. In December 1935 the new group sent me to a conference of communist students in Marx House in London, where I was impressed in particular by the eloquence of John Cornford, a Cambridge student who was killed in Spain just after Christmas a year later.

Unfortunately I was so new to communism that when Jack Cohen, the CP student organiser, referred to 'the Party' as we were walking down Theobald's Road I asked in all innocence 'which party?'. I had still to learn that for communists 'the Party' could only mean the CP. When I got back to Edinburgh I had to confess to my comrades that, as most of the talk about political theory had been couched in a Marxist language I had still to learn, much of it had gone way above my head. I could not give them an intelligible report, except to say that we all had to work a lot harder to build up the communist group and the broad student anti-fascist movement to the dizzy heights apparently reached in Oxford and Cambridge.

It was typical of the systematic, organised way the CP set about things that the first thing it did when it found it had a student group on its hands was to set up some classes for us in Marxism. Our tutor was a friendly engine driver by the name of Crombie, who had a passion for engines and railways and a pawky (Scots for drily humorous) Scottish sense of humour. He was rather shy of the student 'intellectuals' he had taken on, but his tutorial technique was far in advance of anything the university had to offer. He did not expect us to swallow the given message whole but questioned us to draw out our own thoughts.

As important as the CP's education was our encounter with unemployment, poverty and slums at first hand. The young-sters in the Young Communist League with whom we went out selling *Daily Workers*, leafleting and collecting money, were nearly all unemployed working-class boys (with a few girls), although some had dead-end jobs, for example as message delivery boys. Most of them lived in the stone-built tenements in and around the old town, where whole families lived in one or two rooms with neither a toilet nor a bathroom of their own.

They were a bright bunch intellectually, keen to make up for their lack of education, but their health was not so good. I was shocked to discover that their leader, Cecil Thomson, a tall youth of 19 or 20, had lost all his teeth. Further discreet enquiry showed that Cecil, far from being the exception, was nearer the norm. Most of them had lost all or nearly all their teeth long before they were 21. When I was the editor of *The Student* I asked my friend Jim MacGregor, a newly qualified doctor with vaguely radical leanings (and a consuming passion in his own words for painting, reading, girls and booze) to describe his experiences in his first job as a 'locum' standing in for a coal company doctor in Fife. Jim came back full of admiration for the miners and their wives, but he rejected totally the facile argument that the undernourishment of the children was due to the ignorance of the mothers, for it was impossible to provide the food their families needed on the money they got. 'The root of the trouble' he wrote, 'is sheer degradation of poverty, filth and the uncertainty of employment ... Here is disease that no medicine can mend.'

'The Party'

I became a regular visitor at the Communist Party rooms in Edinburgh's High Street, which were inhabited by a changing but invariably friendly and usually talkative population of men and women, mostly unemployed, who seemed to be there as much for a chat as for CP business. My patently middle-class manners, dress and accent did not seem to put them off. On the floor were piles of pamphlets, posters and unsold *Daily Workers*, which were taken on a sale-or-return basis and had to be sent back to London eventually. Stacks of Party banners were piled against the walls in the back room. Somebody, usually a man, would be painfully typing some document or correspondence with two fingers, and the duplicating machine would be running off badly typed and Roneoed leaflets in purple ink. There were dirty cups and saucers, teapots and a kettle on the table. It was an extraordinary mixture of energy and disorder, a condition not unlike that of my own workplace even now.

The newspapers told me that the CP and the *Daily Worker* were paid for by 'Moscow gold', but neither then nor later did I discover any signs of that precious commodity. When Herbert Morrison tried, as Home Secretary in Churchill's government in 1940, to find some evidence before suppressing the *Daily Worker* to substantiate his repeated allegations that it was financed by Russia, he drew a blank. He had to admit in a letter to the Labour MP Lees-Smith that 'we are quite satisfied that they are receiving sufficient financial support in this country to maintain the paper and the Party'. A bit of 'Moscow gold' would, in fact, have come in handy, for the CP was run on something less than a shoestring. As far as I can remember the only paid member of the staff in Edinburgh was Fred Douglas, the organiser, whose forte lay less in organisation than in holding forth with powerful lungs in a rich Edinburgh accent at The Mound on Princes Street and other open-air stances. Fred was a bit of a ranter, but he had a gift of repartee and folksy argument and I respected his integrity. He lived on the miserable Party wage which barely kept him above the poverty line. When I came to earn the Party wage in 1940 Barbara and I each had other sources of income. Fred and many of the full-time Party workers did not.

The other thing that impressed me was that there was no room in the Party for members who did not do some work for it. The Party never ceased to remind us that what distinguished the Communist Party from Labour or Social Democratic Parties was the CP's view of itself as a 'disciplined vanguard' of *active* members, in Stalin's words 'the party of a new type'. At the very least members were expected to distribute and to sell the *Daily Worker*, which had been banned by the newspaper whole-salers since its inception in 1931. The ban, damaging as it was to the *Worker's* sales, helped to cement the Party by involving its members in a task that could not be allowed to slide for a single day. This enabled the *Worker* to build up a most unusual relationship with its readers, who were not only its sellers but also its fund-raisers and 'legmen' – the people who supplied reports and tipped the *Worker* off about the scandals and disputes that were the very stuff of its industrial news. I was also struck by the fact that, whereas the Labour Party seemed to be essentially a vote-getting machine that came to life at election time, the communists believed in developing people's political and class consciousness through systematic political education and by participation in all the issues and grievances that affected their domestic and working lives. People rarely voted for the Communist Party but individual communists were prepared to stick their necks out and incur all the risks of victimisation and to do the donkeywork in community campaigns, and often won large personal followings.

Being a Communist Party member often entailed many other risks and sacrifices. Communists found it hard to get jobs when so many were out of work, and many had been victimised by employers for attempting to unionise the workforce. They were also the target of violence and intimidation by the police who put themselves out to protect the fascists. I organised the defence of Fred Douglas and other communists who were charged with breach of the peace at a fascist meeting held at The Mound in 1936. The police turned out en masse to protect the fascists' 'right' to preach Hitler's doctrine of unadulterated anti-semitism. The communists who protested, almost entirely by shouting and pushing, were arrested and Fred was so badly beaten in the police station that he had to be taken straight to hospital suffering from extensive cuts and bruises. No policemen were charged for this assault but Fred and half a dozen of his comrades were found guilty as charged by a Tory magistrate and fined. The magistrate was simply not interested in the defence evidence which showed, as one of the witnesses reminded me recently, that the fascists had provocatively sung the Nazi anthem, the 'Horst Wessel Song', and had used their loudspeakers to drown the voices of the anti-fascists at a peaceful protest meeting nearby organised by the Youth Peace Assembly. As far as the magistrate was concerned, the police could tell no lies, what happened in the police station was not the issue before the court, and nobody could believe the word of a communist. This sort of incident, reported continually in the communist and left-wing press, convinced me that the communists were the *only* group who felt strongly enough about fascism to resist it not only on paper and in speech, but on the streets of London and other cities where fascists were terrorising Jews and others for whom the police showed little or no concern.

Reforming the University

Inside the university I felt an irresistible urge to push what seemed to me to be a moribund, self-satisfied and reactionary institution into attitudes more appropriate to the middle of the twentieth century. The process was great fun, but the immediate results were meagre in the extreme. I floated the idea that instead of electing retired Tory generals and such like to the post of Lord Rector, the Chairman of the University Court, the students should elect one of their own number. Another 25 years passed before Edinburgh elected Gordon Brown as its first student Lord Rector. We persuaded the Students' Representative Council (SRC) to set up a Reform Committee (known as 'the committee to reform everything') of which I became chairman. It produced a series of constructive reports, none of which look very radical today, which the university authorities resolutely declined to discuss with us. We proposed, for example, that instead of segregating men and women students in separate University Unions there should be one Union offering a wide range of facilities for all students and staff. A single Union for men and women was opened 37 years later. We attacked the meanness of the University Grants' Committee which consistently underfunded Scottish universities by comparison with the English universities – a £29 grant for every Edinburgh student, but £42.25 for every Liverpool student, to take a typical example. Sir Thomas Holland, the Principal of Edinburgh University, smugly asserted in reply that the English universities were far behind, and were only 'catching up' with the Scottish universities.

We attacked the university's disintegrated concept of higher education. We saw the Arts faculty as little more than a factory for the mass production of pass degrees, which were obtained by passing exams in a series of totally unrelated subjects. Arts students were required to take one science subject, but learned nothing about what we would now call ecology, or interrelatedness, or about scientific method or its application in other fields. Students were left in almost total ignorance of

Scottish life, history or culture. Science students were separated physically and culturally from Arts or medical students and barriers were erected between the different branches of science. The medical faculty turned out doctors ignorant of general practice and of the social and economic causes of the symptoms that they were expected to treat, and who had little grounding in preventive medicine, nutrition or public health. We urged, without success, a radical rethinking of these courses and the ending of compulsory lectures, against which students in every faculty were in revolt, and the introduction of a real tutorial system. In *The Student* I also attacked the class nature of the university, drawing attention to the fact that only 2 per cent of the 18–21 age-group in Scotland were then getting any higher education.

Our one real success was to open the men's Union's debates to women, in the teeth of strenuous resistance from the Union committee and its supporters who were centred in the medical faculty and the Rugby Club. The University Union Debates attracted meagre audiences because they debated puerile subjects. My agitation on this issue would not have succeeded had it not been for the tact, popularity and diplomatic skills of David Pitt, a medical student from Grenada who was the first black to be elected a Vice-president of the Students' Representative Council. The mixed debates we initiated under his chairmanship attracted large audiences. Barbara contributed the shortest speech in the first debate to which women were admitted, on the legalisation of abortion, by telling a story about the woman who wanted an abortion and attributed her innumerable pregnancies to the fact that 'it's me 'usband's only 'obby'.

David, better known today as Lord Pitt, scored 'firsts' as a black in British life throughout his career, becoming a Labour Chairman of the Greater London Council and in 1985 the President of the British Medical Association, but his popularity could not obscure the fact that colour prejudice was rampant in the university at that time. When the *Daily Express* gave space to a student's demand that 'coloured' students should be barred from the university the SRC passed a unanimous resolution asserting 'a complete lack of any colour bias' at Edinburgh University. David's own view, expressed in an article in *The Student*, was that 'a most unfriendly welcome' awaited the coloured student who came to Edinburgh.

Student Editor

When I was first asked to edit *The Student* I refused, because I had accepted an invitation to represent the Scottish National Union of Students (NUS) in a debating tour of the Canadian universities with a student from the English and Welsh NUS from October to December 1936. However, when pressed hard to take it on I found an acting editor for the autumn term in the person of Andrew McLaren Young, a gloriously indolent but talented student of Art History who was too lazy to graduate, but nevertheless became in due course Professor of Art History at Glasgow University, and one of the first to recognize the architectural genius of Charles Rennie Macintosh. With the help of a small group of rebellious students (of whom Barbara Stebbing was the only communist) we turned *The Student* into a campaigning journal. We concentrated on university issues and grievances but offered some scope to student writers and poets while taking up wider political and social issues as well. We ran what could be called, not unreasonably, a vendetta against Sir Thomas Holland, the Principal, but when I re-read these pieces today I marvel at the mildness of our comments. Although undeniably tactless they actually understated the case against his blinkered and dictatorial attitudes.

The atmosphere in which we were working can be gauged by the fact that a storm broke out in the Scottish press over a little play called *The Isles of Greece*, written by John D. Scott, who later won a reputation as an official historian, on the theme of a girl student's frustrated crush on another girl in one of the university women's hostels. The word 'lesbian' was not used, and anything less sexually explicit could hardly be imagined, yet Ivor Davies, who combined the roles of Liberal student leader and born-again Christian, denounced the play as 'filth written to satisfy the cravings of a diseased mind' and initiated a 'scandal' in the press by threatening to report us to the Chief Constable. John Scott retorted by admitting that *The Student* was edited by a committee that included the Marquis de Sade, Sigmund Freud, Lady Chatterley's lover, Karl Marx and Francois Rabelais. As for the editor:

It is obvious where his sympathies lie
He reads the *Daily Worker* and wears a red tie.

It was our articles on Spain that provoked the stormiest correspondence. David Mackenzie, an Edinburgh student who had been among the first to volunteer, had rushed to the decisive Madrid front in the autumn of 1936, and wrote a firsthand account for me when he came back. We followed this up with articles on the blatant intervention by Nazi fascist troops from Germany and Italy, the bombing of Guernica, and the reactionary role of the Catholic Church. We also published a chorus of protests from Catholic Tories who regarded the Spanish War not as a revolt against a democratically elected government, but as a holy crusade against atheistic communism that justified the most ferocious repression. Outside Catholic and Tory circles the Spanish Republic was a popular cause but our caustic references to the coronation of King George VI in May 1937 gave far more offence than anything I wrote about Spain. A satirical piece by me called 'King Colorbar's Coronation', which described the coronation of a black king who denied his white subjects any democratic rights, was thought to be particularly outrageous. I was also foolish enough to enrage some of our liberal allies by the ferocity of our attacks on the fund-raising Charities' Week as a form of licensed student hooliganism.

The price I paid for my sectarian tendency to hit out too often at all and sundry was that the Students' Representative Council, while according me unfettered freedom of expression as editor, rejected my recommendation at the end of my term that Andrew Young should succeed me. Ivor Davies, the 'Liberal' scourge of lesbians and freethinkers, took my place. We may have won the arguments, but we lost the battle. It took me another 20 years to learn the lesson that if one's purpose is to get things done (which it was) it can be self-defeating to shout disagreeable things at the top of one's voice at everyone with whom one cannot see eye to eye.

3

Why Communism? Hitler, Abyssinia, and Spain

It is not very difficult to understand why the Communist Party and its Marxist theory had so great an appeal to people like me in 1935 and 1936. It seemed to offer almost everything I was looking for in a desperate situation. Hitler was crushing democracy and the working-class movement in Germany. Mussolini had destroyed democracy and crushed the working-class movement in Italy, and was embarking on a programme of imperialist expansion in Africa. The British ruling class faced no serious opposition in Parliament and seemed determined to collaborate with the Nazi and Fascist governments, with the apparent aim of deflecting their aggression away from the Empire and towards the one socialist country, the Soviet Union. The Labour Party had begun to recover from its crushing defeat in 1931, but only made a very limited advance in the general election of 1935. It seemed far more concerned with purging its ranks of members who wished to set up united movements against fascism than with mobilising the latent strength of the Labour Party and the trade unions. Capitalism seemed unable to offer any path of escape from the appalling Depression, and it did not begin to recover until it was given the stimulus of rearmament followed by war.

I would not dispute for a moment that we held an over-simplified view of both world and domestic politics, but then so did everybody else. Our simplified view had the merit that it pointed clearly to what proved in practice to be the only way to defeat Hitler – the organisation of the entire spectrum of anti-Nazi forces on an international scale from the communists on the left to anti-Nazi Tories on the right. I identified myself at the time very strongly with the ideas of John Strachey, a former Labour MP who joined Oswald Mosley in setting up the New Party in 1931 to attack unemployment, but left Mosley when he went fascist. Strachey was the great populariser of the Marxist analysis of the capitalist system, in a series of books which received wide circulation, particularly after the Left Book Club (for which he served as a selector of books) was formed. Among the largest meetings I can remember in Edinburgh were United Front meetings addressed by Strachey and Sir Stafford Cripps. Strachey's brilliantly logical argument pointed irresistibly to the conclusion that capitalism had nothing to offer but fascism and war, and that the only alternative was communism – even if in the short term the immediate job was to form a popular front that would stop Hitler in his tracks and raise political consciousness to new levels.

The view that capitalism has run into a dead end is very unfashionable today – although I question whether an economic system that is destroying the natural resources that sustain life on earth has found the elixir of eternal growth – but it was widely held in the 1930s. To today's readers it may seem more difficult to understand why we did not recognise the seeds of communist degeneration in Stalinism, for they were obvious enough to some contemporary observers, of whom George Orwell is the outstanding example. I was only half-aware at that time of Orwell's profoundly misanthropic and pessimistic view of people and society, which led him to anticipate, in *Nineteen Eighty Four*, a future in which the human spirit would be totally defeated and left without a glimmer of hope. The same pessimism also led him to underestimate the appeal of Marxism (which as a self-styled anti-intellectual, he never bothered to study seriously) or the positive elements in world communism. I was fascinated when I read his collected writings many years later to find my feeling about Orwell's defeatism confirmed by his diary entry in March 1942 (when Hitler had sustained his first defeat outside Moscow) that 'the Comintern [the Communist International] has always been defeated by the Fascists; therefore we, being tied to them by a species of alliance, shall be defeated with them'.

However, all that came later. *The Road to Wigan Pier*, published by the Left Book Club in 1936, described communists and left-wingers, particularly 'intellectuals', in terms that I could not recognise. They revealed Orwell to be a weird kind of 'socialist' who shared every social prejudice cherished by the most diehard Tories. Was I supposed to recognise myself in his reference to 'astute young social literary climbers who are Communists now, as they will be Fascists five years hence because it is all the go'? Was I supposed to recognise myself in his vituperative references to the 'outer suburban creeping Jesus, a hangover from the William Morris period', or in 'the intellectual, tract-writing type of socialist with his pullover, his fuzzy hair and his Marxian quotation'? Was I 'the intellectual book-trained Socialist, who understands it is necessary to throw civilization down the sink and is quite willing to do so'? Was I part of that 'dreary tribe of high-minded men and women and sandal-wearers and bearded-fruit-juice drinkers who come flocking towards the smell of "progress" like bluebottles towards a dead cat'?

No Colonel Blimp could have been more sweeping in his execration of pacifists, internationalists, humanitarians, feminists, advocates of free love, divorce reformers, birth controllers, Quakers, 'sex maniacs' and atheists, to name but a few of those who figure in Orwell's hate list. He combined this hatred for people who had unorthodox or unfashionable views or habits with a patronising approach to the working class. In *The Road to Wigan Pier* he praised the working-class socialists and communists he met only because he declared them to be incapable of thinking intellectually: 'no genuine working man grasps the deeper implications of Socialism'. He never really grew out of the feeling, which he says he acquired in early boyhood, that working-class people were 'almost sub-human'. They could be warm, friendly and nice to meet: they could even 'improve their minds' provided they did not stop 'labouring with their hands'; but 'where "education" touches their own lives they see through it and reject it'.

I found the very opposite to be true, but Orwell concentrated his venom on the middle-class intellectuals, above all the communists, whose crime was to use their brains instead of their hands. Because we could not recognise ourselves in Orwell's distorted word-pictures we disbelieved much of what he said. After the publication of *The Road to Wigan Pier* I stopped reading his books, although I did read his weekly pieces in *Tribune* in the 1940s. I assumed that his tirades against Stalinism were as lacking in substance as his tirades against all the other objects of his Blimpish prejudices. In short, I and many others refused to take him seriously – and the fault was at least as much his as ours.

Stalin and the Popular Front

I experienced my 'conversion' to communism, to use Orwell's religious idiom, very differently from the way he perceived it. Take, for example, Orwell's claim that we were 'Stalinists' because we wanted 'a Fuehrer'. In 1935 I saw Stalin in much the same way as did those ageing Fabian leaders Beatrice and Sidney Webb in their book *Soviet Communism: A New Civilisation*? – a title from which they removed the question mark in 1937. That is, I saw Stalin at that time as a tough but able and far-sighted leader whose understanding of European politics and the Nazi threat was greatly superior to that of his capitalist contemporaries. Some of his speeches from those days still make good reading, notably the warning he sounded in 1931 in a prophetic speech to Soviet 'business executives' warning them that the Soviet Union had precisely ten years to make itself strong enough to resist the armed invasion he rightly anticipated. Stalin was bringing the 'Five Year Plans' to industrialise Soviet society to a triumphant conclusion, despite the devastation of the Soviet Union in the 1920s by famine, war and epidemic, the total absence of foreign capital and the hostility of the entire capitalist world. What attracted us was the revolution's success in unleashing the constructive potential of the Soviet peoples, and their readiness to accept severe hardship today for peace and prosperity tomorrow. Would Hitler have been defeated without the Five Year Plans?

Communists were undeniably deceived, and deceived themselves, about many aspects of the Soviet system and Stalin's role in it, but we did not flock into the Communist Party to worship a *Führer*. Had we done so we would not have flocked out again when it became incontestable that many of the accusations against Stalin, which we had dismissed as the lies and inventions of our enemies, were true.

In 1935 my hero, if I had one, was not Stalin but George Dimitrov, a Bulgarian communist. He had been working for the Communist International in Germany when the Nazi government charged him with burning down the *Reichstag*, an outrage which had served as the pretext in March 1933 for the unleashing of the Nazi terror. The trial of Dimitrov and others at Leipzig turned out to be a political and propaganda disaster for the Nazis because he had the courage and the skill to turn it into a trial of Herman Goering and his Nazi stormtroopers before a world audience. Dimitrov emerged a free man and became the Secretary of the Communist International, where he was the driving force behind the new Communist International strategy of co-operation with Social Democrats and other anti-fascists in a Popular Front. Ben Pimlott, the Labour historian, said in 1985 that the Communists' work for a popular front was merely 'dancing to Moscow's tune'. In fact the pressure within the Comintern for a popular front came from Dimitrov and the leaders of the French, Spanish and other Communist parties who were appalled by the Nazis' success in destroying the German Communist Party.

The importance of Dimitrov's fight not only lay in the proof it gave me that the Nazis could be exposed and defeated, but also that it was a communist who put a new spirit into the fight against them. Although Social Democrat and trade union leaders had legitimate complaints about the way communists had regarded them until the last minute as 'social fascists', the Social Democrats' performance after President von Hindenburg had appointed Hitler as German Chancellor in January 1933 had been shameful. They hoped, to the last, that some way could be found of leading a legal existence under the Nazis. They even called on their union members to take part in the Nazi May Day parade, for which Hitler rewarded them by contemptuously throwing them into his concentration camps. The communists at least tried to organise underground resistance. It was, paradoxically, the very courage of Dimitrov in the dock at Leipzig that made it impossible for me to believe in 1937 that old Bolsheviks, like Zinoviev or Bukharin, could have confessed to crimes of treason in the dock at the Moscow trials unless they were, in fact, guilty. Their innocence is beyond dispute – but their confessions still puzzle me.

It was above all the campaign for a united front of the working-class parties against fascism, and a broader popular front, launched by Dimitrov at the Seventh Congress of the Communist International in August 1935, that attracted me into the Communist Party. The Popular Front was already taking shape in France and Spain, with collaboration between Socialist, Communist and Liberal parties, but in Britain the Labour Party's anti-communist phobia was so strong that it was expelling Labour Party members who associated with communists in any group or activity, and published an ever-lengthening list of 'proscribed organisations' that no Labour Party member might join under pain of expulsion for doing so. The Labour Party even banned the Relief Committee for the Victims of German Fascism because the communists, as was so often the case, filled the vacuum left by Labour passivity and took the initiative in raising money to relieve the victims of the Nazi terror.

The winters of 1933–4, 1934–5 and 1935–6 saw hunger marches, mass demonstrations and riots on a scale unknown since the Chartist agitation of the 1840s which were twice successful in forcing the government to withdraw punitive scales of unemployment benefit. It was the communists who stepped into the breach and organised the unemployed when the Labour Party and Trades Union Congress (TUC) failed to do so. One might be forgiven when one hears Labour Party speakers today for thinking that the hunger marches were part of the Labour Party's history, yet Wal Hannington, Will Paynter and the other communists in the leadership of the National Unemployed Workers' Movement (NUWM) who fought for the unemployed did so in the teeth of continuous ostracism and sabotage by the official Labour and TUC leadership – even if many local Labour parties and trades councils gave magnificent support. George Orwell had to admit, in *The Road to Wigan Pier*, that 'the best work for the unemployed is being done by the NUWM' which he called 'a revolutionary organisation' under communist leadership whose activists, 'ragged and underfed', he 'greatly admired'.

The Pro-Fascist Alignment

I found the Labour Party's total reliance on parliamentary debates as a means of influencing government policy utterly frustrating. The victory of the 'National government' led by the renegade ex-Labour Premier Ramsay Macdonald had cut its representation to a rump of 50-odd MPs. In the absence of effective opposition inside or outside Parliament, even after the 1935 general election, the Communist Party's emphasis on the need to mobilise the people by extra-parliamentary agitation made good sense. Speeches in Parliament could not by them-

selves defeat the huge Tory majority or deflect the 'National
government' from its clear intention to harry the poor and the
workless and to help both the Nazi and fascist aggressors. In
March 1935 Germany had introduced military conscription
and embarked on a rearmament programme designed to
achieve the plan for conquest spelled out in Hitler's *Mein
Kampf*. France responded by signing the Franco-Soviet mutual
defence treaty in May, but the British government's policy right
down to August 1939 was to resist any system of alliances in
Europe that could deter the fascist powers, or defeat them if
they began a war. On the contrary, within two months of
Hitler's introduction of conscription Britain signed the Anglo-
German Naval Treaty, without even consulting France. This
allowed Hitler to build his submarine fleet up to 45 per cent of
the British level, or to 100 per cent in the event of danger from
the Soviet Union. The treaty was welcomed by the Labour Party
press, but the communist *Daily Worker* opposed it.

Worse was to follow. The cynical fraud of the 1935 general
election and the Tory government's betrayal of Abyssinia that
followed it were the most important formative experiences in
my early political life. It had been known since December 1934
that the Fascist government of Italy under Mussolini was preparing to invade Abyssinia (known today as Ethiopia) to add it
to the Italian colonial empire in north and east Africa. Yet in
April 1935 Ramsay Macdonald, in one of the last acts of his pre-
miership before being succeeded by Stanley Baldwin, met
Mussolini and the French Foreign Minister Laval at Stresa to
proclaim the 'Stresa Front' between them. One purpose of the
Stresa agreement was to shore up the existing order (including
fascism in Italy) in the Mediterranean, where Britain maintained the largest fleet with bases at Gibraltar, Malta and
Alexandria, but its main purpose was to give Mussolini the
green light to invade Abyssinia. He did so in June, confident in
the belief that Britain would neither close the Suez Canal which
it controlled (and through which all Mussolini's supplies
flowed) nor be a party to any serious sanctions by the League of
Nations to punish or defeat Italy's attack on a fellow member of
the League.

Britain, with its massive strength in the Mediterranean, held
the trump cards and Mussolini was hopelessly vulnerable had
Britain been willing to use its strength either to cut Mussolini's

supply line or to cut off the oil on which his Army and Air Force were totally dependent; but the British government's policy was to rearm to defend the Empire, while rejecting any common action against fascist aggression. To have declared its policy openly would have invited disaster in the forthcoming general election, after ten million people had voted for collective security through the League and for disarmament by international agreement in the League of Nations Union Peace Ballot in June 1935. A clear majority – 6³/₄ million – had voted for the use of force if necessary to restrain aggression.

Faced with such a formidable tide of opinion flowing against his policies, Stanley Baldwin, the Tory leader who had succeeded Macdonald as Prime Minister, decided (as he admitted a year later) to deceive the public about his rearmament plans and to present his government as totally committed to collective security. It was one of the most barefaced frauds in British political history, but one which the Labour Party failed to see through or to expose until it was too late. On the eve of the general election in September 1935 Samuel Hoare, the Foreign Secretary, made a sensational speech at the League of Nations, pledging Britain's 'steady and collective resistance' to aggression and to economic sanctions by the League against Italy for its breach of the covenant. The speech won almost unanimous support in the Labour, Liberal and Tory press (but not in the *Daily Worker*). The Tories won the election easily on the fraudulent promise to oppose aggression, and the Labour Party was only able to increase its share of the seats in the House of Commons to 154 out of 615.

Within three weeks of the Tory victory Hoare and Laval agreed to recommend a settlement by which Abyssinia (the victim) would cede half its territory to Italy (the aggressor) while Italy would be given control over the rest of Abyssinia. The leaking of this cynical deal, which broke every undertaking that Hoare had given to the League a few weeks earlier, released such a storm that Hoare was forced to offer himself as a scapegoat, and resigned, although it was the government as a whole that was responsible. However, the Hoare-Laval pact achieved its main objective: sanctions collapsed, Mussolini conquered Abyssinia, the League of Nations was fatally discredited – and Hoare was back in the Cabinet within six months.

The Abyssinian episode taught me that the Tory government

was dishonest and corrupt, and would exploit the people's patriotic and democratic instincts, and their dislike of fascism and war, to pursue selfish, imperialist objectives that had nothing to do with the 'national interest' with which the Tory Party identified itself. It taught me that the Labour Party was politically naive and very weak, for it was taken in by Hoare's transparently fraudulent speech. It taught me to trust the *Daily Worker* and to see the Soviet Union as the one consistent, unwavering supporter of the policy of collective security.

The Spanish War – and Orwell's Fantasies

If the Abyssinian betrayal was the decisive factor in my initial decision to move in a communist direction, the Spanish Civil War completely dominated my political life and thinking, and that of the entire Left movement, for nearly three years from July 1936. The victory in the 1936 election of the centrist Spanish Popular Front government (in which the Communist Party had at first no ministers) and the courage with which the Spanish workers, almost bare-handed defeated the rebellious generals' uprising three months later were an inspiration. It seemed obvious from the start that victory for the Republic in Spain could be a decisive defeat for fascism and for its war plans. Once again in Britain it was the Communist Party that was the first to sense the significance of the event, and to initiate intense political activity in at least three ways.

Communists were very active, although very far from alone, in the movements to raise money for medical aid and to relieve distress in republican Spain. They opposed from the very first the policy of non-intervention by which the British and French governments denied the Spanish Republican government its legal right to buy the arms it needed, even during the brief period between 28 August and 7 October 1936 when the Soviet Union formally observed it, and they took the lead in raising a volunteer force to fight in the International Brigade which saved Madrid in the last months of 1936 and the first months of 1937, despite the British government's use of the Foreign Enlistment Act to make it a crime to recruit volunteers in breach of the Non-Intervention Agreement. The British Communist Party organised 2,300 British volunteers, including many non-communists, who joined the International Brigade and suffered disproportionately heavy casualties. The Brigade members were used as 'shock troops', and were sent to defend the most threatened parts of the front or to take part in the most arduous offensives. In three days alone in the battle of Jarama in February 1937 the British Battalion lost all but 160 of its 500 men.

It is not generally realised, mainly because the most widely sold account of the Spanish War is Orwell's misnamed and misleading *Homage to Catalonia*, that the Independent Labour Party which Orwell joined sent only 40-odd volunteers to Spain (including Orwell). They served on inactive sectors of the front with units of the POUM (Workers' Party of Marxist Unity) which saw little real fighting. Like Orwell they saw their main task not as defeating Franco but as carrying through a revolution in the republican rear. When fighting broke out in Barcelona in May 1937 between Republican government forces and the POUM, Orwell, who had been wounded and was leaving Spain, sided with the POUM on the principle that he always supported 'the worker' against 'his natural enemy the policeman'. When the news reached the British Battalion of the International Brigade at Jarama it was greeted, as Bill Alexander its one-time commander recalls, 'with incredulity, consternation and extreme anger', for 'no supporters of the Popular Front Government could conceive of raising the slogan of "socialist revolution" when that Government was fighting for its life against fascism'.

It was Orwell's misfortune that he landed in the company of men who were undoubtedly idealists but had not the remotest idea of how to win the war, and that he completely misread the political and military situation. It led him to indulge in fantasies, such as his view that a republican victory would also lead to a form of fascism, and to spout pseudo-revolutionary slogans for the next two and a half years to justify his relentless hostility to any kind of popular front against fascism. The sheer political insanity – one might say treachery in the Spanish context – of Orwell's view at this time made it utterly impossible for me (or for anybody else who saw the only hope in unity against fascism) to listen to Orwell's legitimate criticisms of some aspects of the Communist Party's and the Comintern's activities, or to his revelations of the crimes of the KGB. He was in our eyes totally discredited.

Labour and Non-Intervention

After Abyssinia we had no illusions about the Tories, not excluding Churchill who leaned towards Franco until near the end of the Spanish War, but we still expected something better from Labour. Yet Labour initially backed the Non-Intervention Agreement between Britain, France, Germany, Italy, the Soviet Union and other powers on the pretext that it had to do so out of loyalty to the French Popular Front government whose Premier was the Socialist, Leon Blum. The truth, which was known at the time, was that non-intervention was forced on France by crude British blackmail. The Labour leadership rigged the Labour Party Annual Conference, held in Edinburgh early in October 1936 so that the non-intervention issue would be debated on the Monday, before the Spanish Socialist Party delegation arrived. The British government collaborated with the Labour leaders by holding up the Spanish delegation (which included a fiery young Scotswoman married to a Spaniard), so that they could not speak until the Wednesday.

Through this trickery the leadership carried the non-intervention policy on the Monday with the help of the big block votes cast by Ernest Bevin and other right-wing trade union bosses. We followed the proceedings almost word for word and I had never previously known such a sense of betrayal. When the Spaniards spoke two days later they swept the conference off its feet. The delegates, moved by bad consciences as much as by the passionate pleas of the Spaniards to be allowed arms to defend the Republic, forced Attlee and other Labour leaders to set off immediately for Downing Street, with promises to sit there until Italian and German breaches of the agreement were stopped; but it was not until July 1937 that the National Council of Labour finally abandoned its support for a policy whose sole purpose (in which it ultimately succeeded) was to strangle the Spanish Popular Front government.

Politics also helped to bring Barbara and me even closer together. At Liverpool, before I sailed for the Canadian debating tour, we decided to get married. When I asked David Prosser for time off to get married, my reply to his not unreasonable enquiry 'Who is the lucky girl?' was 'A girl I know'. Barbara refused to have an engagement ring, which she regarded as a sign warning men that she was destined to become my property, and we told our parents that we were *not* 'engaged'. We got married in London on 2 April 1937, the date having been influenced by the fact that by getting married before 5 April we could claim a year's marriage allowance off our income tax after three days of married life. We were a practical couple as well as being idealists.

4

Sit-in Strike

It must seem odd given the strength of my detestation of the Labour Party's right wing that one of the first things I did when I returned to Inverness in December 1937 was to join the Labour Party. It would have been pointless to join the Communist Party, which only had two members, and to have done so would have caused terrible ructions in the family firm of Stewart, Rule and Co. Dad's principal partner, Colonel MacArthur, was a Tory who had to put up with the Scottish nationalism of Dad and my brother Robin. He could tolerate a Labour activist in the firm but would have drawn the line at a communist. Nor did I see anything inconsistent in being a Marxist and a member of the Labour Party, for there had always been Marxists in the Labour Party and I identified myself with the numerous members of the Labour Party who saw eye to eye with the CP on the major issues of war, fascism and unemployment. *The Daily Worker* was the voice of the CP, but it was also the daily paper of the Left. I was, if you like, a 'fellow-traveller'.

I would have been astonished if anybody had told me that within a year I would be elected a county councillor and adopted as a prospective Labour candidate for Parliament, for initially I had no political ambitions. I found myself catapulted into these positions mainly due to the accident that Barbara and I went to live in North Kessock, and found ourselves at the centre of a running battle between the people of North Kessock and the proprietor of the ferry that linked the village (and the Black Isle) to Inverness. My parents had bought Kessock House the year before, and we were able to buy the neighbouring gardener's cottage (called Braehead) which had a magical situation looking over Inverness, the Great Glen, the Beauly Firth and the mountains of Ross-shire.

The owner of the Kessock Estate and of the ferry rights was

William (otherwise Bunt) Macdonald, who thought he could make his fortune by introducing a car-carrying chain ferry to replace the old steamboat that had been condemned in 1935 by the Board of Trade. In the course of 1936 he bought three second-hand chain ferries, two from the Clyde and one from Cornwall. It was not really surprising that all three were lost at sea as it calls for a high degree of luck to tow a small chain ferry boat (which is merely a platform open at both ends designed for use in sheltered waters) up to 1,000 miles through some of the stormiest seas in the world. In February 1938, as the supply of second-hand ferryboats had run out, Bunt bought a large, second-hand car ferry in Holland. Its maiden voyage, to which he had invited all the notables (even me), was a disaster. As the Inverness harbour pilots had warned, the boat was too large to make a landing either at North Kessock or at the Inverness side, and had to beat an ignominious retreat into Inverness harbour, where Bunt said goodbye to his last hope of running a modern service at Kessock Ferry.

Victory at Kessock Ferry

In the meantime Bunt had kept the service going with a small, open motor boat, incapable of carrying livestock or carts, by which Dad and I commuted daily to Inverness, exposed as were all the passengers to the wind, the waves, the rain and the snow. For this appalling service Bunt charged fares well above those laid down in the Sheriff's regulations, and crammed twice as many people into the boat as the Board of Trade licence allowed. Only good luck averted a Kessock Ferry disaster.

The long-suffering residents of North Kessock and the Black Isle were clamouring for an end to the deprivations, dangers, miseries and loss of trade inflicted on them for two years. The North Kessock Watch Committee, of which Dad was a prominent member and to which I was soon co-opted, had turned the issue into a public scandal in the local and Scottish press. By 1938 the situation was one of complete deadlock, and the public authorities had done nothing either to put a stop to Bunt's criminal and dangerous behaviour or to provide an alternative service. The Watch Committee wanted Inverness Burgh Council and Ross and Cromarty County Council to buy and run the ferry, but even after the fiasco of the 'maiden voyage' the local authorities were reluctant to act. So, in November 1938, the Watch Committee organised what was probably the world's first sit-in strike in a ferry boat. We tendered the regulation fares for season tickets, Bunt's men refused to issue them, we refused to budge, and Bunt refused to sail. Cars took the commuters the 24 miles to Inverness while a handful of us, fed with coffee and sandwiches by villagers, sat in the boat all day. Bunt won an interim interdict (a Scots Law injunction) in the Sheriff Court ordering us not to run the rival service we laid on, but he had to cave in after a week. He was prosecuted on seven charges, found guilty on all of them and fined a derisory £10, but we had established the principle that the owner must provide the service prescribed by the regulations.

The publicity attracted by these events had two entirely unexpected consequences. One was that when the the Watch Committee decided to contest the county council elections due in December 1938 I found myself regarded as the obvious candidate. Although well-known by then as a Labour man I stood as an Independent with a wide spectrum of support, and defeated the son of a local landowner, Richard Fraser-Mackenzie of Allangrange, by 321 votes to 265. Almost at the same time the prospective Labour parliamentary candidate for Ross and Cromarty resigned. The invitation to take his place came out of the blue, and within days of being elected a councillor I was adopted as the prospective candidate.

At my first meeting of the Ross and Cromarty County Council, just before my twenty-seventh birthday, I was appointed to the Kessock Ferry Joint Committee, which soon recommended that the ferry should be acquired and run jointly by Ross and Cromarty and Inverness councils. The county council approved the recommendation by a majority of four votes in July 1939. The outbreak of war made it impossible to commission a new boat, but after the war the authorities ran an admirable service with a series of modern boats until the Ministry of Transport bridged the crossing in 1982. The Kessock Ferry drama had almost as big an effect on me as my bike crash, for it involved me in what would now be called 'community politics', led to a short but invaluable spell in local government, raised my political profile and taught me a political lesson that proved highly relevant in Exmoor nearly 40 years later – that consensus often has to be fought for by confrontation: the authorities would not listen to the people of Kessock until we had resorted to confrontation and 'illegal' action.

County Councillor

The county council was 'non-political' but essentially conservative in outlook, with a membership dominated by the larger farmers and landowners, a minister of religion or two, and others less easily classified. The only Labour councillors came from the Hebridean island of Lewis. The chairman, Major Stirling, was, almost inevitably, a landowner. The councillors' overriding purpose was to keep expenditure down to a minimum, and thereby to keep the rates as low as possible. Unanimity was achieved when the different factions (including me) banded together to demand more money from the government, and to condemn the feeble policies for Highland development which it announced in the summer of 1939. The county of Ross and Cromarty was a wholly artificial creation whose boundaries looked as if they had been drawn up by an official who had never visited the Highlands. The Lewis councillors, separated from the mainland by a stormy overnight sea crossing, only visited the mainland for meetings, and the mainland councillors rarely visited Lewis. In between the quarterly meetings there was virtually no council business for the ordinary members unless they were, like me, restless busybodies who pried behind the doors where the work of the council went on.

The county council had a very small permanent staff, even the County Clerk (nowadays the Chief Executive) being a part-time Dingwall solicitor who, as I discovered from firsthand experience, used his position to promote the interests of his private practice and his clients. The council had no offices worthy of the name. The Medical Officer of Health had a small temporary hut dating back to the 1914–18 War. A penny rate only raised £700. Major Stirling told the Education Committee at my first meeting that the council could not afford one eighth of a penny on the rates to provide two essential classrooms at Ullapool School. He wanted a cut-price, temporary job. I described this as 'penny-wise, pound foolish', and urged the committee (unsuccessfully) that it would be cheaper in the end to put up a building that would last. That, however, was not the Ross and Cromarty way.

Not only was the full-time council staff cut to the bone, but wages were depressed to the lowest possible levels. The council, far from being a model employer, was one of the worst. The county roadmen had arduous labouring jobs in all kinds of weather, often on exposed hill roads. They suffered from 'broken time' as their nine-hour shifts were spread over twelve hours or more, but they were only paid for the nine hours, and then only at eleven pence an hour, or little more than £110 a year before stoppages – and even that was paid monthly. I argued for minimum wage legislation, because wages in the Highlands were often below subsistence level. I had one case in which a man with a large family, earning £2 a week, was refused a grant of clothing to enable him to send his children to school, although it was admitted that he was below the poverty line, on the ground that it would open the door to too many claims. I failed to persuade the council twice in 1939 to accept the roadmen's claim for another penny an hour and fortnightly payments, and although I succeeded in December, the war had by then inflated prices and depressed their real wages even further.

Agent For the Poor – and the Rich

Nobody had given very much thought to what I would actually do when I took up Dad's offer of a job in the family law firm. The pay of £3 a week was pitched about as low as it could have been, but as Barbara had an income from her investments of twice as much we were relatively well-off. As there was no office to spare for me I was housed in some style in the grandly-named 'board room', a big room with an immensely long table that was used from time to time for meetings of the directors of the companies managed by the firm. Their exotic names (The Deltenne (Ceylon) Tea Estates, Sutherland Trading and Transport Company, Hamilton's Auction Marts, The Highland Bus Company, The Balkan Trading Company, British Gazogenes and many others) made an imposing show on the brass plates outside the front door, and no doubt inspired confidence in the world-wide scope of the business transacted inside.

I did some company work, including a reorganisation of the tea company after some Mincing Lane tea brokers had been called in to rescue it, and picked up some useful knowledge about company law and the hazards and profits of private enterprise, but within days of starting work in January 1938 I found that most of my time was going to be spent working without fee for poor clients. I was appointed by the Inverness Faculty of Solicitors to be one of the 'agents for the poor'. At that time neither England nor Scotland had any statutory system of legal aid supported out of public funds, but in Scotland the local Faculty of Solicitors used to appoint one or more of their members to defend 'poor' people on criminal charges, to give a certain amount of legal advice, and to initiate or defend law suits in matrimonial and similar cases.

The Inverness faculty appointed me precisely because the older men had done their turn, while I was the youngest and least experienced solicitor in town. This was bad luck for those who needed a solicitor, although no doubt better than nothing. Much of my time was spent helping unmarried mothers to compel the alleged fathers of their children to support them. The men, almost invariably young and badly paid or unemployed, were trying to dodge the consequences of their sexual relations, whether these took the form of genuine love affairs or casual copulation. When it came to the point most of them admitted paternity, but the mothers were only awarded a shilling or two a week and it was difficult to get the men to pay.

There were times when I would much rather have been conducting the prosecution than the defence. One of my 'poor' clients was an habitual wife-beater and salmon poacher who promised me two fine salmon if I got him off on a charge of beating his wife. I lost, and was saved the embarassment of having to refuse the salmon. At other times it was difficult to know what to make of the law, or the client, and I found myself involved with clients who really needed psychiatrists or social workers. Stewart, Rule and Co.'s clients ranged right across the social spectrum, from free-riding poachers and careless or trusting girls at one end, to Lord Lovat at the other.

Politics only intruded occasionally, as in the case of Mark Cymbalist, a communist tailor from the East End of London who sold new and second-hand clothes in the poorer end of the town. Mark complained that he was being harassed by the police, and as I thought that the police might have suspected him of trading in stolen goods I went to see Chief Constable Nevile to ask him why the police were harassing him. Nevile listened to me politely enough, and when I had finished said 'Don't you know, the man's a communist?' This told me two things: the first was that Cymbalist was being persecuted for his politics (and probably for his Jewishness); the second was that MI5 or the Special Branch did not seem to have noticed the Edinburgh University branch of the Young Communist League, for if it had, Nevile would surely have been alerted not only to Cymbalist but also to me. The harassment stopped however, and Nevile was eventually exposed as the corrupt policeman he undoubtedly was, and sacked.

At the other end of the social scale I found myself assisting Dad to draft Lord Lovat's marriage contract, which gave me further insights into the working of the capitalist system and the problems of the landed gentry. In June 1938 the young Lord Lovat, who had recently inherited the title, announced his engagement to Rosamund, the daughter of Sir Delves and Lady Broughton of Nantwich. Their marriage in the autumn was a major event in the social season, and it was followed by a tremendous reception when 500 tenants and others were entertained to luncheon in a marquee set up in the grounds of Beaufort Castle. The essence of aristocratic marriage contracts, as I had observed as a law apprentice in Edinburgh, seemed to be that the bride acquired title, status and a country seat, while the bridegroom recouped the family fortunes. Negotiating the Lovat contract seemed to me rather like negotiating an international treaty in which the lofty purposes of the high contracting parties sit uneasily with the tough practical clauses that follow. Sir Delves proved distinctly sluggish in coming up with the cash required to set Lord Lovat up as a Lloyd's 'name', but to everybody's relief he stumped up in time.

5

Moscow and Munich

Like many other left-wingers in the 1930s Barbara and I were determined to go to the Soviet Union to see the new socialist society ('the first stage of communism') for ourselves. The contrast between the Soviet Union's call for a united front against fascism and Chamberlain's policy of appeasement was becoming starker day by day. When Hitler annexed Austria in March 1938 Chamberlain rejected Soviet proposals to concert action in support of Czechoslovakia as 'inopportune'. His response to Franco's victory in Aragon, which cut Republican Spain in two, was to sign the Anglo-Italian Mediterranean Pact, which acquiesced in Mussolini's forces remaining in Spain until Franco won the war. Our enthusiasm for communism was given an immense stimulus by the news seeping out from China of the extraordinary successes of the Chinese Communist Party, led by Mao Tse Tung (to use the old spelling), in building rural Soviets, and winning over the peasantry to resist the Chinese warlords and the invading Japanese armies. The Left Book Club's publication in 1937 of Edgar Snow's classic *Red Star over China*, with its inspiring story of the Red Army's 2,000-mile 'long march', convinced us that in the end communism must win in China too.

When Barbara and I sailed for a four-week trip to the Soviet Union on 21 August 1938 in the Soviet ship SS *Djerzinsky* we underestimated the seriousness of the impending Czechoslovak crisis. I doubt if we would have sailed on a boat that had to pass through Germany by the Kiel Canal if we had thought that we might be trapped in Germany in a Soviet ship on the outbreak of war. As it was, the passage through the Kiel Canal was a chilling reminder of the European reality as we woke up to see swastika-clad Nazi Army officers strutting on the quayside, but what struck us most was the contrast between the

47

overbearing manner of the Nazis and the simple uniforms and comradely ways of the Russian crew.

I wrote a letter home from Leningrad reporting that the six-day trip on a Soviet-built ship had been 'an object lesson in practical comradeship'. There was 'a very pleasant atmosphere on board between passengers and crew, and between members of the crew – no bossiness, no servility, but good service all the same'. The crew neither expected nor received tips, and wore no badges of rank (these were the days before Stalin reintroduced epaulettes and all the other paraphernalia of rank) so it was hard to say at first glance who were the officers and who the ordinary seamen. The second wireless officer was a young woman, something that neither trade unions nor employers would have allowed on a British ship. The crew worked a seven-hour day in shifts, and we could see for ourselves that the stewards who served us worked much shorter hours than the British stewards who had worked 15 to 17 hours a day on my voyages to and from Canada two years before. There was a club room astern, where the crew went when off duty for recreation and education. The crew, I wrote, 'enjoy splendour amidships in cabins the same as the first class', much better equipped than our third-class cabins, in contrast to the universal practice elsewhere of packing seamen into the forecastle. While the first-class passengers had better cabins than the second- and third-class passengers, it was a classless ship as we all used the same public rooms and decks and ate the same food – which was very good indeed.

Limbless in Moscow

At a personal level the trip was something of a disaster for both of us. I slipped in the bathroom of the New Moscow Hotel while hopping on one leg to the bath, and crashed the stump of my amputated leg onto the marble floor. The pain was as bad as anything I'd experienced and I thought I must have fractured the bone. A doctor was sent for and prescribed some pills to relieve the pain. 'Take one, or two, or more' the interpreter told us, and as the first pill had no effect I took a second, a third, and then a fourth, after which I passed out and to Barbara's consternation remained out for 24 hours. When she checked on the prescription she discovered that the doctor had actually said: 'Take one, or two, but on no account more', although why, in that case, he had given us more than two pills we could not fathom. I had to get around Russia on crutches after spending two days in bed, and when I got back an X-ray confirmed a fracture.

Crutches severely limited my walking range, which was already restricted by the overpowering heat of Moscow's hottest summer for 60 years, but my disablement did enable me to get a glimpse of the Soviet health service from the inside when Intourist gave us the free use of a car to take us to a limb-fitting centre to get some crutches. The centre was overcrowded, its equipment simple and the limbs were not up to the standard of the British limbs which were then (but not now) said to be the best in the world. As Britain had no public limb-fitting services before the introduction of the National Health Service in 1948 the mere existence of such a facility was evidence that the Soviet Union was introducing the first national health service in the world.

Russia, on the Webbs' figures, had less than one doctor for 7,000 people before the revolution. The Russian Soviet Republic was aiming at one doctor to 1,000 people, and by 1935 it had already achieved a level of one doctor to 2,000. There were by then 52 schools of medicine compared to six before the revolution. In all probability few of the limbless people crowding the centre would have been able to get a limb in pre-revolutionary times, and certainly not one fitted free. When we visited the motor works in Moscow and Gorki what impressed us far more than the factories – which were examples of American technology built with the help of American engineers – was the enormous scale of the factories' educational and literacy programmes and the service provided by the factory health centres. The factory doctors and nurses were responsible not only for industrial health and injuries, but for promoting the health and welfare of the workers and their families. They gave antenatal care to mothers, and provided creches for the babies of working mothers. The Webbs recorded that the Stalingrad tractor works, which we also saw, employed 110 doctors.

Down the Volga

We were more concerned at the time about our own health than about the Russians'. I was on crutches and Barbara had a recurrence of severe ulcerative colitis. This condition was quiescent when we arrived in Leningrad, and we set out on a four-day trip down the Volga from Gorki to Stalingrad in good spirits. This was in many ways the most rewarding part of the trip, for here were all the outward signs of unchanging, traditional Russia – the small horse-drawn carts, the wooden houses, the men in their Russian blouses and trousers tucked into their boots, and the women in homespun clothes with headscarves.

At every landing stage, whether for cities like Kuibyshev or Ulianovsk (Lenin's birthplace) or rural stops in the back of beyond, peasant families would arrive on foot or in carts with chickens and sacks containing their worldly possessions. The stevedores on the city wharves indulged in harmless horseplay when the gaffers were not looking, but had to carry everything on their backs and clearly belonged to the pre-industrial age from which Russia was emerging. As the boat weaved its way among the sandbanks we understood why the interpreter at the exhibition on the Volga that we had seen in Moscow (which showed the plan to harness the river by a succession of dams for flood control, irrigation, electricity generation and navigation) had ended her presentation by saying: 'and so it was decided, by the Party and the government, completely to reconstruct the Volga'. The 'reconstruction' had already been begun by the opening of the impressive Moscow–Volga canal, the Moscow port of which we had already seen. The idea that 'reconstructing' the Volga might have harmful ecological consequences never occurred to us, or for that matter to the Soviet government, but the Volga is now reported to be in a critical condition as a result of damming and water abstraction.

The boat, in marked contrast to the Baltic vessel, was most emphatically a two-class affair. It reflected a continuing gulf in 'the first or socialist stage of communism' between the habits and living standards of ordinary working folk and the conditions expected by professional people, engineers, government or Party officials and, of course, the curious Intourist foreigners. The second class, the great majority, were packed into the front of the boat, with very little shelter from the weather (which was superb), and seemed to have a very good time with endless tea-making and singing to the accompaniment of mouth organs and accordions. These were not the miserable Russians of anti-Soviet propaganda. By contrast, the Intourist and other first-class passengers – mainly Russian families on holiday with their extraordinarily well-behaved children – had comfortable cabins and excellent food in the restaurant, and they could spend the entire day leaning on the rail and letting Russia slip by.

The boats, shallow-draft vessels with an imposing superstructure built in Austria-Hungary before the First World War, were delightful, but the appalling condition of the toilets was Barbara's undoing. There was shit everywhere and it seemed to be nobody's business either to clean the toilets or to educate passengers or crew in hygiene. The revolution might have provided factory health centres and more general health care, but it was clearly up against the Russian backwardness against which Lenin and Stalin had railed. Barbara, who had already had one mild bout of dysentery in Leningrad was taken really ill and had to spend an entire night running from our cabin to and from the disgusting WC. We were rather a miserable pair when we got to Stalingrad, one hopping and one running. There we saw a doctor who prescribed some medication that helped to stop the dysentery and the bleeding.

Soviet Impressions

Whatever our personal misfortunes, our experiences convinced us that the Soviet Union had made remarkable advances in industry and in the social services in the previous ten years, and that it had only been able to do so because the majority of the people were behind the regime and proud of its achievements. The Soviet Union seemed to be creating the industrial base for a more caring, socialist society, and had a far more enlightened approach to social services than its capitalist counterparts. The first two Five Year Plans were an inspiration to people all over the world who were appalled by the failure of *laissez-faire* capitalism in the great slump that followed the Wall Street crash of 1929. Here, for the first time, a great nation was planning the use of its human and material resources, and carrying the plans out. Our trip also gave us a real feeling for the Russian people, who no longer featured in our minds as slogans, posters or statistics, but as human beings. Up to a point it is true to say that we saw what the government wanted us to see, and that we saw things through red-tinted spectacles, but we were nearer the mark in our assessment of the Soviet

Union than those who were proclaiming its political, social and industrial weakness.

Some people who went out with us returned disillusioned. They had expected to see some sort of workers' paradise but we had no such illusions. We had read widely about Russia and not only from Stalinist or communist sources. We knew we were seeing the painful birth of a new era taking place in the ruins of the past, not a mature socialist society. Some visitors never recovered from the shock of the general air of decay which was particularly noticeable on the bus drive from the Leningrad docks to the superb city centre – the broken and chipped stucco, the unpainted woodwork, the poorly repaired streets and the inferiority of Russian clothing to our own. We attributed this – on the whole correctly – to the diversion of resources to industrialisation, the new social services and defence preparedness. We were impressed by the health and happiness of the children, the crowded cafes, the new blocks of flats springing up in the suburbs of Leningrad and the astonishing scale of new construction in Moscow, which had a tremendous sense of vitality. We were horrified by the plans for the new Palace of Soviets proposed for Moscow (a monster of 1,000 feet or so to be surmounted by a 300-foot statue of Lenin for which the site was already being excavated) not least because it consumed resources badly needed elsewhere. It was stopped by the war, and never built.

We shut our eyes to the signs of Stalinist megalomania which the Palace of Soviets expressed, partly because we could not *see* the Stalinist terror, and partly because we were more impressed by everyday occurrences. Barbara and I visited a People's Court in the company of a Soviet lawyer, and I certainly found the informality and directness with which the three elected judges – a lawyer with two lay assessors deciding cases by a majority – tried to find out the truth about commonplace disputes or crimes in many ways preferable to our adversarial procedures. It was refreshing to see worker-judges sorting out the problems of their own people, instead of the middle- and upper-class magistrates or judges we knew in Britain passing judgment on working people whose lifestyle they did not share. We liked the impeccably clean and tidy parks (which the public clearly respected as *their* property) and the newly literate Russians' unquenchable thirst for information.

Religion – and Self-Deception

Some visitors to Russia were put off by the Soviet attitude to religion, but my reading had convinced me that the Russian Orthodox Church (like the Roman Catholic Church in Spain and Latin America) had been one of the main instruments by which the ruling class maintained its grip by perpetuating ignorance and superstition and preaching subservience. The Webbs attributed the reaction against religion during the revolution, when land was seized and churches converted to secular uses, to the corruption and venality of the Orthodox Church ('Christianity at its worst') of which the Tsar was the autocratic head. The Church had been openly counter-revolutionary, and often unpopular. The Webbs described the wealthy monasteries as 'nests of miracle-mongering', and the village priests who told the peasants to sow and reap according to the calendar of saints' days as 'illiterate and grasping'. The Webbs also concluded that the excesses of the League of the Godless in the early days of the revolution had been severely curbed and that, although organised religion was still severely handicapped, believers were free to worship and were no longer persecuted. If the revolution repressed religion it also taught the churches in the Soviet Union to mend their ways.

We saw enough to satisfy ourselves that religious observances were certainly not forbidden, and that anti-religious propaganda was essentially rational and scientific. Just round the corner from our hotel in Leningrad, for example, old women and the occasional man could often be seen saying their prayers and kissing the stones of a shrine without arousing any interest whatever. We saw similar scenes in other cities. One could hardly miss the Anti-Religious Museum in Leningrad, for it was housed in St Isaac's Cathedral – a change of use comparable to turning St Paul's into a Centre for the Dissemination of Atheism. As I did not believe in God myself I was curious to see how atheism was presented in a cathedral whose rich interior, with its gold leaf and malachite columns, struck us as positively obscene and totally contrary to Christ's teaching of poverty – a point that the exhibition made by showing how the Church had squeezed its riches from the poor. There were exhibits exposing the fraudulent nature of the 'holy relics' in which the

Church traded and the absurdity of the superstitions (including the idea that the sun rotated round the earth) that religious mysticism fostered. These exhibits were still thought to be necessary in 1938 because 70–80 per cent of the population had been illiterate when the Communists took over in 1917.

I suppose that our most obvious failure lay in our inability, and in some ways our unwillingness, to probe beneath the surface of Soviet life. The surface can, of course, tell one a great deal. Visitors to Germany at that time could hardly fail to see the character of the Nazi regime as it was displayed by the storm-troopers, the swastika flags, the Hitler salutes, the anti-Jewish slogans, the closure of Jewish shops and the all-pervading atmosphere of jingoistic German nationalism. The emphasis in the Soviet Union, equally obviously, was over-whelmingly on the need for peace in which to complete the tasks of industrial and social construction of which the people themselves seemed to be immensely proud. Russians feared war; they did not want it.

However, we spoke no Russian so we relied on Intourist to lay on interviews and excursions and never met people who were either critics or victims of the Stalinist regime. We were conned (or conned ourselves) into accepting the official version of Soviet democracy. The Soviet state was, after all, only 21 years old; it had only known peace for 17 years, and throughout that time it had had to face the boycotts and hostility of almost the entire capitalist world. The obstacles it had overcome were immense and the Five Year Plans created the new industries without which the Soviet Union would have been defeated by the Nazis in 1941–2. The Soviet system had (and probably still has) elements of popular administration and justice, social control of resources and a socialist orientation in its domestic policies that helped to give the impression that a new form of socialist democracy was taking shape. It seemed reasonable to think that this would continue to develop if the economy grew stronger, conditions improved and external pressures eased. Perhaps because there are none so blind as those who do not wish to see, we failed to see the many signs that the system lacked the freedom of speech, press and opinion and the access to information without which no political system, capitalist or socialist, can correct its mistakes. We glossed over the hero-worship of Stalin, whose achievements and clear-sighted leadership we genuinely admired, while refusing to believe his detractors, and we could not have forseen the ultimate failure of the centralised command economy.

We did not question, in particular, the trials of the Bolshevik leaders, culminating in the executions of Bukharin and others, that did enormous damage to the Soviet Union and to its reputation abroad in 1937. We had no inkling of the terror that Stalin had unleashed, let alone of its scale. But the Soviet Union is a vast country and I was interested to learn from a TV programme by Charles Wheeler in September 1989 that many Soviet people were totally committed to Soviet reconstruction and unaware of the extent of the terror. It now looks naive, but, as the communists we knew were good people, unselfish idealists, the very kind of people who later formed the kernel of the anti-Nazi resistance in Europe, it was inconceivable to us that communist leaders could murder, torture and imprison their own Party comrades. Good communists seem, in fact, to have been Stalin's main victims. Moreover, people who knew Russia vastly better than we did had attended the trials and vouched for the authenticity of the confessions made publicly in the dock. We were not to know that the Webbs knew the truth about the trials and the use of torture but preferred to keep silent. We saw enough of the really enormous achievements of the Soviet Union, and of its everyday life, to know that the enemies of the Soviet Union were lying or mistaken about many things. It was not so unreasonable to think that they were lying or mistaken about the trials and the prison camps too.

The Czechoslovak Crisis

On our last days in Leningrad we heard for the first time that the simmering Czechoslovak crisis had been brought to the boil on 7 September by Hitler's ranting, hysterical speech at the Nazi rally in the Nuremberg Olympic Stadium. We had planned to spend our last morning in the Hermitage Museum, but no sooner had we arrived there than the air-raid sirens went and everybody was ordered to go down to the cellars. At first we thought that the war had begun, but before long we were told that it was only a realistic air-raid rehearsal. We emerged from the cellars several hours later, without having seen a single picture, to find air-raid wardens in gas masks washing down streets. We got back to London on 22 September, the day on which Chamberlain flew to Bad Godesberg for his second meeting with Hitler. Trenches were being dug in the London parks, gas masks were being issued and evacuation plans were being put into operation, and we returned to Inverness a day or two later in an almost hysterical atmosphere of war preparations.

The trench-digging and the gas masks were indeed part of a war of nerves, but it was directed against the British public, not Hitler. Without creating an atmosphere of imminent war Chamberlain could not have sold his deal with Hitler to the public nor presented himself in the guise of the saviour of the world, 'the man of peace'. This is not hindsight, for we had only to read the speech made by Maxim Litvinov, the Soviet Foreign Minister, to the League of Nations on 21 September, published fully only in the *Daily Worker*, to understand what Chamberlain was up to. The Soviet Government was ready to fulfil its treaty obligations to France and Czechoslovakia, and had already proposed an immediate conference between the Soviet, Czech and French general staffs to concert appropriate military measures. A few days later, when France had reneged on its treaty obligations at Chamberlain's instigation, the Soviet Union even undertook to stand by Czechoslovakia although the treaty no longer obliged it to do so. But on 21 September Litvinov also spelt out, nine days before Munich, the fact that Britain and France had *already* betrayed Czechoslovakia and taken steps 'which have led, and could not but lead, to a certain, large-scale war tomorrow'.

Litvinov knew, though we did not, that Chamberlain and Hitler had agreed at their first meeting on 15 September that the Sudetenland should be ceded to Germany, and that Chamberlain had undertaken to persuade France and Czechoslovakia to accept the dismemberment of Czecho-slovakia and the handing over of all its fortifications to Hitler. This was the betrayal that made war inevitable. Munich merely confirmed it. France presented no problem but Chamberlain had to deliver three ultimatums to Czechslovakia, each telling Czechoslovakia that if it did not yield up the Sudetenland on Hitler's terms it would be left to fight Germany alone. One of them was delivered to an exhausted President Benes in the middle of the night. When Chamberlain met Hitler for the second time on 21 September and told him that France and Czechoslovakia had both accepted his terms, he found that Hitler had characteristically raised his price. He wanted more territory, and he wanted it within a week. Chamberlain's response, of course, was not to turn against Hitler but to blackmail Czechoslovakia into yielding more.

The Munich Betrayal

I still find it hard to credit the readiness of the Labour and Liberal leaders in the House of Commons to believe that the cynical charade in which Chamberlain was engaged was a peaceful mission. When Chamberlain announced on 28 September that Mussolini and Hitler had agreed to meet him and Daladier at Munich the following day, his intention was already clear to those of us who read the *Daily Worker*. A.J.P. Taylor in his *English History 1914–45* records the scene in the House of Commons in these words: 'members rose to their feet, cheering and sobbing. Attlee, Sinclair the Liberal leader, and Maxton of the ILP [Independent Labour Party] blessed Chamberlain's mission. Only Gallacher, the communist, spoke harshly against it.' Gallacher's actual words were 'I would not be a party to what has been going on here ... and I protest against the dismemberment of Czechoslovakia.' The ILP, whose leader 'blessed Chamberlain', was Orwell's party. Churchill is said to have remained seated, and he did not utter a word, just as he never once voted against the appeasement he criticised. When the four-power conference met at Munich to put the formal seal of approval on the act of betrayal, neither Czechoslovakia nor the Soviet Union were invited or consulted. Czechoslovakia was merely told to send two representatives, to whom the conference's decision would be communicated.

Munich was the supreme moment of Chamberlain's career. He had secured Hitler's signature to a worthless piece of paper proclaiming 'the desire of our two peoples never to go to war with one another again'. He told the crowds 'it is peace in our time' and 'peace with honour'. He had begun to establish, he thought, a four-power anti-communist block in which Britain and France would in future work with the two fascist states,

Germany and Italy. The Soviet Union was blackballed: it was not eligible for membership of the exclusive Hitler-Chamberlain club, for the role assigned to it was that of enemy, not partner. In his 'New Year Message' three months later Chamberlain declared that 'no one would have dared to prophesy that the four great European powers would have advanced so far along the road to conciliation'. The Soviet Union, it will be noted, was not even regarded by Chamberlain as 'a great European power'. Munich was interpreted in Moscow as an anti-Soviet coup which robbed the Soviet Union of its French and Czechoslovak alliances, added immensely to Hitler's military and economic strength and opened the way for Hitler to realise his oft-proclaimed intention of expanding the Greater German Reich into Eastern Europe. The record shows that Chamberlain got Hitler off the hook. His generals were opposed to a war for which Germany was not ready, and had war come Germany could have been defeated. Stalin must have got the message that signing a non-aggression pact with Hitler was a game that two could play.

Unlike the majority who thought that Munich had lifted the shadow of imminent war, we on the Left saw it as a betrayal that made war all but inevitable. On returning to Inverness I organised a meeting to protest against Munich, at which I spoke alongside John McCormick, the Scottish Nationalist. The organisation of a non-party meeting annoyed the Labour parliamentary candidate for Inverness, Hugh Fraser, who was far more interested in defeating McCormick than in defeating Hitler, and John could not resist the temptation to blow his own party's trumpet by pointing out that not only had the Labour Party blessed Chamberlain's mission to Munich in advance, but that at least one Labour MP, Ernest Thurtle, had publicly blessed him on his return. My difficulty was that he was right and the Labour Party wrong. I was beginning to feel distinctly uncomfortable in the Inverness Labour Party, when Alex Mathieson, the stationmaster at Dingwall and chairman of the divisional Labour Party, asked me to become the Labour Party's prospective parliamentary candidate in Ross and Cromarty.

6

Phoney Peace to Phoney War

The pictures that come to mind when I look back on the time between Munich and the outbreak of the war eleven months later seem to have a surreal quality about them, as if several different people were remembering different things. I remember very well the strong intellectual, or political, conviction that war had become almost inevitable. Although peace hung by a thread and our hopes were repeatedly shattered by events Barbara and I were very, very happy most of the time. Kessock was a beautiful and friendly place in which to live, Barbara was busy transforming our little house and garden into a home of unforgettable joy and beauty, and from April onwards we were elated by Barbara's pregnancy.

She was determined to enjoy it despite the special risks that she ran on account of her diabetes and other health problems. In one of her letters to her sister Hilary she describes how a terrific struggle with an intimidating maternity corset reduced us to hysterics:

It does up down the back, with yards and yards of tape, I suppose to allow for the Growing Figure – but if it's really all necessary I shall be giving birth to an Elephant at least. Malcolm has to go outside the bedroom and into the passage in order to get the two ends equal

– a problem illustrated with a sketch of Barbara in her corset hanging on to a chair, and grinning broadly, while I stand yards away pulling on the tapes. She made endless fun of the sillier recommendations of the maternity 'experts':

One must NOT stretch up during pregnancy, apparently even to reach up to put a plate on a high shelf is quite fatal, and instantly ties the cord round the baby's neck so that it's strangled at birth ... Have you ever heard this? How do monkeys manage?

– this with a picture of a pregnant monkey hanging from a branch, or 'reaching up to it', with both hands. For both of us 1939 was at least as much 'the year of the baby' as the year of the war, although the expected baby also heightened our anxieties.

The ghastly news from Spain, in the final agonies of the civil war, broke through all our emotional defences. I can still see, as if it were yesterday, a picture on the front page of the *News Chronicle* one morning at the end of January 1939 of a crippled Spaniard, one of a long column of weary, hungry, broken refugees, hobbling over the frontier into France. That night I spoke at a crowded Labour Party meeting at Avoch, a little fishing village a few miles from Inverness. What struck me was the feeling that my sense of grief and anger was shared by the people who packed the hall. I looked up the file of the *Ross-shire Journal* recently and found that it estimated the attendance at 300 people, equivalent to half the adult population of the village and its immediate area.

Meetings of this kind convinced me that, although Munich was only three months behind us, the public was no longer swallowing the line that Chamberlain had brought peace by appeasing the fascists. Nevertheless appeasement continued. Chamberlain recognised Franco on 17 March, a month before the fall of Madrid. His treachery was completed by his failure to keep the promise he made at Munich to guarantee the integrity of what was left of Czechoslovakia, when Hitler seized Czechoslovakia on 15 March 1939 and with it the arms plants that supplied a third of the tanks with which he invaded France a year later. The Soviet Union, despite all the rebuffs it had received, immediately proposed a conference between Britain, France, the Soviet Union, Poland and Romania to concert appropriate measures, but Chamberlain rejected the suggestion as 'premature'.

Over Christmas and New Year we planned a winter campaign that had no precedent in Ross-shire outside election-time – four or even five meetings a week, to be held in every burgh and all the largest villages coast to coast. I found in the party chairman, Alex Mathieson the Dingwall stationmaster, a warmth of friendship and a breadth of political toleration that was lacking in the Inverness Labour Party. With his waxed moustaches and his immaculate uniform Alex exuded pride in the railway and in his job. He used the National Union of Railwaymen to create what amounted to a 'linear' party branch. When envelopes had to be addressed Alex sent them 'up the line' in the guard's van, to be addressed by the railwaymen, or more likely by their wives. We held nine meetings in midwinter in the first ten days, and another 14 in the next two months, most of them packed to overflowing. We followed this up with a summer campaign on the west coast in July and August when we held 31 open-air meetings in six days.

The German-Soviet Pact

Barbara and I were staying with her mother in Berkshire when the crisis broke with the signature of the German-Soviet Pact on 21 August, the Nazi invasion of Poland on 1 September and Chamberlain's declaration of war two days later. My first reaction to the news of the German-Soviet Pact was one of shock and disbelief. It shattered our world. I was revolted by the parade of Nazi emblems and the playing of the storm-troopers' 'Horst Wessel' anthem for the Nazi leaders in Moscow, and shocked by the obvious consequences. War was inevitable, for even if Chamberlain reneged (as I thought he might) on the guarantee he had given to Poland, Hitler would turn his forces against Britain and France and not, as the Right in these countries had hoped and planned, against the Soviet Union. The first outraged reactions showed that the unity of the Left was shattered beyond repair. The hope of forming a popular or united front against fascism lay in ruins.

I saw (and still see) the Soviet-German Pact as the bitterest fruit of Chamberlain's policy. His patent insincerity in the negotiations for a Franco-British-Soviet alliance in July and August must have convinced Stalin that no alliance with Britain was on offer. Chamberlain made no serious attempt to negotiate the military alliance with the Soviet Union without which his 'guarantee' to Poland was worthless. Although he negotiated directly with Hitler and Mussolini, he sent only 'a clerk in the Foreign Office' (Lloyd George's words) to Moscow. While Hitler's threats against Poland became daily more menacing Chamberlain's military mission took 19 days to get to Moscow by the slowest conceivable route – a slow, chartered steamer. When the mission arrived the Russians found that it had no authority to conclude a treaty. The Polish government refused to accept Soviet aid in any shape or form. Chamberlain, who never hesitated to threaten Czechoslovakia with the direst ultimatums to force compliance with Hitler's demands exerted no pressure whatever on Poland.

A.J.P. Taylor summarised the negotiations in his *English History 1914–1945* by saying:

> No alliance has been pursued less enthusiastically ... They did not at any time seek Soviet military aid in practical terms ... They were hoping all along to strike a bargain with Hitler ... and kept the door open for agreement. They ... thought of proposing a sort of Anglo-German economic partnership; Germany to be predominant in eastern and south-eastern Europe; a colonial condominium for the exploitation of tropical Africa; and a British loan to Germany of £1,000 million ... These projects were repeatedly aired to the Germans in the course of the summer ...'

Poland was in fact hopelessly ill-prepared for war, militarily, economically, and psychologically. The claims of its nationalistic generals that Poland could be defended without Soviet help turned out to be hollow boasts, and neither Britain nor France lifted a finger to implement their treaty promises to intervene militarily on Poland's side. It made headlines when the first British soldier was killed in France. The British government had neither war aims nor a credible war-winning strategy. It failed to mobilise industry, agriculture or labour or to capitalise on the anti-fascist mood in the country. Life was essentially 'business as usual'. Neither the Labour Party nor the Liberal Party would join a government dominated by the 'Men of Munich'.

If the British war effort was phoney, the French government made war not on the Nazis but on the communists and their sympathisers. It suppressed the communist newspaper *l'Humanité* even before war had broken out, and although the French Communist Party, like the British, supported the war at that time, the party was declared illegal on 26 September 1939. About half its 70 'deputies' (MPs) were arrested and the remainder went underground. Some 500 trade union organisations under communist leadership were dissolved. A hundred local councils were replaced by government commissioners. Deputies, councillors and others were herded with 15,000

Spanish republican and other anti-fascist refugees into concentration camps. Here, as the November *Labour Monthly* (a communist publication) pointed out, was 'unanswerable proof' that the war was not 'a war against fascism'.

When war was declared on 3 September my overriding feeling was one of immense relief. At last instead of endlessly appeasing the Nazis and retreating before them we were going to fight them. I agreed with the line initially taken by the Communist Party that socialists should support the war while trying at the same time to remove the 'Men of Munich' and turn it into a genuine 'people's war'. I enquired whether I could rejoin the Territorial Army artillery brigade from which I had been invalided out after losing my leg, but my inquiry was treated as an absurdity. The rejection of my initial impulse to take part in the fight against fascism helped to focus my mind on the character of the 'phoney war' which I had begun to question even before the British Communist Party denounced it on 6 October, on the instructions of the Comintern, as an 'imperialist war'.

The Soviet-German Pact: Was There an Alternative?

I soon came to the conclusion that the Soviet government, having been denied the anti-fascist alliance for which it had striven for years, had been left with no alternative but to buy space and time as best it could to enable it to repel any future Nazi attack. In the nature of things, it could hardly proclaim this strategy publicly. It seemed to me legitimate, if this was the purpose, to go through the motions of the diplomatic game, even if that involved flying the swastika at Moscow airport. As I could see no hope of ever defeating Hitler or sustaining socialism unless the Soviet Union survived and became, in time, our ally I was ready to give it the benefit of my often considerable doubt.

Hugh Dalton, speaking for the Labour Party, had warned Chamberlain on 31 July that the government would be guilty of 'an intolerable betrayal of the cause of peace' if it refused immediately to conclude a Franco-British-Soviet Pact. But when the House of Commons was recalled on 24 August for an emergency session Stalin, not Chamberlain, was Labour's villain. Aneurin

Bevan certainly spoke for me when he pointed his finger directly at Chamberlain and cried 'he is the man upon whom Hitler relies; he is the man responsible for the situation', but what seemed to me the most shocking aspect of that emergency session, as we saw at Munich and at the time of the Falklands War, was the 'patriotic' hysteria that grips the Commons and the media on these occasions. Nye Bevan was subjected to angry protests from the Tory benches; but he was also highly unpopular with the leaders of the Parliamentary Labour Party, which signally failed to examine Chamberlain's responsibility for forcing the Soviet Union to seek a way out by coming to terms with Germany, or the consequences for Britain.

I do not accept the view that by concluding the Soviet-German Pact Stalin deliberately unleashed war in Europe. Hitler had gone too far in working up hysteria in Germany over his claims to the 'Polish corridor' and Danzig to be able to pull back. He was already committed to war. The real question is whether Stalin had any realistic alternative to a deal with Hitler. In 1939 hardly anybody answered, or even asked, the question put at the time by Professor Berriedale Keith (a Scottish Professor of International Law for whom I had a high regard) in *The Manchester Guardian* and *The Scotsman*: what was the Soviet Union supposed to do, after all the rebuffs it had received at the hands of Britain and France? It is worth looking at Stalin's options.

One was to do nothing, and to let Hitler occupy the whole of Poland, thereby outflanking the Baltic states and exposing the Soviet Union to the risk of war at the time of Hitler's choosing under the most unfavourable possible conditions. Another was to send the Red Army into Poland, with the aim of recovering the western parts of the Ukraine and Byelorussia, thereby risking an immediate war with Germany in which the Soviet Union had no allies. I find it inconceivable that in the latter event Chamberlain would have hailed the Soviet Union as an ally, as Churchill did in 1941 when Britain was fighting Germany single-handed. The only other option was to conclude the Soviet-German Pact with its secret protocol, which enabled the Soviet Union to enter eastern Poland without opposition on 17 November and to control the Baltic states. The Soviet-German treaty of 'amity and frontier' signed on 28 September 1939 restored the Soviet Union's eastern frontier on the 'Curzon line' of 1920, named after the then British Foreign Secretary, which defined the linguistic frontier between Poland and the Ukrainian or Byelorussian-speaking peoples. The Soviet Union did not annexe Polish territory: it recovered Ukrainian and Byelorussian lands that Poland had seized in 1920, but the treaty extinguished the Polish state whose 'indefeasible right to independence' the Soviet government had recognized in 1918. Nevertheless when I thought it over I came to the conclusion that Stalin had no alternative. I knew nothing, and suspected nothing, of the brutality with which the Soviet Union treated its Polish prisoners and imposed its rule on the Baltic states, but its behaviour does not invalidate its right to protect itself. It is also true that Stalin threw away in 1941 most of the advantages of time and space that he gained in 1939–40, but that could not have been foreseen in 1939 and the space gained in 1939–40 almost certainly saved both Leningrad and Moscow in 1941 – and so helped to determine the outcome of the war.

Anti-Soviet Hysteria – and Finland

The wave of anti-Soviet propaganda and anti-communist hysteria let loose by the Soviet-German Pact and the occupation of 'Polish' territory, rose to even greater heights as the Soviet Union systematically set about protecting its western frontiers in the autumn of 1939. Diplomatic pressure and (no doubt) threats of force were used to secure Soviet bases in Estonia, Latvia and Lithuania and then to incorporate them in the USSR. Their annexation was a violation of their national sovereignty, but they were potential German bases, and it is worth recalling that at the Teheran summit in 1943 Churchill and Roosevelt endorsed their incorporation in the Soviet Union. Stalin tried to complete the protection of his Baltic flank by securing a strip of Finnish territory by negotiation. When this failed, the Soviet Union attacked Finland on 30 November. One trivial consequence was to be my resignation from the Labour Party.

The British government, which never tried to expel either Germany or Italy from the League of Nations, voted for the instant expulsion of the Soviet Union on 14 December. But Britain's hypocritical espousal of the League Covenant came too late. Experience had taught the Soviet Union not to rely on covenants or International Law or high-sounding statements of principle emanating from British politicians, but to rely on force. The argument that Leningrad could not be defended so long as it could be bombarded from the Finnish frontier only 20 miles away was unanswerable.

I did not credit at the time the lurid press stories of immense Soviet defeats, gross incompetence, low morale and rotten equipment (even cardboard tanks!), which created the impression that the Red Army was not only uniquely wicked and cruel but also worthless militarily. I took the Soviet side, on the ground that Finland, whose leader Field Marshall Mannerheim was an extreme anti-communist and friend of the Nazis, was potentially a Nazi ally. So it proved to be in 1941, but I now realise that the Soviet invasion was a military disaster. Stalin underestimated Finland's strength, the Red Army had not recovered from the purge of its officers in the terror, and the Soviet troops suffered heavy losses through the incompetence of their commanders. One consequence seems to have been to convince Hitler that his *Blitzkrieg* could defeat the Red Army; another was to feed the anti-Soviet obsession of the capitalist world.

Anti-communist politicians created a united front, from the fascists to the centre of the Labour Party. Although, as Churchill was to say in April 1940, a million heavily-armed German troops were poised to launch a *Blitzkrieg* on the Western Front, supplies of badly needed planes, guns and munitions were sent from Britain and France to Finland. A recruiting office run by a British Army major was opened in London to recruit volunteers. The Foreign Enlistment Act, which had been used to make the recruitment of volunteers for Spain illegal, was used to encourage volunteering for Finland. In stark contrast to its long support for non-intervention in Spain (and its total failure ever to organise practical help) the National Council for Labour issued a call on 7 December 1939 to 'the free nations of the world' to give every practical help to Finland.

The Labour Party and Finland

Barbara Gould, the Chairman of the Labour Party, sat on the Finnish Aid Committee with Lord Plymouth, who had represented Britain on the Non-Intervention Committee, and Lord

Phillimore who was one of General Franco's most ardent admirers. A Labour Party-Trades Union Congress mission headed by Philip Noel-Baker MP and Sir Walter Citrine visited Finland and exhorted the British government to give all possible military aid. Mussolini sent 'volunteers' and aircraft with pilots. Franco sent 'volunteers' and candles from the Catholic faithful. The Pope gave his blessing to the crusade, and the *Catholic Herald* declared that the 'paramount purpose' of the war with Germany (apart from reviving faith in Almighty God) was 'resistance to the Godless, Asiatic, purely destructive Soviet menace'. President Reagan was singing a very old tune in 1985 when he described the Soviet Union as 'the evil Empire'.

The final lunacy was the decision to organise a Franco-British Expeditionary Force of 100,000 fully equipped men with an escort of 40 destroyers to seize the Swedish iron ore fields which kept Hitler supplied, and to fight the Soviet Union in Finland. Churchill took on the job of publicly upbraiding the neutrals for their failure to join the allies' fight for 'democracy'. The French government made no secret of its desire to use Polish destroyers based in Britain to attack Soviet forces in the Arctic, and to bomb the Soviet oil fields in Baku. On 5 February 1940 the Allied Supreme War Council agreed to send the Expeditionary Force, the British Chiefs of Staff having already advised the War Cabinet (as we now know) that, notwithstanding the British policy of 'avoiding war with Russia', they were 'prepared to take the risk of war with Russia and to weaken our forces on the Western Front'. Chamberlain advanced the extraordinary argument, as the official history of the war shows, that as the force would consist of regular divisions in the guise of 'volunteers' (on the analogy of the Italians in Spain!): 'Russia need not declare war against the Allies unless she wishes to do so.' It was only Sweden and Norway's repeated refusals to allow the passage of the Expeditionary Force through their territory that frustrated the plan. The acceptance by Finland of the Soviet peace terms on 13 March was a severe defeat for the British government, which foolishly perceived that its interest lay in the continuation and the extension of the Soviet–Finnish war.

There is a tendency nowadays to skate over the attitude adopted by the Labour Party and the Chamberlain government towards the Soviet Union at the time of the Finnish

War. A.J.P. Taylor observes, in *English History 1914–1945*, that 'the motives for the projected expedition to Finland defy rational analysis. For Great Britain and France to provoke war with Soviet Russia when already at war with Germany seems the product of a madhouse.' Paul Addison in *The Road to 1945* also describes the episode as 'wholly irrational' as indeed it was. But one has to look for the explanation of these attitudes not in the actual situation confronting Britain in 1940–41 but in a pathological anti-Soviet phobia that deprived those infected by it of the ability to think rationally.

It was impossible for me to remain a member of a Labour Party that was actively supporting war against the Soviet Union and seemed to be conspiring with the government to commit the suicidal folly of waging war against Germany and the Soviet Union at the same time. I announced my resignation in a letter to the local newspapers, in which I attacked the Labour Party's (and Chamberlain's) readiness to seize on the Finnish War as an excuse to provoke a war against the Soviet Union. Within four weeks of the Finnish surrender on 14 March Hitler invaded Norway and the phoney war came to an end. Finland was forgotten, and with the invasion and fall of France any idea of a campaign to explain my position lost whatever meaning it had.

Dashed Hopes – and a New Life

Barbara and I had by then a more pressing problem on our hands and in our minds. We had been overjoyed when Barbara, despite all the risks, gave birth in November 1939 to a baby girl, whom we called Anne. But our joy was short-lived. It soon became clear that, although apparently healthy, she was not responsive to light, and did not seem to be able to identify objects. Cataracts in both eyes were diagnosed, and we made two hasty trips to Edinburgh to see a specialist who confirmed the diagnosis and agreed to operate. Once again we were buoyed up, but the operations were a failure, and we were told that nothing more could be done. We steeled ourselves to face the problem of bringing up a blind girl, but by then it was becoming obvious that Anne was also very seriously disabled (I think the word 'spastic', a new one to us, was used) and mentally retarded as well.

Barbara, who never ceased to amaze me, suffered acutely but never gave in. She was the bravest person I have ever known, and her response to set-backs or defeats was always to 'accentuate the positive'. She was troubled throughout 1940 by recurrences of her colitis which were debilitating and exhausting and, when our birth-control technique failed, had to have an abortion, which was only allowed at that time for acute medical need. Having dropped out of political activity I was so preoccupied with Barbara and the baby that the awesome events of 1940 – the Norwegian disaster, Dunkirk, the fall of France, the Battle of Britain and the Blitz on London – seemed extraordinarily remote.

Barbara was well enough in September for us to take a short, unforgettable holiday on the west coast of Inverness-shire, which was at that time in the military 'Protected Area' north of the Caledonian Canal from which (for security reasons) all visitors were excluded. As we lived north of the canal, inside the area, we could move freely within it as 'local residents'. One summer evening, against the backdrop of Loch Duich and those superb mountains, the Seven Sisters of Kintail, we heard on a crackling radio the news of the first German air-raids on London. The nightmare we had so long anticipated had begun. When we got home we agreed that, much as we loved Kessock, we ought to look for a new life somewhere else. There was no longer enough work for me in Stewart, Rule and Co., the county council had settled down to a wartime routine and the Labour Party (of which I was no longer a member) had virtually folded up. By November 1940 I had almost concluded negotiations to join a legal firm with strong trade union connections in the south of Scotland, and resigned from the county council 'to take up a business appointment in the south'.

Then, out of the blue, came an urgent letter from William Rust, the editor of the *Daily Worker*, asking me to join its new Scottish edition in Glasgow as its legal adviser. He had been unable to find a single Scottish lawyer who would take the job on, perhaps because the *Daily Worker* had been threatened with suppression in July 1940, although the Home Secretary, Sir John Anderson, had flatly refused to specify the items that he regarded as 'subversive' or 'seditious'. However, the *Daily Worker* appealed to us precisely because it was both anti-fascist and 'subversive' of the established order.

Barbara and I felt elated at the prospect that I might work for a paper and a political party with which we could fully identify. She was about to return to hospital for more treatment but insisted that I should respond positively to Bill Rust's appeal, although the pay was rock-bottom and the job, in conventional terms, offered no 'prospects' in terms of salary, job security or promotion. It was not unlike volunteering for the services, although the impulse in our case was political rather than 'patriotic'.

By the end of November I found myself installed as the *Daily Worker's* legal 'vet' in Kirkwood's Print Shop on the quay of Glasgow's Broomielaw, lodging with Bill McGeachy, a young communist doctor with a practice in Glasgow's East End. Barbara was unable to come with me, and it was nine months before she was well enough for us to live together again. Joining the *Daily Worker* was the beginning of an association with the Communist Party and its newspaper that was to last for 16 years, and completely changed the pattern of our lives.

7

Exit from a Blind Alley

I did not realise it at the time, but in moving from a solicitor's desk in Inverness to work for a paper that was teetering on the brink of illegality I was crossing my Rubicon. I found myself in the company not of cautious county councillors, conventional Labour Party workers and country solicitors but of people dedicated to working-class militancy, for whom even the threat of imprisonment held no terrors. Bill Rust himself had been jailed twice. Both he and J.R. (or 'Johnny') Campbell (whom I met almost as soon as I arrived in Glasgow and who became the main influence on my work for the Communist Party) had been among the twelve communist leaders sent to prison for 'seditious conspiracy' in 1925, when Bill was given twelve months and Johnny six. The chief sub-editor on the Scottish edition was Bill Shepherd, a cheerful cockney woodworker-turned-journalist who had been given 18 months in 1931. His 'crime' had been to distribute a 'subversive' leaflet about the cuts in service pay that provoked the Invergordon Mutiny in 1931. Harry McShane, our one Scottish reporter, had been jailed more than once, most recently only a year previously when he was given six weeks for peacefully resisting an eviction.

I doubt whether the *Daily Worker* really needed a lawyer in Scotland, or whether as its legal 'vet' I was of much use to it. In trying to steer the Scottish edition clear of prosecution or suppression my problem was that what is 'legal' depends not so much on the law, which is open to many interpretations, but the prevailing political climate. What passes for 'fair comment' at one time is 'sedition' at another. At the trial of the communist leaders in 1925 the Attorney-General argued (and the judge supported him) that the Communist Party was an 'illegal' organisation. Its illegality was forgotten once the General Strike had been defeated in 1926.

The People's Convention

After resigning from the Labour Party, but before joining the *Daily Worker*, I had been one of the 500 signatories of an appeal to support the People's Convention, which met in London in January 1941. It is fashionable nowadays to dismiss the People's Convention as an insignificant event inspired by the CP (as indeed it was) that was completely out of tune with 'Britain's Finest Hour'. Paul Addison in his penetrating study *The Road to 1945*, Ben Pimlott in his biography of Hugh Dalton, and Michael Foot in his *Life of Aneurin Bevan* do not so much as mention it. In fact, the support it attracted was significant evidence of a strong trend of dissatisfaction with both the aims and the conduct of the war.

To assemble over 2,200 people in London during the Blitz on Sunday 12 January (half of them from outside London, over 600 straight from the factory floor and 665 from trade unions) was an extraordinary feat of organisation. It could not have been achieved without a high degree of political commitment and widespread support. Only three weeks before the event the Manchester Free Trade Hall, in which it was to have taken place, was destroyed in an air-raid, yet the organisers were able to shift the convention to the Royal Hotel and the Conway Halls in London, to notify all concerned through the *Daily Worker*, to find beds for all who needed them, and to attract enormous press coverage. The delegates got there on a railway system that was disrupted nightly by bombing, and during the night before the convention met there was an alert and bombs were dropped on London.

I was carried away by the size and enthusiasm of the meeting and by Dennis Pritt's keynote speech attacking the Men of Munich. A characteristically fiery contribution from Krishna Menon of the India League (a Labour candidate for Dundee until his expulsion from the Labour Party in 1940, and later India's Defence Minister) reminded us that if Britain was free India was in chains. The point was emphasised by the presence of Indira Gandhi (later India's Prime Minister), whose father Pandit Nehru was at that moment in jail with other Indian nationalist leaders. What united the convention was the feeling that some way had to be found out of a war for which we could see no end, and whose only aim, beyond immediate survival, seemed to be to hang on to the Empire. Next day I picked my way through the ruins of the City of London around St Paul's, admiring the courage and competence of those who had fought the fires and were now clearing up the mess, but I came away strengthened in my conviction that unless there was some radical change in policy the war would become an endless nightmare of death and destruction, of which the City was only a foretaste.

Through rejecting the Soviet alliance year after year Britain seemed to me to have got itself into a blind alley. It was very heroic to be 'standing alone' and Britain might be able to hold out for years against a Nazi Europe, although at a terrible cost, but alone it had no chance whatever of defeating fascism. When Churchill raised hopes of victory he was fantasising, or gambling on the ultimate intervention of the United States although I question whether even the intervention of the US would have been enough either to defeat fascism in Europe or to give the war a genuinely anti-fascist character. Whatever the People's Convention was, it was not a gathering of Fifth Columnists or pro-fascists. The *Daily Mirror's* verdict the next day, that 90 per cent of the delegates were opponents of Hitler who were turning to the Communist Party because they were disillusioned with the Labour ministers, was nearer the truth.

If the idea that Britain alone could defeat a Nazified Europe was a fantasy so was the programme of the People's Convention. I was still blinded by my distrust of Churchill, the Labour leaders and the 'Men of Munich', and unable to grasp the reality of our situation. The People's Convention wanted 'friendship with the Soviet Union', which did indeed prove to be the key to the defeat of fascism, but we had no idea how to shift the Soviet Union away from the neutrality into which Chamberlain had driven it. The Convention wanted a 'people's government', which clearly implied a government not only shorn of the 'Men of Munich' but also well to the left of the wartime coalition, but such a government had no basis in the relationship of political forces in Parliament or in the country. The convention's idea that a 'people's government' would conclude 'a people's peace that gets rid of the causes of war' was another of our fantasies, although one that appealed to pacifists. A 'people's peace' was caricatured by the anti-communists as a sell-out to Hitler. That was a falsehood, but we were

deluded by our belief that the German workers would respond
to the establishment of an anti-imperialist British government
by overthrowing Hitler. We did not realise (and we were very
far from alone in this) the degree to which the Nazis had captured the minds of the German working class and, by their
terror, destroyed nearly every vestige of opposition.

The Scottish *Daily Worker*

At this time I was, in any case, utterly absorbed in my new job
on the *Daily Worker*. I remained with the paper for the next 16
years, apart from two and a half years after the ban when I
worked directly for the Communist Party. Even now I cannot
imagine a more satisfying or enjoyable job – until, towards the
end, political disillusionment and conflict set in. The job on
the Scottish edition was not, in reality, vetting the paper for
libel or sedition. With a total editorial staff of five or six in
Glasgow to bring out a daily newspaper we were desperately
short-handed so, as I loved writing, I began to transform myself
from a solicitor into a journalist and in the process made
friends as well as learning new skills. From Bill Shepherd,
Jimmy James the head printer and Phil Bolsover (honoured in
1985 when Michael Heseltine, then Minister of Defence, listed
him as one of the Campaign for Nuclear Disarmament's 'sub-
versives') I began to get the hang of newspaper journalism.

The idea of attempting to print in London and Glasgow,
which was already normal practice in the mass circulation
dailies, would not have occurred to Bill Rust had it not been for
the impossible conditions being created by the German air-
raids. Production was being interrupted continuously by loss of
gas or electricity supplies; trains never ran to time, if they ran at
all, and key workers were bombed out and living in tube stations. Ironically, the *Daily Worker's* London plant in Cayton
Street was destroyed in an air-raid in January 1941, a few days
after Herbert Morrison had banned it. Supplies to Scotland,
which the Party regarded as a key industrial area, were increasingly irregular. The Scottish edition had to be launched, as the
Daily Worker itself had been launched in 1930, with resources
of people and money that a commercial publisher would have
regarded as absurdly small.

The Scottish edition was printed on an old flat-bed press,

which was so slow that we had to go to press in the afternoon to print the normal run of 12,000 to 14,000 copies. We had no news agency services or technology to transmit print or pictures. Leading articles and a few major reports were telephoned from London when our one telephone was free. Feature articles and much else were taken from the London edition published one or more days previously. For Scottish material we relied on worker-correspondents in the factories and shipyards, and on Harry McShane. Harry was a boilermaker with a heart of gold, who had been the ardent lieutenant of John Maclean, the revolutionary teacher who was jailed for opposing the First World War and was later appointed Soviet Consul in Glasgow by Lenin. Harry was an ebullient, ruddy-complexioned stoutish man, immensely friendly and good-humoured despite (or perhaps because of) a long history of militant activity, victimisation and imprisonment, who liked nothing better than to regale us with his stories. Bill Shepherd too carried with him the romantic aura of ten years' service on the *Worker* from its foundation, with a jail sentence thrown in. I got a new and vivid impression (even if a highly-coloured one) of the previous 20 years from these two communist workers who had lived through them.

The Ban

The ban on the *Daily Worker* on 21 January 1941 should not have come as a surprise, for the possibility was often discussed and the Party had made preparations for it. The appointment of Herbert Morrison (the supreme anti-communist of the Labour Party) to succeed Sir John Anderson as Home Secretary a few days before I joined the *Daily Worker* was a clear danger signal. On the other hand the *Daily Worker* had just emerged the moral victor in an action for damages brought by Sir Walter Citrine and six other trade union leaders in which the judge restricted the damages to £300 or so apiece on the ground that punitive damages should not be used to prevent the legitimate expression of communist views. The ban was a gross abuse of 'Defence Regulation 20', which had been rushed through Parliament in the summer of 1940 to deal with a situation that might arise in the event of an invasion. The Home Secretary had no need to give any reasons for closing down the *Daily*

Worker, because 'Regulation 20' allowed him to ban any 'newspaper' (although not a leaflet) without evidence, trial or right of appeal. He was judge, jury and executioner. But if one thing was clear by 1941 it was that no invasion was likely.

The ban clearly had nothing to do with whether or not the *Daily Worker* was 'systematically fomenting opposition to the successful prosecution of the war' as the banning order asserted. I believed at the time that it was the success of the People's Convention that prompted Morrison's action. From the government's point of view the *Daily Worker's* line in January 1941 was much less objectionable than it had been in, say, the summer of 1940 when invasion was a real possibility. The *Daily Worker's* attitude to the war was ambiguous (being opposed both to British imperialism and to any deal with the Nazis) and its main campaigns were to re-invigorate a paralysed Labour movement and to remove the 'Men of Munich' who stood in the way of a genuinely anti-fascist war effort. The ban remained in force for more than a year after the German attack on Russia on 22 June 1941 that led the British Communist Party to give unreserved support to the war. Morrison even continued the ban after the Labour Party Conference had voted against it in May 1942, and only yielded on 26 August 1942 when he realised that the Trades Union Congress in September would vote for lifting the ban. Morrison lifted the ban because it had ceased to be politically productive for the Labour leadership, just as he imposed it because he saw a never-to-be-repeated chance to disarm the Communist Party by depriving it of its main propaganda and organisational tool.

I had not really expected the ban and had made no plans for it, but events moved so fast that I never had to decide whether or not to go back to the law. At almost the same time as the ban a by-election was announced in East Dunbartonshire, a scattered urban and rural constituency which included the shipbuilding town of Clydebank and the coalfields between Glasgow and Stirling. It was a Labour seat with a large majority, and under the wartime electoral truce the Labour candidate would not be opposed by a Tory or a Liberal. The Communist Party decided to put up a candidate who would campaign on the People's Convention programme. The election would also be the first shot in the Party's campaign to lift the ban on the *Daily Worker*.

The Crypto–Communist Candidate

The suggestion that I should be the candidate came from Johnny Campbell, who had been removed from the *Daily Worker's* editorial chair and exiled to Glasgow for his unsuccessful opposition to the Communist International's line that the Party must oppose the 'imperialist war'. Johnny remained the Party's most senior member in Scotland, a veteran campaigner who had won the loyalty and affection of the Party in Scotland. Although we had not met very often Johnny and I had taken an instant liking to each other. He thought that as an ex-Labour Party man, a backer of the People's Convention, a worker on the banned *Daily Worker* and a recent convert to the Communist Party with an impeccable middle-class background I would be the best candidate to attract a broad spectrum of support. In addition the Party had a strong organisational base in the constituency, with a councillor in Clydebank, groups of members in the shipyards and mines, and one of those rare 'little Moscows' in the industrial Vale of Leven, between Loch Lomond and the Clyde, where there were several Communist councillors. The Labour Party section of the Vale of Leven Trades Council voted unanimously to support me and one of the communist councillors, Hughie McIntyre, a Co-op insurance agent, proved to be a tireless, endlessly good-humoured and highly efficient election agent.

Johnny's assessment was sound enough, and flattering too, and I agreed to stand, but he had got one thing wrong. Although I was willing to stand as a communist, I had not in fact joined the Party. Nobody had asked me to join, on the assumption that as I was on the staff of the *Worker* I must already be a member. Johnny himself must have made the same mistake. Even when the Political Bureau in London approved my candidature and I was formally adopted by a large meeting of Party members in the Vale of Leven, it never occurred to me to apply for membership. I had to own up after the election, when Johnny asked me to work with him in the Scottish office of the CP, and I then got my Party card. I have the distinction of having stood for Parliament as a unique crypto-communist – not one who concealed his membership, but one who concealed the fact that he was *not* a member!

I must divert at this point to say a few words about Johnny Campbell, because it was almost entirely due to him that I became in the CP jargon a Party 'cadre'. He was the economic specialist of the *Daily Worker*, and twice its editor over a period of many years. He was the well-read working-class intellectual despised by Orwell, with a passion for poetry (he liked to recite Burns' 'Holy Willy's Prayer') and a sense of fun. He could take a government White Paper, skim over it page by page, and write a cogent, accurate leader or summary against a tight deadline in the huge, childish hand that was the only sign of his lack of education. He was a slight, untidy, self-effacing man who walked with a marked limp caused by the loss of all his toes from 'trench foot' in the First World War, in which he had been awarded the Military Medal.

Like all the original leaders of the Party, to which he dedicated his life Johnny had been through the mill of prosecution and imprisonment and had become notorious nationally as the central figure in the 'Campbell case' which brought the first Labour government down in 1924. As editor of the *Sunday Worker* Johnny published an article headed 'Don't Shoot', which called on soldiers not to fire on striking workers. Ramsay Macdonald's Attorney-General brought a prosecution for 'sedition'. When faced by a storm of protest from Labour parties and trade unions the government withdrew the prosecution on the pretext that it was 'fair comment', coupled with the maudlin statement that Johnny was a disabled ex-serviceman with a good war record. The Liberals, who held the balance of power, voted for the Tory motion of 'no confidence' and, thanks to the Zinoviev or 'Red Letter' forgery, the Tories won the ensuing election.

With Pollitt and Gallacher, Campbell had voted against the line of 'imperialist war' in the Central Committee in October 1939, arguing that the Party should support the war but oppose the government and try to change it. Two months later he and Pollitt published a recantation (in which neither of them believed). It took me another 15 years to realise that they were moved by the same misplaced sense of loyalty to the Party and the Soviet Union that may have led Bukharin and others to confess to non-existent crimes in the Soviet Union. In the East Dunbartonshire by-election Johnny went as far as he could towards his (private, unspoken) opinion, and approved my election address without submitting it to London. Had he done so somebody would have drawn attention to one extraordinary omission which Peter Kerrigan, the Party's industrial organiser and one-time political commissar in the International Brigade, spotted immediately. Why, 'Big Peter' asked me, did the address nowhere mention the Soviet Union when friendship with the Soviet Union was one of the main planks in the Party's and the People's Convention's platforms? I told Kerrigan that it was 'just one of those things', the result of haste and pressure, but the truth was, as the Party would not let us say the one thing that would have made sense – that fascism could only be defeated through an alliance with the Soviet Union – Johnny thought it was better to say nothing than to repeat the convention's vague formula about 'friendship with the Soviet Union'.

War and the 'Party Line'

Harry McShane wrote in his memoirs that 'in order to pursue the anti-war line we [the CP] ran Malcolm MacEwen as a peace candidate' in Dunbartonshire, but I do not think he accurately reflected the point of view presented by the Party in my campaign. *Mass Observation*, which made a detailed survey of the candidates' views and the reaction of the electorate, concluded that our campaign was *not* anti-war. I argued in my election address that 'a successful defence of the people against fascism abroad' depended on raising the people's morale through a 'people's government' that would provide air-raid shelters, take action against the vested interests and profiteers who were responsible for waste and inefficiency in industry, and create a democratic Army. I characterised the war as a struggle for world domination between the ruling classes of Germany and Britain but I rejected any idea of a 'deal' with Hitler. Communists, I said, knew from bitter experience far better than any other party what fascism was and I went on to say:

> To seek a way out of this war by surrender to Hitler would be an unspeakable crime. To seek a way out as the Coalition Government does is to sacrifice untold millions of lives for imperialist ends. There is a third way out ... a People's Government which will defend us from fascism at home and abroad ... Such a Government ... would lay the basis for a new social order in time of war.

There is not a trace here of 'revolutionary defeatism', or of Lenin's axiom that 'a revolutionary class in a reactionary war cannot but desire the defeat of its own government', and should transform war between governments into civil war. In my address the idea of taking arms against one's own government only applied to Nazi-occupied Europe. I argued that an anti-fascist government in Britain could stimulate the growing discontent in Europe (which was true) and encourage the movement for a 'people's government' in Germany (which was sheer delusion). The Party had, in fact, moved a long way by 1941 from the simple 'anti-war' line which, whatever Palme Dutt might be saying in *Labour Monthly*, no longer reflected the feelings of the Communist Party members who worked for us in East Dunbartonshire, if it ever did. The ingrained habits of loyalty to the Communist International and to the Party leadership prevented most communists from saying in public what many of them thought in private, but the Party's suspicions about the government's real war aims were shared by a large section of the public. War Office surveys in the first half of 1941, quoted by Andrew Davies in *Where did the Forties go?* (Pluto Press 1984) revealed that the morale of the forces generally was very low – and this was attributed to 'the troops' suspicion of the military leaders and their enthusiasm for engaging in this anti-fascist war'.

The By-Election

My experience in the by-election confirms this assessment of the public's feelings on the war. There were no demonstrations of hostility towards me or any of the supporting speakers in the course of many dozens of open-air and indoor meetings. In the Roman Catholic mining village of Croy the priest preached a sermon against communism, holding a copy of the *Daily Worker* with a pair of tongs to avoid soiling his hands, but we got the votes of some Catholic miners. There were no anti-communist patriotic mobs; it was no longer possible to whip up hysteria against an imaginary communist enemy when Hitler's armies stood on the Channel and British cities burned. Harry Pollitt, whom I found to be immensely helpful to an inexperienced candidate, did counsel me, however, to lower my voice when I was holding forth about the iniquity of the class system in the Army while a group of officers were eating a meal at the next table.

My biggest problem was trying to find some food that was acceptable to Krishna Menon, the Indian National Congress representative in London, who came up to speak about India's struggle for freedom against the British Raj. I failed completely, and I do not think that Krishna ate a bite in the course of 24 hours, which probably made him speak with even greater asperity than usual about the imperialist aims of the government. The press ignored the election, except when my brother Robin (at that time a private in the Army) agreed to stand against me as a Scottish Nationalist. A fratricidal struggle was 'news' whereas the Communist Party's policies were not. Luckily for us the Army refused to give Robin leave (and Robin knew that leave would be refused), which left the Nationalists without a candidate and gave me a useful stick with which to belabour the government for refusing to let a serviceman stand in the election.

Polling was on 29 February. The result when it came next day was not, perhaps, the 'victory' that Hughie McIntyre immediately proclaimed with the irrepressible optimism of the militant who perceives a victory in every defeat, but by polling 3,862 votes against the 21,900 for the successful Labour candidate we saved our deposit handsomely and raised the Party's vote to 15 per cent. We proved that those who had predicted the collapse of the Communist Party after October 1939 were wrong. The Party was in fact gaining members at this time – largely, I suspect, because many people in the Labour movement could see no end to the struggle other than a betrayal like that which had followed the war of 1914–18.

An Anti-Fascist War

After the election I took Barbara from Kessock to her mother's home in Berkshire where she and our baby Anne could more easily be looked after, although getting them there was a hair-raising business. The night we spent en route in Glasgow happened to be the night of the Clydeside Blitz, and the journey from Glasgow to Oxford with an air-raid en route was a nightmare for a sick woman. After a few days with Barbara I went back to Glasgow and worked for the next seven months with

Johnny Campbell in the Scottish office of the Communist Party
in Glasgow. My job was to bring out small news- or propa-
ganda-sheets, with a different title every week to avoid the
charge that we were producing a 'newspaper' that could be
banned. Any spare time, apart from a short holiday visiting
Barbara in the summer, was spent speaking at meetings and discovering for the first time what the inner life of the
Communist Party was like. I had barely settled in when Hitler
attacked the Soviet Union on 22 June. Nobody doubted that it
was the duty of communists to stand solidly for the defence of
the Soviet Union, but not many of us anticipated that
Churchill would come out, as he did on the radio that evening,
100 per cent for treating the Soviet Union as Britain's comrade-
in-arms in the war against Hitler. I was astonished, although
delighted, when he did, painful as it was to swallow the idea
that the only way to help the Soviet Union was to give our
support unequivocally to Churchill.

The change in the Party 'line' lifted an enormous burden of
doubt from the consciences of most Party members. There was
no longer any need to hedge or equivocate. There was a clear
job to be done, and the Party set about doing it with even
greater zest and enthusiasm than it had put into its campaigns
for the unemployed, for Spain or for the Popular Front. It
redoubled its efforts to rid Britain's government of the
remaining 'Men of Munich'. But it was not just our perception
of the war that had changed. For the first time there were military and political reasons for thinking that fascism could be
defeated, and the CP was not alone in making a U-turn.
Churchill called in John Platts-Mills a near-communist Labour
barrister to run a pro-Soviet campaign, and used these words:
'I've been teaching the British people since 1918 that the
Russians eat their young. Take as much money as you need and
change the public perception of them.'

I had to go back to Inverness two weeks later for the funeral
of my father, who had died after a long illness. Crossing over to
Inverness on the Kessock ferry the day after his funeral there
was only one subject of discussion: could Russia hold out? And
what did I think of the extraordinary speech that Stalin had
made on the Soviet radio, after a silence of two weeks since the
invasion of Russia? What struck everybody was not so much
Stalin's admission of the 'grave danger' the Soviet Union faced,

or even the implication that the Soviet Union had been caught only half-prepared by a fully mobilized Nazi Germany; it was the call for a 'scorched-earth policy', for the 'total war' that Britain had so far failed to wage. Stalin spoke of war in a way never before heard in response to a Nazi invasion. Nothing was to be left for the Germans. The land was to be turned into a desert. Everything that could be moved was to be moved to the rear. Everything else was to be destroyed. Everywhere guerrilla movements were to make life for the enemy 'unbearable'. This unquenchable spirit of resistance had impressed my fellow passengers. Anti-Soviet prejudice was already giving way to the hope that the Soviet system would prove to be the stronger. They realised that 'we' might win the war, if 'they' could beat Hitler's *Wehrmacht*.

Hitler's pathological, anti-communist and racist vision of Germany conquering Russia and winning 'living space' for the 'Teutons' had opened the door at the end of the blind alley in which we were all trapped. When I look back on it I share the conclusion reached by Isaac Deutscher in his political biography *Stalin* – that although Stalin threw away many of the advantages in space, time and war preparation that the German-Soviet Pact had gained, it was the very outrage and perfidy of the German attack that united the Soviet peoples and made their epic resistance and victories possible. Deutscher believed that in 1939 the Soviet peoples strongly supported Stalin's decision to keep them out of the war. They had been fully stretched for 25 years by war, civil war, famine, and never-ending efforts at reconstruction (and, I would now add by Stalin's purges) and their efforts to prevent war had been spurned by the Western European governments. Their strongest feeling, wrote Deutscher, 'was probably the urge to escape the inexorable destiny of war', but 'the fact that the war for national survival was forced upon Russia brought out the best qualities in the Russian soldier in the years that followed'. The Soviet-German Pact, by thrusting the responsibility unequivocally on Hitler, may well have proved to be one decisive factor in the Soviet victory, and Stalin's will-power, personifying the national will, was undeniably another. It is one of the paradoxes of history that, monstrous criminal though I now know him to have been, there was no other national leader on earth except Mao Tse Tung (as we then knew him) who could have responded to Hitler as Stalin did on 3 July 1941.

Part 2
The Party

8

Party Cadre

In September 1941, when the ability of the Red Army to hold out before Moscow seemed to be hanging in the balance, Johnny Campbell asked me if I would take the place of John Gollan the District Secretary of the Communist Party in the North-East of England who had been appointed Scottish District Secretary. The North-East was a key industrial area, embracing the shipyards of the Tyne and Wear, the Vickers tank and armament factories at Elswick and Scotswood in Newcastle, the chemical and steel plants of Teesside, the coalfields of Durham and Northumberland and the railway workshops at Darlington and Carlisle.

In normal times the Party would not have dreamed of asking somebody with my background and lack of experience to take on such a responsible job. For the 'Secretary' in the CP was not so much a secretary as a political leader: Gorbachev, like Stalin, was the 'Secretary' of the Communist Party. As I was technically 'disabled' I was one of the few people available to organise the new members who were flooding into the Party by the thousand in the atmosphere of enthusiasm for the war and for the Soviet Union.

It never occurred to me to refuse the chance to lead the Party in the North-East, particularly as it meant that Barbara and I could set up a home again after living apart for nearly a year. She had made what seemed to be a good recovery during the spring and summer and we were overjoyed by the prospect of taking over the flat vacated by John and Elsie Gollan in Newcastle. Working for the Party would help to fill the void in our lives – but most of all in Barbara's – created by the decision, which we had taken in June, to have our little girl Anne cared for in a home. She was now two and not only blind but severely incapacitated, both physically and mentally. In

October we were able to secure a place for Anne, on terms we could afford, in a small private home for blind and 'backward' children in Reigate. I have asked myself many times whether we were right to send Anne to a home, but I still believe that Barbara's health and the lack of supporting services gave us no alternative. Barbara joined me in Glasgow in October and we moved to Newcastle soon afterwards.

Back to School

I set off almost immediately for a Party school in London which reflected the transitional phase through which the Party was passing. One of our tutors was Robbie Robson, one-time National Organiser who had been jailed for six weeks during the General Strike for carrying a copy of *The Workers' Bulletin*. Robbie, although a neatly-dressed man, exuded the spirit of revolution and illegality. He had organised the recruitment of British volunteers for Spain after the government had declared it to be illegal, and did his best to freeze the blood of the new organisers by telling us that every Party member should seize the chance to be trained in the use of arms. In fact the course was designed to train us to organise and educate the new members to whom many of the ways of the CP were distinctly foreign, and who had not the slightest thought of an armed 'revolution' in Robbie's terms.

Raji Palme Dutt and Emile Burns, the two leading theoreticians in the Party apparatus, put us through a concentrated course in Marxism-Leninism or, more accurately, Stalinism. The main set book was the *History of the Communist Party of the Soviet Union (Bolsheviks) (Short Course)*, which had become the CP's bible. It was supposed to have been written by a committee of Soviet historians but was actually Stalin's one-sided version of history in which Trotsky emerged as the villain and Stalin as the hero of the revolution and of the early years of the USSR. Its value to the Party leadership lay in its dogmatic presentation of Stalin's concept of the centralised, disciplined, 'monolithic' Party run on the principles of 'democratic centralism' – whose members must speak with one voice in support of the Party line, and for whom trade unions and other working-class organisations are seen as the 'transmission belts' through which the Party's policies are communicated to the masses. I took it all as gospel, partly because the 'Party of a new type' seemed to me to be both more democratic and more effective than the Labour Party. The school gave us a first-class grounding in leadership and administration that has been of immense value to me ever since.

The air-raids had stopped but London was a strange place in the blackout and I didn't get to know it much better as any spare time I had was taken up with reading. I stayed at first with Allen Hutt, whom I only knew by reputation as the author of *The Post-War History of the British Working Class* which the Left Book Club had published in 1937. In 1941 Allen was chief sub-editor on the co-operative, left-wing Sunday newspaper *Reynolds News*, which provided a second job for several *Daily Worker* journalists. Staying with him should have been a delight, but it was not. Allen, his second wife Sheena and their baby Sam (who is now a doctor and delights me and many others by his performance as Hank Wangford, the 'country and western' musician) shared a house at Chalk Farm with Irma Lloyd, the wife from whom he had only recently been divorced, and her new husband Bert Lloyd who became Britain's best-known folk singer. The sharing cannot have done either marriage much good. Sheena felt under no obligation to soften her ways on account of my presence, and I was amazed to discover when I rejoined the *Worker* that the Allen who could not say 'boo' to Sheena's goose was himself an abusive, if talented, tyrant in the office.

Two-Way Culture Shock

By November we had moved to Newcastle and had taken over an upper flat in a semi-detached house. We soon acquired a lodger in the person of Margaret Johnson, a lively 16-year-old County Durham girl who had just got her first job as a shorthand typist with the Fire Brigades' Union through the CP's 'old comrades' network. Margaret's dad was an ex-miner from County Durham who had been victimised after the General Strike. Margaret had never mixed with middle-class people and the result was a bit of a culture shock on both sides. To begin with she was somewhat overawed by us and found me particularly intimidating. I felt obliged to play the 'father' role, and Margaret had some difficulty in convincing me of her innocence when she stayed out all night whitewashing 'Second Front' slogans for the Young Communist League.

My conviction that I was always right combined with my Scottish chauvinism to create an unwholesomely aggressive mixture. I even objected to Margaret adding sugar to the well-salted porridge I made every morning for breakfast, although I had to give in when Barbara took Margaret's side. But Margaret was a spirited girl who could give as good as she got. When I complained, as I did most mornings, about the house-shaking snores that came from the man in the flat below she retorted that *he* could hardly enjoy *me* clattering up the uncarpeted staircase on my tin leg when I came back from Party meetings late at night! It was, in her eyes, typically middle-class not to bother to carpet the staircase when we could perfectly well afford to do so.

Margaret remembers me as a workaholic who seemed to have almost no life outside the Party. I worked all week and every weekend, Saturdays and Sundays being my busiest days. In the two years we were in Newcastle I can only remember one trip into the countryside and we had one week's holiday on Speyside in August 1942, when we heard a BBC announcer telling us through a crofter's open window that the ban on the *Daily Worker* had been lifted. What surprised Margaret most was the fact that Barbara seemed to work as hard as I did despite the poor health of which she never complained. Barbara would not hear of being a 'housewife', and worked initially as the office messenger-girl before throwing herself into the work of the Women's Committee, rejoicing in what she called 'a real job' which was virtually full-time although unpaid. She was very well-liked by all her comrades, as the many letters I received when she died in 1944 testify. As a result the flat was always in a mess – again, in Margaret's eyes a typically middle-class failing. Her critical eye was certainly a factor in forcing us to roll our sleeves up every now and then to tidy the place up. However, we survived the culture shock. Margaret and her husband Solly Kaye, the one-time Communist councillor in Stepney, have been my good friends for nearly half a century.

'A Happy Ship'

My new job was totally absorbing and enormous fun, but I cannot have been entirely welcome for at least two reasons. Joe Waters (like myself a recent recruit from the Labour Party) and

Hymie Lee the other two full-time political workers in the District office, must have hoped for the job when Johnny Gollan left for London. It had nothing to do with money, for we all had the same low pay (roughly equal to a skilled worker's pay without overtime) but to be the District Secretary and a member of the Central Committee conferred status. I only discovered the second reason in 1985 when Charlie Woods, a retired miner who had been the District Secretary in 1936–7, told me that he had regarded my appointment as a clear sign that the Party leadership did not take the key North-East industrial district seriously enough. It was not my youth that he objected to (I was 30) but my lack of industrial, trade union, cooperative or Party experience. Charlie had a point. I was so middle-class that I struck Alan Brien, the writer who was then a precocious schoolboy in Sunderland and an activist in the Young Communist League, as not only very 'tough', but also 'very posh' and an obvious 'intellectual'.

I remember the District office, marvellously situated overlooking Newcastle's Eldon Square (now vandalised by redevelopment), as a very 'happy ship'. Everybody worked almost unlimited hours and Joe Waters and Hymie Lee proved to be good comrades in every sense. Joe, our industrial organiser, measured his success by the formation of factory groups, the election of communists to trade union posts and the number of resolutions passed in support of CP policies. Our unpaid Treasurer worked by day for the Midland Bank in Gosforth and led a double life for the rest of the week by working for the Party as 'Frank Thornton'. Hymie Lee was responsible for 'agitprop' and 'education' (propaganda and educating the new Party members). Hymie, a larger-than-life East End of London Jew – stout, puffing, loquacious, untidy, funny and totally unselfish – was a favourite at the Bigg Market, Newcastle's equivalent of Hyde Park's Speaker's Corner, where the crowd would only listen to speakers who could garnish politics with wit and entertainment. Hymie lived with Maggie Airey, another Tynesider whose fiancé Wilf Jobling had been killed in Spain. Maggie, warm, intelligent and hard-working, ran the Workers' Bookshop in Westgate Road, where miners and shipyard workers as well as academics and intellectuals could be found poring over the books and pamphlets.

I did all my own typing and we only kept enough records to

enable us to follow up decisions because 20 years of police raids, prosecutions and the threat of 'illegality' had generated long-standing habits of secrecy and security. The membership list for example was never kept in the office. By keeping paperwork down we created the time to organise factory and professional groups and local branches, and to arrange an endless series of education classes and public meetings which ranged from open-air meetings to major rallies in the biggest halls. The pressure on our tiny staff was enormous. New branches were formed in the most unlikely places, even in Hexham, a country town on the Tyne, and in Wordsworth's birthplace, Cockermouth.

Industrial Headaches

In Carlisle we were strongly organised, both in the railway and in the town where I used to speak at large open-air meetings on Sunday evenings below the castle walls. I became very friendly with Isaac Norman, a well-read engine driver and a jolly companion, with whom I stayed in a terrace of railway houses where the night watchman still 'knocked up' the men for the early shifts by tapping on their bedroom windows with a pole. Isaac had been for many years a fireman on the beautiful Carlisle–Settle line over the Pennines and the Yorkshire Dales. He was as dedicated to the railway as he was to the Communist Party and took enormous pride in keeping his trains on time – which had meant, when he was a fireman, shovelling coal non-stop to the limit of his strength to push his heavily-loaded train over the Pennines. Recalling Isaac's name reminds me of the problems the Party faced in a region largely unscathed by war, where industrial relations had been soured by years of unemployment, victimisation, low pay and degrading working conditions. Full employment gave the workers an industrial clout they had not known for years, and industry was seething with dissatisfaction.

The miners were tied to their jobs by wartime orders but hardly a week passed in 1942–3 without strikes in protest against low wages (still held at levels determined by the private coal-owners when the miners were on their backs after the 1926 General Strike and the Depression), appalling conditions, lack of baths and canteens, gross mismanagement and continuous fines and even imprisonment for absenteeism. Nearly half the North-East pits were out at one time in support of two 18-year-olds who had been sent to prison for non-payment of a fine imposed for their refusal (on genuine health grounds) to go underground. An 80-year-old miner was fined for absenteeism. Miners' wives, daughters and sisters were earning more making munitions than their men could make in the pits. The Party walked a tightrope, exposing the conditions and backing the men's demands but opposing strikes because our political priority was victory over fascism. Miners listened to me politely enough at our meetings but went on strike all the same, and we were wise enough never to ask (let alone to order) our Party members to blackleg. It was not until 1943 that the government took the management of the pits out of the coal-owners' hands.

The 'total time strike' in the Tyne shipyards in October 1942 was my worst experience as District Secretary. The shortage of pay clerks in the yards was so acute that the workers' pay fell three days in arrears. The employers' sudden announcement that the men would be paid a week in arrears triggered off strikes in every yard but one, over grievances that had been accumulating for years. The trade unions were also to blame for they had approved the scheme without consulting their members. The government could have prevented the strike had it listened to the CP's proposal, backed by the shop stewards, to set up an immediate Court of Inquiry into pay, failure to employ women, mismanagement and waste of resources. Two-thirds of the workforce came out in defiance of their unions, which did nothing throughout the dispute. It seemed to me unthinkable for communists to hold up ship production when the submarines were still inflicting huge losses on the Russian convoys, and the battles for Stalingrad and North Africa were undecided, but it seemed equally unthinkable for communists to defy a majority decision to strike.

Our members spoke and voted against the strikes (which were 'unofficial') but we would have advised them to come out with the strikers if they lost the vote had Harry Pollitt not come up and instructed them to go to work. I did not quarrel with his decision but it was an emotional not a political one. The Party shop stewards who worked through the strike were isolated and instantly deprived of their positions, yet the workers would have been willing to listen to them had they not black-legged. The *Daily Worker* (which had reappeared in September of that year) was the only newspaper to put the strikers' case; indeed it was the only paper to report the strike at all as it had been blacked out by the rest of the press and the radio. I spoke every day at yard-gate meetings but never experienced any hostility. The strike was called off after a week without winning any immediate concessions, but it was a pyrrhic victory for the Party. Few of the Party stewards were reinstated after the strike and the Party never regained the influence it had previously exercised on the Tyne.

The Red Tide at High Water

The Party's 'no strike' policy and its determination to push the concept of 'national unity' to extremes created problems of our own making, but the political tide was flowing the CP's way and reached its highest mark about the time I left for London in September 1943. Doors that had been closed to the CP for years suddenly opened. Although the government tried to out-flank the CP by promoting official Anglo-Soviet Committees there was enormous enthusiasm at the grass roots for the Soviet Union. During 'Tanks for Russia Week' tanks from the Vickers factory were taken on test through Newcastle flying the Red Flag and bearing slogans like 'Good Old Joe'. Our 'Second Front' and *Daily Worker* rallies pulled in huge audiences despite the blackout and the curtailment of public transport, and raised very large sums of money. Our meetings, big and small, were designed to boost morale, to recruit members and to promote our policies, but they also satisfied people's craving, in the wartime blackout, for participation and entertainment.

We filled the City Hall and Stoll Theatre in Newcastle twice in three months early in 1942; 3,000 people in the City Hall paid sixpence or a shilling for admission and contributed over £100 (over £3,000 in 1989 money) to the collection. Harry Pollitt was the star attraction, but we could fill large halls with such lesser lights as Isabel Brown (a superbly gutsy, earthy, prol-etarian speaker) or Ted Willis (later famous as the creator of 'Dixon of Dock Green', now a Lord but then the leader of the Young Communist League). Joe Waters, who took the collec-tions, had acquired the art, first developed by Isabel Brown during the Spanish War, of turning the collection into a political event that was at one and the same time a first-class comedy turn and an uplifting evangelical experience. He would ask first for fivers to be handed up to the platform, then for one pound notes and then for ten shilling notes, all to a continuous comic patter, and passed round the boxes for loose change only when the last note had been extracted. The higher the total rose the greater the enthusiasm, and the announcement of the final total used to send the audience home with a sense of elation and achievement.

The Labour Party in the North-East was moribund in 1942–3, and we were able to forge stronger links than ever before with the local miners' leaders – with Jim Bowman (later Chairman of the National Coal Board) in Northumberland and with Sam Watson (later Chairman of the Labour Party and a strident anti-communist) in Durham. The Labour Party Conference voted in May 1942 by a narrow majority for the ban on the *Daily Worker* to be lifted, and the fear of an overwhelming defeat at the Trades Union Congress finally forced Herbert Morrison to lift the ban in August. The *Worker* reappeared on 7 September all the stronger for the ban, and we raised £50,000 in two months (say £1.5 million today) to relaunch it. However, all our attempts to achieve any kind of unity or even co-operation with the Labour Party or the TUC were defeated. We underestimated the degree of distrust that had been generated by the Soviet-German Pact of 1939 and the CP's automatic acceptance of Soviet leadership, and the Labour leadership was so paranoid about communism that it detected 'an almost Nazi purpose' in Anglo-Soviet Committees.

'Professional Revolutionaries'

As a newly co-opted member of the CP's Central Committee I travelled overnight to London on desperately overcrowded trains for the monthly meetings at Friends' House in Euston Road on Sundays. I was the new boy in an outfit dominated by seasoned veterans, most of whom had been in the Party since its foundation in 1920 or had been jailed at the time of the General Strike. Several, including our tutor Robbie, had been in the Communist International in Moscow. Pollitt, having been humiliated in 1939 for supporting the war, now dominated the

committee and seemed to have buried the hatchet competely
with those, like Palme Dutt, who had carried through the
Comintern line. There were some very able trade unionists, like
the Welsh miners Arthur Horner and Will Paynter and the engineer George Crane, who had been Shop Stewards' Convenor at
Rover Cars, and some legendary figures from the Invergordon
Mutiny (Fred Copeman) and the International Brigade (Dave
Springhall the National Organiser, and 'Big Peter' Kerrigan), but
there was not one worker from the shop floor on the Central
Committee at that time, although several were elected at later
congresses. No less than 16 of the 26 members of the Central
Committee were full-time 'professional revolutionaries', nearly
all of whom were working men (plus two or maybe three
working women) who had dedicated their lives to the Party
without any thought of financial rewards. It was not unlike a
religious community.

When I came into political conflict with Pollitt and the leadership in 1955–6 I saw the flaw in a Party led by a totally
dedicated professional elite, but my overpowering memory of
the two years I spent on the Central Committee was one of a
friendly, comradely atmosphere in which I acquired great
respect for my colleagues' unselfishness, integrity and intelligence. None of them was 'in it' for themselves, and the same
was true of the great majority of Party members. Meeting Willie
Gallacher was like meeting a living legend – the man who went
to Moscow from Red Clydeside to confront Lenin, and returned
with Lenin's praises ringing in his ears along with Lenin's criticism of his ultra-leftism. Yet when one got to know him Willie
turned out to be a lovely, modest man with a warm personality,
who could always see the funny side of things except where the
'Demon Drink' was concerned – for Willie was such a staunch
teetotaller that as an MP he even tried to have pubs banned
from new towns.

Our minds were so dominated by the need for unity and an
all-out effort to win the war (and initially to avert the total disaster of a Soviet defeat) that there was little political argument.
The report on 'the political situation', with which Pollitt
opened every meeting, was not so much the occasion for a
searching debate as an uplifting *tour de force* whose purpose was
to communicate his unquenchable confidence in Soviet victory
to the Party at large. It is not surprising in these circumstances,

that we misread the changing public mood in 1942–3. The by-election victories of Independent and Common Wealth candidates reflected the growing distrust of Churchill and the Tories that was to lead to their defeat in 1945, but our initial response was not to question our policy of supporting government candidates (whether Tory, Labour or Liberal) in by-elections; it was to attack the Common Wealth Party ('Welcomed by Pro-Fascists'; 'Splitting Unity'), and so to weaken our links with the new radical Left.

The End of the Comintern

On 22 May 1943 the Presidium of the Executive Committee of the Communist International announced its decision recommending its immediate dissolution. Within two days an emergency meeting of our Central Committee had unanimously accepted the recommendation and a telegram was on its way to Dimitrov, the Secretary of the Comintern, endorsing the Presidium's resolution. So strong was the ingrained habit of accepting the Moscow line that neither I nor anybody else remarked that the dissolution was utterly unconstitutional, and that the 'consultation' with other Communist Parties in wartime (when many Communist Parties were underground) was an empty formality. The British CP was the only one in Europe whose Central Committee was able to meet, but we did not publish the Comintern resolution until 29 May, five days after we had telegraphed our agreement! We gave our members no chance to express an opinion on a fundamental change in the constitution of the world communist movement and of the CP itself.

There were in fact very cogent reasons for reforming the Comintern, if not for dissolving it. The idea of a centralised world movement operating on the basis of democratic centralism, in which the constituent parties were bound to obey instructions from the centre, was unworkable and undesirable. It was obvious that the Comintern had become a diplomatic embarrassment to the Soviet Union at a time when Stalin was trying to forge a post-war settlement with Churchill and Roosevelt. After the traumatic experience of following the Comintern line on 'imperialist war' in 1939 most of us heaved a sigh of relief at the prospect of never having to toe the

Comintern line again. I immediately rode off on my personal hobby-horse. Why not, I suggested, replace the awful Comintern jargon 'Political Bureau', 'Secretariat', 'agitprop' and so on with good English words, drop the words 'of Great Britain' from the Party's name and redirect the education of our members away from Soviet history to our own? My proposals were published in the Party press and agreed to by the 1943 Party Congress. The dissolution of the Comintern removed one of the main arguments against the affiliation of the CP to the Labour Party, and we used it to put new life into our unity campaign, but in reality we continued to act as if Stalin's word was holy writ, and the Soviet Party continued to dominate the world communist movement.

The Ethics of Spying

A few weeks later we were shocked by the arrest of Dave Springhall, the National Organiser to whom I was personally responsible, on a charge of espionage for the Soviet Union. He was sentenced to seven years imprisonment in October 1943. Pollitt was telling the truth when he told the next meeting of the Central Committee that neither he nor anybody else in the Political Bureau knew what Springhall was doing, and that he was guilty of a gross breach of Party discipline. I had a personal reason for feeling that 'Springie', as we all knew him, had let the Party down. He came up to Newcastle fairly often, and I used to breakfast with him at Lyons Corner House at Tottenham Court Road before Central Committee meetings. Springie was a burly, bullet-headed, tough communist in the old Bolshevik mould who had been a Political Commissar in the International Brigade. I took a great liking to him, and he gave me excellent down-to-earth advice on how to run the Party. He warned me against trying to get results by laying down the line and telling the comrades to get on with it. His advice was to treat members as human beings and, if a comrade let the Party down, to look for an explanation in his personal life before firing off charges of disloyalty – for, as he put it, the bus driver who failed to turn up at Party meetings might be in trouble with his wife because he was having it off with the conductress, not because he was 'disloyal' to the Party.

Not long after Springie's warning that members might come to me with some very unexpected problems a master at Bede's School in Sunderland (whose name I forget) came to see me one day, twittering with worry. He said he had passed on some blueprints of a warship design from a draughtsman in one of the shipyards to a Soviet agent. What, he asked me (rather late in the day I thought) should he do? He did not realise, though I did, that by telling me he had made me a party to his crime, and my advice was to have nothing more to do with spying and to keep his mouth firmly shut if the police or anybody else ever asked him about it. The next time I saw Springie I asked him if I was right in thinking that Party members should not get involved in espionage for the Soviet Union, and if I'd given good advice. 'Absolutely right, Malcolm' he replied.

I saw nothing wrong, let alone treasonable, in passing military or naval information to our Soviet ally, nor do I believe in 'my country right or wrong' – particularly as it often *is* wrong. I have no sympathy for the 'cash spy', and not much for the Anthony Blunts who lack the courage of their earlier political convictions when found out, but if it is true (as we are constantly told) that 'mutual deterrence' has prevented nuclear war for the past 30 years, the physicist 'spies' Klaus Fuchs and Nunn May, far from being traitors, helped to make the world (and Britain) a safer place by helping the Soviet Union to acquire the means of deterring the US sooner than it would otherwise have done.

Back to the Daily Worker

I would have continued to work for the Party as North-East District Secretary for much longer had Barbara's health not begun to deteriorate. She continued to suffer from ulcerative colitis and internal bleeding and was having increasing difficulty in balancing her blood sugar against the insulin she injected twice a day. She began to suffer from what I can only describe as 'fits', a terrifying experience brought on in the middle of the night by an excess of sugar in her blood. She would be semi-conscious, her back would arch and her jaw would lock, and I had to bring her back to consciousness by inserting a sugar solution between her teeth. There was no National Health Service in those days, and nobody in

Newcastle seemed to know how to treat her condition. I told Harry Pollitt about it, and asked if I could be transferred to London in the hope of getting suitable treatment there. Harry's response was typically generous and practical. He arranged immediately with Bill Rust for me to rejoin the *Daily Worker*, which no longer had a Scottish edition, in London. Thanks to the Blitz and evacuation many London houses were standing empty, and within a few days we had bought a house at 31 Tanza Road in the unfashionable end of Hampstead, overlooking Parliament Hill. By the end of September 1943 we had moved to London and I was once more on the staff of the *Daily Worker* – but this time as a journalist.

9

Life (and Death) on the *Daily Worker*

The move to London coincided with a temporary improvement in Barbara's health (although the London doctors had no more idea what to do than those in Newcastle) and she thoroughly enjoyed the experience of making 31 Tanza Road fit to live in under wartime conditions. Socially the area has been transformed. In the 1940s it was a lowish middle-class area, the unfashionable end of Hampstead with families and bedsitters and anti-fascist German refugees; the Party branch included a teacher, a plumber, an architect, a salesman for Russian Oil Products and intellectuals like Emile and Elinor Burns.

The only restaurant I can remember was a publicly-owned British restaurant selling subsidised meals for a shilling. There were few consumer goods and clothing was rationed, but nobody went hungry or ill-fed, and empty houses (including the one opposite us) were requisitioned for the homeless. There were no off-licences, whereas now there are three, but despite the black-out the pubs did a roaring trade when they could get beer. The three butchers (where we queued for scraps of offal 'off the ration'), the two general grocers and a fishmonger have all gone; so have those marvellously silent, fumeless trolley buses which had replaced the trams before the war on the run from South End Green to Blackfriars and the City. The tram-lines were still in the road and without them I could never have found my way home by car in the pea-souper fogs which as late as 1952 killed 4,000 people in London in a few days – for we were all burning raw coal in open fires in houses in which refrigerators were a luxury and washing machines unknown, and the household equipment consisted of an earthenware sink and a crude gas cooker. Hampstead Heath was half-covered with allotments, wire fences and rabbit hutches. The site for the famous Fair was occupied by an anti-aircraft battery, whose rockets went off with a fearsome but reassuring 'whoosh' during air raids. Women 'manned' the barrage balloons that floated from their moorings on the Heath, one of them at the bottom of Tanza Road.

Number 31, with four storeys, was far too large for Barbara and me, so we offered the top two floors (which had to share a tiny new kitchen and bathroom) to the *Daily Worker* for low rents, and for a few years there was a *Daily Worker* colony in Tanza Road. The first floor was taken by Jack Owen, a toolmaker, trade unionist and city councillor from Manchester who had been expelled from the Labour Party and had become an industrial and political reporter and a member of the *Daily Worker* editorial board. The top floor was taken by George and Betty Tate, a young middle-class couple who had met when they were students and members of the communist 'October Club' at Oxford before the war. George, a historian, was a sub-editor and Betty was about to give birth to their first daughter. Nat Rothman, a deputy chief sub-editor, and his wife Betty, who ran Mrs Churchill's Aid to Russia Fund, were living next door.

I knew that D-Day had come when Barbara heard the Normandy-bound planes overhead in the small hours of 6 June 1944 and rushed to the window crying out that the Second Front had opened. An air-raid alert followed and a bomb fell half a mile away on the Heath, but it was an odd kind of raid: we never got the 'all-clear' because these were not true air-raids but 'buzz-bombs': the small pilotless aircraft launched from sites in Normandy which bombarded London at random for the next two months. They fell to the ground and exploded when the engine cut out, but as they were visible – the glow from the exhaust could be seen at night – people felt safer if they could see them. The top of Parliament Hill (just beside our house) was an amazing sight, a grandstand thronged with spectators day and night because it was the best viewpoint in London. Hundreds of people sat in deck chairs or lay on the ground watching the bombs and trying to guess where they would fall. Although one hit the paddling pool at the bottom of Tanza Road and brought half our ceilings down, the risk in Hampstead was negligible, but Londoners were on alert 24 hours a day and could expect bombs to go off virtually without warning at any time. One of our printers lost a leg when he was hit on the way home. Claud Cockburn, with whom I worked very closely when I became foreign editor and he was the diplomatic and political correspondent, lost his house in St John's Wood, although the only casualty was his cat.

Life and Death

Barbara and I treated the buzz-bombs as little more than a nuisance for, short of living in the tube station, nothing could be done apart from making our wills. Barbara was determined to stick it out with me although she was having a rough time, with a recurrence of the periodical 'fits' caused by hyperglycaemia, and continuous bleeding from ulcerative colitis. But she did not seem to be worse than usual when she went to spend a few days with her mother in Sutton Courtenay in Berkshire towards the end of July. The next thing I heard was that Barbara had been taken in an emergency to the Acland Nursing Home in Oxford, where the surgeon decided to carry out a colostomy – the operation by which much of the intestines are removed and what is left discharges into a bag through a hole in the stomach. It was typical of Barbara's courage that she agreed to the operation, which (quite apart from its horrendous implications) was doubly dangerous for a diabetic. I concluded afterwards that it was a typical case of doctors performing a technically interesting operation but failing to consider whether it would have been preferable to let a patient with a short expectation of life die in peace. Duncan Leys, who had been Barbara's doctor in Inverness, wrote to me after her death to say 'you will feel rather bitter towards the doctors: we are indeed a damned ignorant lot, who blunder about like the early physicists but with people instead of things for our clumsy experiments'.

I went up whenever I could on the appallingly crowded trains to see her in the nursing home, but she was highly sedated, barely able to talk and (as her nurse told me after her death) in great pain, although she gave no sign of it. The surgeon was invariably non-committal, and it was only when Barbara was dead that her nurse told me that she never had a chance. For three weeks I clung to the hope that she would recover, and she even seemed to be a little better the last time I saw her. I was shocked when her sister Hilary rang me up on the morning of 16 August to tell me that Barbara had died. I went up immediately to Oxford, to see her mother and to save her the anguish of registering the death and arranging the cremation. Barbara herself had had no illusions and her mother told me she had said that she did not want me to go to her funeral – I suspect because she knew I would have been appalled (as she would have been) by the religious ritual with its meaningless phrases about everlasting life. I didn't go and the funeral service was, in her mother's words, 'dreadful' – adding that telling me to stay away was 'a typical Barby thing to do'.

There is one postcript to be written to our marriage. In March 1945 I was given a month's notice to remove our daughter Anne from the home for handicapped blind children in Essex to which she had been transferred. The home was intended for disabled but educable children, and Anne had proved to be totally ineducable. I could not find a place for her in a private home at a price that I could afford. I was incapable of looking after her myself, even temporarily. The home was in Essex but Essex County Council had no places in mental hospitals. The London County Council told me that its institutions for mental defectives were reserved for 'London cases', but they found a way through the bureaucratic maze: Anne was moved to a private nursing home in Kensington, thereby becoming a 'London case', and within four days the London County Council admitted her to the Fountains Hospital where she was detained as a certified mental defective. I never saw her again, although she lived to be nearly 28. As I could neither communicate with her nor help her, seeing her was pointless. She could never see, speak, sit up, recognise people or do anything beyond playing with baby toys or smiling when she heard voices. When she died from bronchial pneumonia she had been ill for years.

Comradeship

When I came back to the *Daily Worker* office from Oxford I said to myself that the only thing to do was to immerse myself in my work. The Party and the *Daily Worker* gave me unstinting support. Letters came from comrades with whom Barbara and I had worked, from Newcastle, the Scottish CP office, the Party centre, the Colonial Committee, local branches in Durham and Northumberland, academics in Durham and Newcastle universities, individual miners and shipyard workers and their wives. There were two common themes: one was the affection and admiration that Barbara had inspired and the feeling that her heroic, uncomplaining, unselfish dedication to the movement would be an example to others, and in particular to me; the other was that working for the cause would help, as one miner put it, 'to ease my sorrow', or as a vicar and his wife (who were both in the Party) said, would give me 'the only relief possible'. Marca Burns, who had recruited us to the Party in Edinburgh University and regarded Barbara as her closest friend and confidante, told me that 'Barbara's sunset precedes the dawn of great days in this troubled world – days that will bring us very near to Socialism.'

Passages like these sound naive or maudlin, particularly in the light of subsequent events, but I quote them because they reflected our shared faith in communism and the Party and the comradeship that gave members of the CP a passport to friendships the whole world over at that time. Years after we had both left the Party, Christopher Hill (the great historian of the Cromwellian period and later Master of Balliol who was my closest comrade in the fight for inner party democracy in 1956 [see Chapter 16]) told me that he still missed the comradeship that the Party and its historians' group had given him. Our blind, unshakeable confidence in the Party and our tendency to confine our friendships to communists or sympathisers were, in the end, among the causes of our failure and self-deception, but at the time they gave us strength out of all proportion to our numbers and helped me to survive the most traumatic experience of my life.

The Reborn *Daily Worker*

Rejoining the *Daily Worker* in London in September 1943 was an exhilarating experience. The atmosphere was euphoric because the paper had pulled off the greatest feat in its history when it reappeared in September 1942 after the lifting of the ban, and all the talk was about the coming victory over fascism and the plans for a post-war mass circulation paper of the left. The re-publication of the *Daily Worker* by a small editorial team led by Bill Rust remains an achievement without parallel in the history of the British press. The press in Cayton Street had been destroyed in the Blitz, yet within ten days a completely new four-page paper with a full range of news, features, arts and sport was produced on an unsuitable and unfamiliar press (rented from the steelworkers' union) without a single trained sub-editor and only one trained reporter. There was not at first even an editorial office, and the first issues were produced with the help of communist or sympathetic journalists from other newspapers, working without pay wherever they could find a chair or a table in passages and corridors. Barristers and solicitors volunteered to form a rota of lawyers to vet the paper for libel.

A new staff had to be recruited, most of whom were disabled in one way or another, and all of whom had to be trained in the basic skills of sub-editing, reporting or feature writing. Paul Terry, our air correspondent, was an ex-RAF airline pilot who had been crippled by the rheumatoid arthritis which killed him a few years later. It was all he could do to hold a pencil in his hand, but he was always cheerful and turned in good copy on time. Lieutenant Colonel Hans Kahle, our military correspondent, was very fit physically but disabled politically, for he was an ex-Prussian officer who had fought (on the German side) in the First World War, and for republican Spain in the International Brigade. He joined the Communist Party and found refuge in Britain when the International Brigade was disbanded in 1938. Like most anti-Nazi Germans he was deported to Canada in the shameful 1940 panic, and when he came back the government rejected all his offers to fight against the Nazis. The British Army's loss was the *Daily Worker's* gain, for in Hans we had one of the best critics of military strategy and probably the most popular man in the office. Hans would never have been given a job after the war in West Germany where denazification was never taken seriously. He went to East Germany in August 1945 to put his anti-Nazi principles into practice as a provincial chief of police. Sadly, he died within a few months from an infectious disease.

The reborn *Daily Worker* was, for the first time in its history, a real newspaper. The immense political pressure from the Labour movement that had forced Herbert Morrison to lift the ban had also broken down other major barriers. The whole-salers lifted the ban which they had imposed in 1930 forbidding the distribution of the paper by their newspaper trains and trucks, which made it possible for the *Worker* to reach most newsagents' shops before breakfast. This in turn made it worthwhile for the paper to subscribe to the three main news agencies: Reuters for overseas news, the Press Assocation for home news and The Exchange Telegraph for parliamentary reports. The *Daily Worker* was allowed into Parliament, with a reporter in the Press Gallery and its political correspondent in the Lobby. By its previous standards the paper had plenty of money, as advertisement revenue began to come in to supplement the sales revenues. £4,000 was raised every month for the 'Fighting Fund' through personal donations and workshop collections. The fund was run by Barbara Niven, who sacrificed her real interest in life – she was a gifted painter – for the *Worker*, and established an extraordinary rapport with thousands of readers. More than anyone else she forged the personal links that enabled the *Worker* to transform itself in 1946 into a co-operative society with thousands of shareholders, and to translate into reality the slogan 'the only paper owned by its readers'.

Bans and discrimination remained, of course. The export of the paper was forbidden for the best part of a year after republication. Herbert Morrison, furious at having to lift the ban on the *Worker*, carried his spite to the point of absurdity by excluding us from Ministry of Home Security briefings on the heavy air-raids that were anticipated when the Second Front opened in 1944 – presumably on the principle that *Daily Worker* readers were better dead than red. The Labour Party still forbade its members and affiliated unions to attend *Daily Worker* conferences, which nevertheless attracted enormous attendances. The government refused to accredit any *Daily Worker* war correspondents until the war ended in August 1945, not because (as it claimed) communists could not be trusted but because it did not want our reporters to expose Churchill's support of royalist and fascist personalities in Greece or Italy. I told a conference on the post-war *Daily Worker* in May 1945 that 'if Generals are shaking hands with Goering, we want the *Daily Worker* correspondent to see it'. Claud Cockburn was admitted to Algiers as the newspaper's reporter by De Gaulle's Free French in 1943 only to be deported within 24 hours by the

British Command. Clemens Dutt landed in the South of France in June 1944 with the invading Free French Forces, but he too was deported by the British Command.

By tying the *Worker's* paper rations to its pre-war consumption, when it's circulation was tiny and it was small in size, the government prevented the *Worker* from increasing its share of the market at the time of its greatest popularity. By 1945 the *Daily Worker* had a circulation of 104,000, but it was only able to reach this figure by keeping the paper down to four pages in a very small format with very small type. The demand for the paper far exceeded the supply, and we were unable to give news or features anything like the space available in other papers.

The Two Als

I had no idea what job I would be offered when I arrived at the office in September 1943. I had a smattering of experience in Glasgow but I was totally untrained as a sub-editor or a reporter, and ignorant of the basic procedures for newspaper production. I was put through a crash course in sub-editing under the eyes of Allen Hutt the chief sub-editor and his deputy Alan Winnington. As every piece of copy has to pass through the sub-editors' hands the subs' table is the best place from which to get the feel of a newspaper and the people who run it. It was immediately obvious that despite its handicaps the paper was efficiently run.

Bill Rust was a decisive editor (unlike Johnny Campbell who dithered in times of crisis) and left nobody in any doubt that he was the boss, although he in turn was responsible to the Party's Political Committee. But he was also a listener, and as a newcomer I was fascinated by the often heated discussions of the editorial committee (of which I soon became a member) and the meetings at which editions were planned. The tape boys (who took the tapes from the teleprinters to the news editor) addressed the editor as 'Bill' and took part, along with secretaries and other non-editorial staff, in the morning conference at which the previous day's issue was criticised. Douglas Hyde, the news editor who turned Catholic and deserted the paper in a blaze of publicity in 1948, asserted in his confessional memoirs that the *Daily Worker* staff lived in 'a loose amoral atmosphere that was supercharged with sex'. I got a different impression, partly because I do not equate all extra-marital sex with immorality. There were, of course, affairs and liaisons among the staff, but what bound us together was essentially moral principle: we had all decided to work, not for money, but for what we conceived (sometimes mistakenly) to be the betterment of mankind.

My mentors as chief sub and deputy chief sub, the two Als, were close buddies and drinking companions, but as different as chalk from cheese. Allen Hutt was a Cambridge man, and a lifelong communist who rejected many lucrative offers to work for the press barons. Alan Winnington was a buccaneering, hard-drinking, hard-working, cockney who also remained a communist to the end of his life. He was a full-time press officer for the CP when Hutt pulled him into the relaunched *Daily Worker* and, as Alan recalled, 'in two terrible and almost sleepless weeks trained me as his deputy in the most exacting and expert editorial job of all – chief sub-editor – usually regarded on the British press as needing years of tempering'. Alan proved himself to be a first-class chief sub and, when he reported the Korean War (as we will see in Chapter 14), a fearless and brilliant reporter.

It was only when I was sitting at the subs' table that I realised how much I had to learn from Allen Hutt. It was Allen more than anybody else who turned a squad of unqualified and in some cases poorly educated people into journalists whose product could stand comparison with the best in Fleet Street – and proved it by winning the newspaper design prize in 1954 and 1956 when anti-communist prejudice was near its peak. He wrote what was for some years the standard work on newspaper typography, and even *The Times* felt obliged to call Allen in when it wanted a new look. It was Allen who insisted on (and got) the highest standards of typography and layout and achieved miracles in producing a richly varied and visually interesting newspaper within a tiny space.

The training manual Allen wrote for his staff of novices, nick-named the 'subs' bible', became a collector's piece in Fleet Street because it was the best manual written up to that time. With its help Allen taught us the abc of popular journalism: the facts and figures must be accurate; the first sentence must catch the readers' interest; the first short paragraph must convey the gist of the story and throw up a punchy headline; the story must be clearly told and fit the space allotted to it, and the copy must be written so that it can be cut paragraph by paragraph from the end and still make sense if space has to be found for a major story that breaks just as the paper is being put to bed. Subbing is the art of translating these apparently simple rules into practice by transforming even the crudest reports into crisp, accurate copy of precisely the right length, capped with a headline in the typeface, and within the space limitations, prescribed by the chief sub.

Allen's achievement can be understood better if I explain that many of our reporters had started life as industrial workers and had left school before they were 14. They had an immense advantage because they knew industry and the conditions in which the working class lived from firsthand experience. They knew their way around the Labour Party and trade union scene and they could communicate easily with working people. They were one of the paper's greatest assets – people like George Sinfield who doubled as industrial correspondent and sports editor and enjoyed an immense popularity in trade union circles; Jack Owen, the toolmaker who specialised in industrial and trade union stories; Harry McShane, the boilermaker who reported from Scotland; Rose Smith, a one-time textile worker who focused on women's and social issues; and Ben Francis, a miner disabled by lung disease (and always short of breath) who was our forces correspondent but also covered industrial stories.

Some of them – Johnny Campbell, George Sinfield and others – became first-class writers. Bill Rust, although a dominant editor, had the humility to ask Claud Cockburn to help him to master the journalist's craft and he became a forceful, though not a subtle, writer. Others were less successful and it was painful to see them trying to find the right words to give their stories the heavy punch, the light touch, the fun, the sharp jab or the appeal to the heart that they needed. The shortage of space made it doubly difficult for them to compress their stories into the allotted space.

The potential in these circumstances for tensions between reporters and sub-editors is notorious. Reporters see the subs mangling their stories and cutting out 'the best bits', and (most galling of all) writing headlines that (they think) distort the reports that carry their names. Subs see their job as turning tedious, inaccurate, badly-written reports into good copy with strong headlines that will make the reader sit up and take notice. At Allen's subs' table we were taught to respect our reporters, and the reporters were taught to respect the sub-editor who could make a poor story good and a good story better.

Foreign Editor

I had the advantage that I was not entirely new to the game, and I suppose that I thought I had an exceptional status because I had been a parliamentary candidate and a member of the Party's Central Committee. It would not surprise me now to be told that I was too cocky by half. Whatever the reason, although I was a quick learner Allen was clearly determined to cut me down to size. I discovered in the first five minutes that Allen was a hyperactive extrovert, who poured out an unending stream of praise and blame for everyone to hear, heavily loaded with sarcasm and frequent jokes at other people's expense – too often, I thought, at mine. It certainly made the office a lively and entertaining place. There was no real malice in Allen's performance, which was often very funny, and he was always at the centre of the merry crowd (including several of those who had been the butts of his wit) which went to the pub when the edition had been put to bed. But I only went to the pub occasionally, mainly because I have never been a regular drinker, much as I like a drink, and I have always grudged the cost of paying for endless rounds of pints when I rarely take more than half a pint myself. I had already discovered that alcoholism is the journalist's industrial disease. I admired Allen, but I found him increasingly hard to take. After a month on the subs' table I stormed into Bill Rust's office after a flaming row and presented an absurd ultimatum: either Allen would stop abusing me or I would leave the *Worker*.

Nobody could change Allen's ways and I had not the slightest intention of leaving the *Worker*, with which I had fallen in love. As a months' subbing was a long training by *Daily Worker* standards Bill gave me a job as foreign editor, for which I had no qualifications except an absorbing interest in foreign affairs. It was characteristic of the shortage of suitable people at that time that the *Worker* should have appointed a foreign editor whose only foreign language was indifferent French and whose experience of the world was limited to a month in Russia, a trip across Canada and occasional visits to France. I jumped at the idea. The job had the immense attraction that I would work very closely with the legendary Claud Cockburn, alias 'Frank Pitcairn', the *Worker's* star reporter and editor of his own private political scandal sheet *The Week*. Claud had been attempting the impossible task of combining the jobs of political correspondent and diplomatic correspondent. He was to continue to do both jobs, but I would relieve him of most of the responsibility for foreign affairs. A desk was found for me and I became foreign editor the next day.

10

Foreign Editor

My arrival at the foreign desk coincided with radical changes in the fortunes of war and the attitude of the CP and the *Daily Worker*. The enormous Soviet advances on the eastern front and the British victory in North Africa had transformed the military situation. Churchill had frustrated the pressure for an early Second Front at the Quebec meeting with Roosevelt in August 1943, but when the 'Big Three' met in December in Teheran Roosevelt and Stalin insisted on a binding agreement to open the Second Front in 1944. The communique recording their 'full accord' on the blows to be struck 'from East, West and South' in 1944 suddenly made the CP's long-sustained campaign for the opening of a Second Front in the west almost redundant. We became conscious of the fact that victory, if not round the corner, would come in 1944 or 1945, and we turned our minds increasingly to the shape of the post-war world.

As foreign editor I found myself handling a series of crises – Italy, Yugoslavia, Greece and Poland to name the most acute – in which virulent anti-communism tried to turn back the course of history and foreshadowed the Cold War. I picked up enough information through months of reading, and by developing personal contacts, to write articles on an astonishing number of countries that I had never seen, including East Prussia, Poland, Romania, Belgium, Nigeria and the Middle East. I was primarily a desk man whose job was to assess and report the incoming foreign news. Claud Cockburn and I both used the 'Diplomatic Correspondent' byline when it suited us.

The title of 'foreign editor' conveys an exaggerated impression of my importance in the scheme of things on the *Daily Worker*. We gave a bigger proportion of our space to foreign affairs than other newspapers, partly because communism is an international movement, but also because we were the only political party firmly committed to independence for India and the Colonies and to social revolution in the countries that had been under fascist dictatorships. On tricky policy issues I would consult Bill Rust or Johnny Campbell, both of whom were members of the CP's Political Committee. In many cases we followed the lead of the Soviet Union in its role as the leading Communist Party, but on many critical issues such as events in Italy and Greece the Soviet Union often preferred to remain silent – at least as far as I was aware. We formed our own judgements after consulting communists from the countries concerned wherever this was possible, for we believed that communists should have a united approach to any issue.

Neither the Party nor the *Daily Worker* deferred to the Soviet Union on Colonial or Indian matters, for the simple reason that we knew far more than they did. The British Party had the best-informed specialists (like Palme Dutt on India or Ben Bradley on the Colonies) who were in very close touch with local communist parties or trade unions. When S.A. Dange, the Communist President of the All-India Trades Union Congress, was freed from jail in June 1944 and came to Britain – a tiny man with a big brain and enormous energy – almost the first thing he did was to come to the *Worker* office to be interviewed by me. This kind of firsthand contact with the people who had been in the Colonial jails throughout the war gave me a vivid picture of the mood of India in the final days of the British Raj. It also helped us to distinguish our unqualified support for the independence of the Colonies from the Labour Party's talk of freedom within the British Commonwealth, which led in practice to the continuation of British Colonial rule (except in India) when Labour won power.

London: A Journalist's Paradise

London at that time was a journalist's paradise, as it was the hub of the Allied war effort in Western Europe and awash with rumours and experts (or people who claimed to be experts) on every country under the sun. The exiled European governments were based in London, and so were their opponents in the emigré population. There was a superabundance of ministers and ambassadors who wanted to promote their interests through the press. There was a strong feeling in liberal and socialist circles that the habits of co-operation forged in the course of the resistance should continue in the new Europe to be created on the ruins of the old. Their hopes were to be disappointed in many cases. We had a resident Czechoslovak expert in Ludwig Freund, whose desk was next to mine. Ludwig was a Sudeten German communist who, like Hans Kahle, had been detained as an 'enemy' alien and only released after a sustained campaign to free 'Morrison's anti-fascist prisoners'. When President Benes's Czechoslovak government in exile asked Ludwig to study British journalism he chose to work in the *Daily Worker* office, where he lived up to his name – *Freund* is the German for friend – being universally popular, well-informed, a good journalist and a useful source of information. When Ludwig went back to Czechoslovakia he adopted the Czech surname Frieka to distinguish himself from the Sudeten Germans who were expelled to Germany.

The two experts with whom I worked most closely were Claud Cockburn and the Honourable Ivor Montagu, the son of Lord Swaythling, a rich City financier. Ivor was the very prototype of the aristocrat-turned-communist. He had a degree in science and was a good investigative journalist with a special interest in Germany and in the roots of fascism. He did a splendid job in Germany after the war as the first of our war correspondents, reporting conditions there and covering the opening stages of the Nuremberg Trial of the Nazi leaders. He was at different times our diplomatic and our political correspondent, but he always had so many irons in the fire that he never did any one job for long.

From being The *Observer's* film critic he became involved in film-making as editor, screen-writer, director and producer. He was one of the pioneers of the British documentary film, a producer for Ealing Studios and a close associate of the great Soviet director Eisenstein with whom he worked both in the Soviet Union and in Hollywood. Ivor was a table tennis champion and the chairman for many years of the international table tennis federation. He invented 'ping-pong diplomacy' by arranging matches between China and Western countries to break through the political boycott of China by the US after the Korean War. He was a Stalinist in politics, but a genius in his own way and a charmer too.

It was part of my job to attend the daily Foreign Office (FO) and War Office press briefings in the London University Senate House in Malet Street, which was then London's only building with more than ten storeys. I soon discovered that these briefings were intended primarily for the provincial and foreign press. *The Times* and other diplomatic correspondents were given the government line (and supposedly the *real* story) by senior officials or by ministers. Foreigners were amazed by the informality of the proceedings, for officials sat on a table swinging their legs and drawing on their fags as they read out the official communiques and answered questions. The senior Foreign Office spokesman, whose name I forget, was married to a woman from Reuters who, it was said, had only to turn over in bed to get the Foreign Office's 'reaction' to the latest news if it broke in the middle of the night. Then there was Guy Burgess, who was a regular spokesman for the Foreign Office throughout my time as foreign editor.

When the press conference was over Guy liked to come with a clique of reporters, mainly American, to a pub a couple of hundred yards away in Store Street. I can't say that I either liked or disliked him. He had a barbed and cynical wit and made a point of asking me difficult questions about Soviet or CP policy. As he had a sharp brain I enjoyed the political or intellectual sparring this led to, but it left me with the feeling (which was probably his intention) that he shared the Foreign Office's basically anti-communist stance – so much so that when the press reported that Burgess and Maclean had disappeared, and were probably Soviet agents, I wrote a piece for the *Worker* recalling our meetings and saying that I found it hard to believe.

Claud Cockburn

The main attraction in the pub was not Guy but Claud Cockburn who dropped in to swap information with American reporters, using the 'barter' technique that had built up the reputation of *The Week* for telling the stories that nobody else dared to print. The Americans liked Claud because, quite apart from his value as a source of information, he made their day by regaling them with an unending flow of funny stories, which became funnier as he elaborated them with repetition. My favourite was the one about Claud's interview with Al Capone, the Chicago gangster, in the days of the Prohibition in the

1930s when Claud was a reporter for *The Times*. The head of *The Times's* Washington Bureau was so taken aback when Claud suggested interviewing Capone – *The Times* never reported crime – that he cabled London to seek higher authority. Back came the cable: 'by all means Cockburn Chicagowards. Welcome stories ex-Chicago not unduly emphasising crime'. When Claud eventually reached the mobster in his Chicago fortress, surrounded by guards with sub-machine-guns, Al Capone launched into a lyrical defence of 'the American system'. He praised freedom, enterprise and the pioneers and referred with contemptuous disgust to socialism and anarchism, saying:

> My rackets are run on strictly American lines and they're going to stay that way ... This American system of ours, call it capitalism, call it what you like, gives to each and every one of us the opportunity if we only seize it with both hands and make the most of it.

Claud had worked for *The Times* in Berlin and Washington before going over to the *Daily Worker*, and he had reported the Spanish War for the *Worker* under his pen-name 'Frank Pitcairn'. He had a raffish, cosmopolitan lifestyle and an uproarious sense of the comedy or farce in political life. He was almost invariably unshaven, untidy and shabbily dressed, and already late for some urgent appointment. Claud had become a legend before the war because his mimeographed newsletter *The Week* created the legend of the 'Cliveden set', a group of right-wing Tories centred in Lord and Lady Astor's house at Cliveden on the Thames who were sympathetic to Nazi policies. *The Week* became compulsory reading for British, French and even German politicians because Claud had a genius for giving his readers the feeling that they were being let into the innermost secrets of the great and the bad. He could spot stories that nobody else could see, or slants on them that would enable him to make his points through ridicule, sarcasm or irony – as he did by using Al Capone to illuminate the gangster character of American capitalism in the columns of *The Times*.

The Week so enraged Dr Goebbels that the Nazi government described it as 'the source of all anti-Nazi lies in Britain' and put Claud on its death-list for the British invasion. It so enraged Herbert Morrison that he banned it in 1941, along with the *Daily Worker*. *The Week* was run in practical terms by Miriam

Risner, the wife of a communist Savile Row tailor whose gifts to the Party leaders included sartorial elegance, and she and I brought out *The Week* together when Claud went to the founding of the United Nations in San Francisco in 1945, but by that time *The Week's* best days were over and I was no Claud.

One of the secrets of Claud's success was the extraordinary range of his pre-war contacts which stretched from Robert Boothby, in Churchill's circle, to the top of the Labour Party. The CP's opposition to the war had damaged some of these links and after 1945 the Cold War severed most of them. By 1948 Claud's commitment to communism had been undermined: he could no longer afford to work for the *Daily Worker* and dropped out without a murmur. But in 1943 *The Week* was back after the ban (although financially rocky and with a much reduced circulation) and at the age of 39 Claud was still a force to be reckoned with: although his range of contacts no longer extended to Churchill's circle they went as high as General de Gaulle, who was reputed to like him.

The Cold War in the Hot War

My central preoccupation as foreign editor was the continuing struggle that would shape the post-war settlement. We had, I believe, a basically sound perception of the conflict between the fascist and the anti-fascist forces, and of Churchill's reactionary aims, but we had a misplaced confidence in the willingness of the Western powers to maintain friendly relations with the Soviet Union after the war, and we blinded ourelves to the realities of Stalinism – although it is interesting to speculate whether Stalin would have imposed such ruthless regimes in Eastern Europe had it not been for the Cold War launched by the Western powers. The crises in Italy, Yugoslavia, Greece and Poland revealed the conflicts that were to decide what kinds of regime would replace fascism at the end of the war.

The Italian crisis was at its height when I became foreign editor in September 1943. The *Worker* consistently attacked Churchill's obsessive anti-communism and his love for royalty, which were responsible for his failure to grasp the opportunities created by the fall of Mussolini and the revolutionary upsurge in Italy in July 1943. When the King and the Fascist government led by Marshal Badoglio (Italy's number one war criminal responsible for using poison gas in Abyssinia) came over to the Allies, Churchill gave them unstinting support 'as the only ,bulwark against "Bolshevism"'. It was not until 1989 that a BBC 'Timewatch' programme revealed, from British Foreign Office records, that from then onwards British governments (including the Labour post-war government) ensured that not one of many hundreds of proven Italian war criminals was handed over to Yugoslavia, Greece or Ethiopia for trial.

Churchill's monarchist and anti-communist obsessions also led him to give his support initially to the Yugoslav royalist Mihailovich, whose anti-communist and Serbian nationalist 'resistance' movement had degenerated by 1943 into collaboration with the fascists. The only effective resistance movement was that led by the communist 'Tito' who was recognised as an Allied Commander in December 1943. Churchill was sufficiently realistic to see, long before the meeting in Moscow in November 1944, that nothing that Britain could do would restore the fortunes of the discredited monarchy. Churchill, who was already planning to restore the Greek monarchy and crush the left-wing Greek National Liberation Front (EAM), slipped Stalin a note cynically offering the Soviet Union a 90 per cent influence in Yugoslavia in return for a 90 per cent British influence in Greece. Stalin, who had no intention of intervening in Greece, accepted by ticking the figures. Through this cynical deal Churchill accepted the incorporation of Eastern Europe in the Soviet sphere, and helped to create the division of Europe against which he subsequently railed.

The Betrayal of Greece*

Greece was my main preoccupation throughout 1944, when the various factions in Greek politics manoeuvred for position as the moment for liberation drew nearer, and Churchill's plans

*The reader who is interested in discovering the truth is referred to: General Stefanos Sarafis, *ELAS, The Greek Resistance Army* (Merlin Press); P. Papastratis, *British Policy Towards Greece during the Second World War 1941–4* (Cambridge University Press); Heinz Richter, *British Intervention in Greece* (Merlin Press); Marion Sarafis (ed.), *Greece: from Resistance to Civil War* (Spokesman); and to P. Grambas, 'The Greek Communist Party: divided opinions 1941–5', in Marion Safaris (ed.), *Background to Contemporary Greece* (Merlin Press, 1990) which is based on the archives of the Greek Communist Party (KKE).

to restore the pre-war monarcho-fascist regime culminated in the war he launched against the Greek National Liberation Army (ELAS). After so many years it is impossible to put the record straight in a personal memoir of this kind.

At the time Churchill tried to conceal the truth by censoring Middle East news, including reports of the 'mutinies' in the royalist Greek Army and Navy in which soldiers and sailors who supported EAM were sentenced to death. The BBC was explicitly instructed not to make any favourable references to EAM or its military wing ELAS, except with the permission of the Foreign Office, but we had excellent sources of information, not least through the Greek seamen's unions based in Cardiff where Betty Bartlett, the CP District Secretary whom I had met as a fellow pupil at the Party school in 1941, had met Tony Ambatielos, a communist and one of the seamen's leaders, whom she married and who later spent years in Greek jails under sentence of death.

Today two things strike me about our coverage of Greece in 1944–5. I am proud of the way in which the accuracy of our reports and the pertinency of our comments – about the internal resistance movement, the 'mutinies' in the Greek forces in protest against the reactionary policies of the royalist government in exile, and the bloody repression of EAM and ELAS by Churchill in December 1944 – stand up today in the light of later information. The other is our misreading of the signals that can now be seen to have pointed to the final tragic outcome. We did not appreciate the lengths to which Churchill would go to crush the liberation movement and to hand power to those who had imposed a fascist dictatorship in 1936 and collaborated with the Nazis during the German occupation. We hailed as positive achievements the agreements by which, in the summer of 1944, EAM accepted a mere five ministries (none of them in key posts) in a new Greek government in exile and agreed to place ELAS under the command of the British General Scobie – thereby placing itself at the mercy of its enemies and sealing the fate of Greek democracy and independence.

Churchill Destroys the Liberation Army

ELAS controlled most of Greece in October 1944 when the Germans retreated, and the British hardly fired a shot to liberate the country. When the British forces arrived they marched into peaceful cities controlled by ELAS and were greeted by wildly-cheering crowds waving EAM banners. EAM proposed the replacement of all the existing armed forces of Left and Right by democratically-recruited security forces, and believed that it had reached agreement with Premier Papandreou, but a crisis was precipitated on 30 November when Papandreou issued a decree, accompanied by the false statement that the EAM ministers had consented to it, ordering a solution in which the royalist forces were kept intact. General Scobie, going far beyond his powers as Commander-in-Chief, and in breach of the agreement by which ELAS had accepted his command, ordered ELAS to disarm in accordance with the decree.

The EAM ministers resigned, and (according to Reuters eye-witness account) the collaborationist Greek police fired from concealed positions into an unarmed protest by EAM in Athens on 5 December, killing 23 men, women and children and wounding over 100. ELAS's urban guerrillas in Athens seized the police stations and EAM announced its readiness to serve in a new broadly-based government. Churchill forbade any change in government, rejected all overtures for a settlement and gave Scobie carte blanche to use all the means at his disposal – including air bombardment – to drive the 'ruffians and bandits' (as he called ELAS) from the Greek capital – even stooping to the charge that Germans had penetrated ELAS. As in any civil war atrocities were committed on both sides, but the essence of the situation, as I said in an article on 9 January, was that 'British bayonets prop a Greek dictator'.*

The reports of British forces bombing and fighting the main Greek resistance army provoked an explosion of anger in Britain, which manifested itself in a massive press campaign led by *The Times* and in a huge midwinter demonstration in Trafalgar Square. At the height of the fighting the Labour Party Conference called for an immediate armistice. Churchill could have been forced to change course had the Labour ministers in the War Cabinet opposed him, but Ernest Bevin saved Churchill in the critical debate in the Commons, betraying

*For a detailed account see G. Alexander, 'The Demobilization Crisis of November 1944' in *Greece in the 1940s: A Nation in Crisis* (University Press of New England, 1980).

Greece in much the same way as he had betrayed republican Spain in 1936.

Eden lied when he told the Commons on 21 December 1944 that the British wanted EAM to be included in 'a representative Greek Government' for Churchill had decided as far back as 1943 to destroy EAM. He made no secret in his speeches of his prior instructions to Scobie to be ready to crush EAM and the communists whom he falsely accused of preparing to seize power. The documents now available show that neither the Greek Communist Party (KKE) nor EAM ever had any such intention. On the contrary they put too much trust in Britain's good faith, and by making too many concessions in the interests of national unity (which was the current communist 'line') they opened the way to their own destruction. EAM was initiated by communists but it was genuinely a leftish, republican democratic coalition in which the communists were no longer in the majority. General Sarafis, the commander of ELAS, was a regular officer with liberal views and strong democratic instincts, who was elected as a deputy of the United Democratic Left in 1951 and run down by an American truck in 1957 – in the opinion of most Greeks and his English wife, probably murdered by the CIA. In the liberated areas EAM had for the first time given the Greek people the opportunity to govern themselves. Some undisciplined fanatics in the Greek Communist Party had been guilty of atrocities and bloody feuding, but ELAS had developed into a disciplined army.

Churchill's success in destroying ELAS resulted in a right-wing terror of which the resistance fighters were the main victims, as I was to see for myself when I visited Greece at the end of 1945. It led directly to the restoration of the monarchy, to the Greek Civil War and to the fascist dictatorship of the colonels in the 1960s.

The Warsaw Uprising – the Crime and the Tragedy

The legend that the Red Army stood aside and allowed the Nazis to crush the Warsaw Rising of 1 August 1944 is still widely accepted as the truth. It is one of the most successful of the false, anti-Soviet atrocity stories although its falsity has always been obvious to anybody who took the trouble to check the facts. The uprising ordered by the exiled Polish government in London took the Soviet government and its High Command completely by surprise. Only the day before the uprising I had published an article in which I asserted, with tragic inaccuracy, that 'Warsaw is in sight of the end of its prolonged and terrible ordeal.' In the *Worker* office we shared the general belief that the sweeping advance of the Red Army would culminate in the crossing of the Vistula and the liberation of Warsaw within the next few days. In fact the Red Army had outrun its supplies and the Germans were able to launch a counter-attack that delayed the taking of Warsaw for five months. The rising was one of the most heroic, futile, cynical, bloody and destructive episodes of the war. In *The Road to Berlin* John Erickson estimates that when the rising was finally put down 'after 62 days of unending horror and atrocity' 15,000 of the 30–40,000 men in the Polish Home Army were dead. The wounded were slaughtered, the survivors were deported or sent to the gas chambers, up to 200,000 civilians had been 'immolated' and 'the Germans bent to the maniacal labour of levelling Warsaw to the ground'.

The motives of those who ordered the rising could only be understood in a political context that Claud and I explained in *The Worker* over the next few weeks. Churchill had been trying for months to persuade the London Polish government to grasp the unpalatable fact that Poland owed its very existence entirely to the Soviet victories, and would have to live on friendly terms with the Soviet Union in future. But history and the conflicting attitudes of the Polish and Soviet peoples virtually guaranteed a conflict. The rival Polish partisan groups, some fighting to restore the old, reactionary, clerical order, others fighting for a social revolution and a national reorientation friendly to the Soviet Union, were already at each other's throats. The crossing of the old Polish–Soviet frontier on 3 July by the Red Army raised the immediate question: which Polish grouping would administer the liberated territory?

The London Poles had allowed their traditional hatred and suspicion of the Soviet Union to cloud their political judgment. They accepted without investigation a Nazi report that the Soviet Union had massacred thousands of Polish officers at Katyn. The Soviet government now admits that the KGB was responsible for the massacre, and the full truth came out in 1990 when the Soviet government carried out the inquiry requested by the Solidarity-based Polish government. At the time, however, not only was it inconceivable to me that the Soviet government had massacred the Polish officers, but the British government also rejected the Nazi version, and continued to do so for over 40 years. The Soviet government broke off diplomatic relations with the Polish government in London, and on 24 July a provisional government called the Polish Committee for National Liberation, consisting of communists and other opponents of the old dictatorship, was established on Polish soil with Soviet blessing. Its manifesto, which I reported in the *Daily Worker* on 25 July, struck all the right popular and democratic notes. The Liberation Committee simultaneously invited Mikolajczyk, the London Polish Premier, to head a new, united provisional government in Poland with elements from the London and the Polish centres.

The Real Purpose of the Uprising

These developments split the London Polish government, and led to a belated decision – by a small majority and on Churchill's insistence – to send Mikolajczyk to Moscow to discuss the situation with Stalin. Mikolajczyk reached Moscow on 28 July but before leaving he gave General Bor-Komarowski, the commander of the 'Home Army' in Warsaw, full authority to launch an uprising which was doomed militarily before it began. Although the Polish Commander-in-Chief General Sosnowski had advised that an armed rising without the co-operation of the Red Army would be 'an act of despair', no attempt was made to contact the Red Army. On 28 July Sir Anthony Eden, the Foreign Secretary, categorically rejected a request by the London Polish government for Britain to drop a parachute brigade and supplies, and to bomb targets.

In the *Daily Worker* our first reaction to the news of the Warsaw Rising was one of mystification, for the only information came from the Polish government in London, which we regarded as a totally untrustworthy source. But within a few days the political and opportunist nature of the rising had become all too clear. In *Barbarossa*, his history of the German–Soviet conflict, Alan Clark makes it clear that the London Polish government's aim was to establish itself in Warsaw before the Red Army could enter the city. The RAF, it hoped, would then have flown the London Polish government in, which would have been able to install itself in the Polish capital with the prestige of military achievement and backed by a powerful local force.

This scenario was pure fantasy – I might even say typical Polish fantasy. Churchill would not have imperilled his relations with the Soviet Union by dropping the London Polish government into Warsaw, and Stalin would not have tolerated such an anti-Soviet coup. The criminal folly of the rising is obvious: responsibility for the fate of Warsaw and its people lies squarely with the anti-Soviet Poles who ordered the rising and the Nazis whose cruelty in repressing it plumbed new depths of barbarism. It is argued that the Soviet Union should nevertheless have done everything in its power, on humanitarian if not on military grounds, to assist the Home Army. Even now I am haunted by the cynicism with which all those concerned pursued their political objectives regardless of the fate of the innocent victims. Stalin was right, if cynical, when he told Mikolajczyk on 13 August that the rising was 'a reckless adventure causing useless victims among the inhabitants'. The British government itself reproved the London Poles (though not in public) for their decision to start a general uprising wthout any prior consultation. Eden demanded, although he failed to secure, the resignation of the Polish Commander-in-Chief Geneneral Sosnowski for issuing an Order of the Day on 1 September castigating Britain for abandoning her Polish ally.

I hoped that the shared experience of German nationalism in its brutal Nazi form had laid the basis for a new friendship between the Russians and the Poles, to which the Soviet-backed programme of the National Liberation Committee gave a positive expression. The Warsaw Rising and the Katyn massacre soured these hopes even before Poland was liberated. After the war, although Warsaw was rebuilt in a heroic reconstruction effort, the promise of a new Poland could not be realised in the context of a Cold War in which the US policy proclaimed by Foster Dulles was to 'roll back' the new frontiers on which peace and friendship depended. Real friendship also required the Soviet Union to behave with extraordinary patience and understanding. What Poland got was the Stalinist reaction, intensified by the Cold War.

11

Labour Victory – and the A-bomb

At the time the most uplifting events of 1945 seemed to me to be the end of the wars against Germany and Japan, Labour's sensational victory in the general election in July and the emergence of the Communist Party at the top of the poll in the French general election. But 1945 was above all the year of the full revelation of the holocaust and of the atom bomb; the year, as John Berger has put it, that changed the basic political question for socialists from 'who governs whom?' to 'the more fundamental and organic one "how to survive?"'. However, it was the Labour victory in the general election that seemed to me at the time to be the event that broke the pre-war mould. It was a 'little Englander' view.

I had been the Communist prospective parliamentary candidate for Leith (the port of Edinburgh) since April 1944, when the Executive Committee of the Party decided to contest about 50 seats. Its electoral strategy was a confused mixture of a sensible aim – getting more Communists into Parliament – and a foolish one – staging 'propaganda campaigns' against Tory leaders for whom we had a special aversion. The CP decided to contest Leith because it wanted to expose the sitting MP, Ernest Brown, a Tory masquerading as a National Liberal who had a particularly black pre-war record as a former Minister for Labour.

For nearly a year I spent most of my weekends in Leith, and Friday and Sunday nights in the train, but only the *Daily Worker* reported these campaigns, and they were bad propaganda. Leith was a hopeless seat because the CP was very weak on the ground, and when the CP decided in March 1945 to withdraw its candidates 'in seats where a split progressive vote could lead to the return of a Tory candidate' Leith was inevitably one of the 30 constituencies to be cut. I shed no tears and the CP helped the Labour candidate to defeat Brown. Had we split the vote Brown might have survived.

A month later I was pitchforked into the Parliamentary Press Gallery when our young Parliamentary correspondent, Gerry Wolfson, dropped dead of a totally unexpected heart attack. I jumped at the job because I was fascinated by the idea of reporting Parliament, which promised to be of enormous interest whatever the outcome of the election – as indeed it proved to be. As I had no shorthand I was singularly ill-equipped to report debates in Parliament or anywhere else, so I took a crash course at the Gregg school for shorthand typists at Swiss Cottage, with crowds of 15-year-old girls. It took me some weeks to reach the dizzy speed of 100 words a minute, which may be OK for shorthand typists but is far too slow for verbatim reporting. Anthony Eden often exceeded 200 words a minute. Leslie Hale, a quick-witted, wisecracking and progressive Labour MP, spoke at more than 300, and was unreportable. A group of reporters would get together and sort out an agreed text for any difficult speaker, which may or may not have been accurate but could not be disputed. Although I lacked Gerry Wolfson's skill I was admitted to the charmed circle that decided what MPs who gabble have actually said. Thanks to the Exchange Telegraph tape and the camaraderie of the Gallery – somebody would always help me out if I was stuck – I was able to get away with a speed of 150.

The General Election

The House of Commons elected in 1935 was dying on its feet when I arrived there in April 1945. The final victory in Europe was only days away and a general election was imminent. There was nothing for the Commons to do except to provide a platform for Churchill to announce the victory. I got my first insight into the way in which new, radically-minded MPs are forced to accept the House of Commons's stifling protocols on my very first day. Dr Robert McIntyre, a former comrade of mine in Edinburgh University's Socialist Society, had won a by-election in Motherwell to become (for two months) the first Scottish Nationalist MP. The sitting was held up for two hours because the Speaker refused to allow Robert to take his seat unless he was formally 'introduced' by two MPs, while Robert refused to be introduced on the ground that as he had been elected he was entitled to take his seat without being 'introduced' by anyone. Robert would have won if he had held out, but by giving in he denied himself a victory over Churchill who had insisted on protocol.

The election was in a very real sense a referendum for or against Winston Churchill. He had won an unshakeable place in British history, whatever his faults and mistakes, as the man who stood up against Hitler and led the nation through the anti-Nazi war, but his ferocity in crushing the Greek Resistance had horrified the left, and I detected a sinister undertone of anti-communism in the speech he gave from a Whitehall balcony to the enormous crowd that was celebrating VE day. Nine years later, when I reviewed *Triumph and Tragedy*, the final volume of Churchill's war memoirs, I discovered that my suspicions had not gone nearly far enough: in this book Churchill reveals himself as a hypocritical double-dealer whose main preoccupation from June 1944 onwards had been the defeat not of fascism but of 'the Soviet peril'. His secretary, Sir John Colville, even records that Churchill himself described his attitude to the Russians as 'double-dealing'.

He was telling Stalin at Yalta in February 1945 that 'common dangers have wiped out past misunderstandings' but he was telling President Truman and Anthony Eden at the same time that the Soviet Union was 'a mortal danger to the world', against whom 'a new front' must be created as far east as possible. He was scheming to get British and American troops into Prague, Vienna and Berlin before the Red Army, and even told Field Marshal Montgomery to stockpile captured German arms in case German troops should need to be used against the Red Army. On VE day he told Eden that in his eyes 'the Soviet menace' had already replaced 'the German foe', and nine days later he was talking of a 'go slow' on demobilisation in readiness for his 'showdown'. Lord Aldington, in a recent libel case, said that the Army's main concern in Austria in May 1945 was preparing to fight the Yugoslav partisans. My conclusion on reading *Triumph and Tragedy* was that Churchill himself had put an end to the lie that the Soviet Union had rejected co-operation after the war. Since Stalin himself must have known all about Churchill's deceitfulness, thanks to Philby, Burgess and others, it is not surprising that Stalin became increasingly uncooperative.

The Labour Party was pledged by its historic manifesto for the 1945 election 'Let us Face the Future' to consolidate 'the great wartime association' of the British Commonwealth with the US and the USSR. It went on to say 'Let it not be forgotten that in the years leading up to the war the Tories were so scared of Russia that they missed the chance to establish a partnership which might well have prevented the war.' Nearly all Labour candidates proclaimed the need for a lasting friendship with the Soviet Union, and even Bevin declared that only the Left could speak to the Left. Communists were welcomed with open arms in most Labour committee rooms, and in many cases were the shock troops of Labour's electoral army, but Labour's posture of friendship for the Soviet Union was electoral eyewash. Attlee's memoirs show that he was treating the Soviet Union as an enemy when he took Churchill's place at the Potsdam conference in July 1945.

Churchill's hysterical speeches revived the Tory tradition of dirty electioneering, and his attempt to present Professor Harold Laski, the Chairman of the Labour Party, as its evil genius smelt of anti-semitism. His opening broadcast, in which he raved that Labour 'would have to fall back on some form of Gestapo' while small savers might see their nest eggs 'shrivel before their eyes' won him the praises of the fascist paper *ABC* in Franco's Spain. On 22 June I heard him assert that 'the sacred right of collective bargaining, largely promoted by the Conservative Party' was threatened by socialism. Stafford Cripps, he alleged, had made it clear that 'Parliament will be curtailed or swept out of their way' if it resists the orders given by 'Cripps and his kind'. He accused Cripps and others of advocating 'violence' and predicted a period of disorder such as had never been seen in British history if these 'autocratic philanthropists' attempted to make 'us' conform to 'their' ideas. Churchill the statesman was replaced by Churchill the unscrupulous demagogue, the gangster politician.

Labour's Victory

On 1 July I accompanied Churchill's election cavalcade round London and described it as 'the Tories' biggest defeat', under the headline 'London Did Not Heil Fuehrer Winston'. Except in a couple of Tory strongholds there were more boos than cheers, and Churchill's cavalcade drew huge crowds for the Labour candidates to address when he had moved on. I was surprised by the bitterness of the feeling shown, not so much towards Churchill personally (many of those who stayed to cheer the Labour candidates had given Churchill a cheer for his war record) as towards the Tories, particularly by women. At his eve-of-poll rally in Walthamstow only 20,000 people turned up instead of the 50,000 expected, and they drowned his speech with boos and cries of 'We want Labour'.

Churchill had no coherent policy to set against Labour's commitment to full employment, social security, a free health service, the planned use of land, 'fair shares for all' and industrial reconstruction. He could not respond to the yearning for Britain to turn its back on the miseries of the pre-war years. But the optimism of my reports and articles did not reflect my private fears. I found it hard to believe that Churchill's rabble-rousing was falling on stony ground. Despite the evidence of my eyes I asked myself if Churchill could really lose. The new Gallup poll predicted a Labour victory, but polls were a new-fangled invention and I did not believe them. I thought the election could go either way – with Labour possibly having the edge. The euphoria surrounding the Communist campaign led me to think that the CP would hold Willie Gallacher's seat in West Fife and win at least four more – including Hackney, where Bill Rust was very confident of being elected, and the Rhondda where communists led the Welsh miners and sat on the local council and Harry Pollitt had a big following.

We had to wait three weeks for the votes of the men and women in the forces all over the world to come in and tip the scales in Labour's favour. I was sitting in a cottage by the Sussex Downs where I was taking a short holiday when, to my astonishment, the radio began to report one 'Labour Gain' after another in 'safe' Tory seats. I rushed into the village street to tell the good news to my communist neighbour Tom Poulton, only to collapse laughing into the road as we collided head-on as Tom was rushing to tell *me*. I have never felt so politically elated in my life.

Later in the day we realised that although the CP had done far better than it had ever done before it had failed to make the political breakthrough we had hoped for. Willie Gallacher held his seat in West Fife with a bigger majority and so did Dennis

Pritt who stood as a Labour Independent in North Hammersmith on a platform that was indistinguishable from the CP's. Phil Piratin won Mile End in Stepney (where the Blitz had turned the constituency into a rotten borough by driving away many of the voters), but Pollitt lost in the Rhondda by a handful of votes and none of our other candidates came near to winning. In the *Daily Worker* I attributed the Party's relatively poor showing to the grossly undemocratic British electoral system which excludes the smaller parties from Parliament (except where they have a very strong local base) and enables individual candidates to win seats, and parties to win power, with a minority of votes. Labour's majority (393 seats to the Tories' 213) grossly exaggerated the support for Labour (with 48 per cent of the vote) and the Tories' failure (with 40 per cent). The result confirmed me in my long-standing support for proportional representation (PR). Had there been PR in 1945 the CP might well have gained 5 per cent or more of the first-preference votes and perhaps 15 or 20 seats in Parliament.

The voting system faced the CP with an insoluble dilemma. The CP's campaign for unity with the Labour Party had only been narrowly defeated and our primary aim was to secure the victory of the Labour Party. The only hope of any of our 21 candidates winning any seats lay in defeating Labour candidates in safe Labour seats. The CP had the impossible job of being anti-Labour in 21 seats and pro-Labour everywhere else and there was no way within the existing electoral system in which this inherent contradiction could be resolved.

However, there were other, and in the long run more important, reasons for the CP's electoral failure, although I did not appreciate them fully at the time. The CP's switch from supporting the war to opposing it on Stalin's orders in 1939 had not been forgotten; enthusiasm for Russia was already waning and did not in any event translate automatically into support for the CP. Despite the abolition of the Comintern many voters saw us (not without reason) as the 'Soviet Party', uncritically accepting Soviet policy and admiring everything Soviet. The CP had also alienated many people on Labour's left by carrying its all-out support for the war and for 'national unity' to politically suicidal extremes, as in its total opposition to strikes, however severe the provocation, and for a time backing Tory candidates in Tory-held seats in by-elections. It handed the chance to represent the many voters who were turning against the Tories to the Independent and Common Wealth Party candidates, and so eventually to the Labour Party.

The CP's most catastrophic error was the announcement by its Executive Committee on 20 March 1945 (without consulting the membership) that it wanted the coalition with the Tories to continue after the war in a new 'Government of National Unity' based on a majority of Labour and Communist MPs. This struck me as an extraordinary idea, and it aroused such a wave of spontaneous indignation that it was dropped within three weeks. By that time the damage had been done, and Herbert Morrison for one lost no opportunity to remind the voters that the CP had been willing to have Tories in a post-war government. This blunder was a characteristic example of the British CP leaders being more Stalinist than Stalin. It was Dutt, not Stalin, who argued that the Yalta principle of post-war co-operation between states with different political systems called for Labour and the CP to work with the Tories.

The New House of Commons

I came back to a very different House of Commons when the new Parliament met. When I went down to the House I kept on running into old friends or acquaintances who had become Labour MPs and continued to disguise themselves as Captain this or Major that. The atmosphere in the House was totally changed from what it had been two months earlier. Japan had surrendered the day before, the war was over and the place was bubbling with excitement. The Tories were still in a state of shock, the Labour MPs sang 'The Red Flag' in the lobby, and the crowds in Whitehall cheered the new Labour ministers. So great was the euphoria that even such a case-hardened cynic as Claud Cockburn was ecstatic when the King's Speech promised in the first year to nationalise the Bank of England and the mines, to control investment, to repeal the Trade Disputes Act of 1927 and to speed up parliamentary business. At last, it seemed, a Labour government was going to carry out a radical programme and the *Daily Worker* could not have been more generous: the speech was a 'historic announcement' and 'could

... reasonably be described as epoch-making'. Victory in the war and the election of a Labour government had ushered in 'the age of the common man' and 'the triumph of democracy'.

Nor was the support of the Party and the *Daily Worker* for the government limited to words. Within days of the Japanese surrender the US government plunged Britain into a financial crisis by suspending the Lend-Lease arrangements by which the US paid for Britain's essential imports of food and raw materials while its industry was turned over to war production. The American terms for a loan confirmed the accuracy of our initial reaction that Wall Street was determined to use Britain's financial crisis to open its Empire markets to American trade, capital and political influence. Nevertheless, despite profound misgivings, the two Communist MPs Gallacher and Piratin voted in November 1945 for the American loan negotiated by Maynard Keynes to save Britain from imminent bankruptcy, in the belief that there was no alternative. The *Daily Worker* made its support conditional on the government using the breathing space it had won to build up British industry. In the event most of the loan was squandered within 18 months on maintaining armed forces abroad and allowing holders of sterling to convert it into dollars. The resulting dollar crisis in 1947 shook the government to its foundations.

The Atom Bomb and After

The sequence of events that followed the dropping of the first atomic bomb on Hiroshima on 6 August 1945 is critical to an understanding of the Cold War. On 8 August the Soviet Union declared war on Japan in fulfilment of an agreement made with Churchill and Roosevelt. On 9 August the Red Army invaded Manchuria, and Nagasaki was wiped out by another atom bomb. On 14 August the Japanese government surrendered unconditionally to the United States. On 13 August, only a week after Hiroshima, the *Daily Worker* published a leader expressing our shock that the Tory press, notably the *Daily Mail* and *The Observer* (no liberal in those days) should be speculating on the advantages of the A-bomb as a threat against our ally the Soviet Union, which was at that moment destroying the Japanese Army. American reaction emphasised the need to retain an American monopoly of the atom 'secret'.

On 16 August, on the second day of the debate on Labour's programme Churchill let loose all his powers of invective against communism in what I called 'an irresponsible piece of demagoguery'. He hinted openly that the American monopoly of the Bomb might be of use in dealing with 'passionate differences in ideologies' and it seemed to me, as I wrote in my report, that the election had stripped him not only of office but also of all sense of responsibility or restraint. It was a revelation not only of the 'new' Churchill but also of the appalling possibilities inherent in the American monopoly of the Bomb. Churchill's theme was taken up in the House by his acolyte Robert Boothby and by others who shared his wish to use the Bomb to force the Soviet Union to abandon its political and territorial positions.

When Ernest Bevin replied to the debate on 20 August, in a speech that was punctuated by Tory cheers, he failed to repudiate Churchill. On the contrary he was congratulated by Anthony Eden for announcing his intention to continue unchanged the Tories' foreign policy in Greece and elsewhere. Three days later Bevin announced the government's refusal to share atomic secrets with the Soviet Union 'for the time being' – a statement that prompted Konni Zilliacus, a former League of Nations official and the best-informed expert on foreign affairs on the Labour benches, to warn prophetically that his attitude would lead to a fiendish new atomic arms race. But 'Zilli's' appeal to the government to dissociate itself from an Anglo-American 'atomic bloc' against the Soviet Union fell on deaf ears. Within days of the end of the war the Labour government had taken the first steps to form an unacknowledged alliance with Churchill in waging a nuclear-backed Cold War against the Soviet Union.

It took some time before we realised that President Truman had been lying when he claimed that the Bomb had been dropped to cut short the war and to save 'thousands of young American lives'. The truth was that the US had not planned to invade Japan until 1 November, and would not have suffered large-scale casualties until then. The decisive factor in the choice of 6 August for dropping the bomb was the knowledge that on 8 August the Soviet Union would keep Stalin's promise to declare war on Japan three months after the defeat of Germany, and would win a quick and decisive victory. The report on the Pacific War by the US Strategic Bombing Survey concluded (in 1947) that Japan would have had to surrender by December 1945 'even if the atomic bombs had not been dropped, even if Russia had not entered the war, and even if no invasion had been planned or contemplated'.

Japan was already on the verge of surrender in July, the main sticking point being the Japanese insistence that the Emperor must retain his throne. There can be little doubt that the Bomb was dropped as a demonstration of American power to obliterate cities and to prevent the political disaster of a Japanese surrender to the Soviet Union. In this it was supremely successful, for by conceding the Emperor's immunity from prosecution as a war criminal the US secured an immediate Japanese surrender and total control of Japan. Professor P.M.S. Blackett, the British physicist who was a member of the government's advisory committee on nuclear matters, provided convincing evidence in his book *Military and Political Consequences of Atomic Energy* (1948) for his view that the Hiroshima bomb was not so much the last shot in the Second World War as the first shot in the Cold War against the Soviet Union. We in the *Daily Worker* had no inkling of these facts at the time. Our editorial on Hiroshima said that nuclear energy could prove to be a blessing or a curse, but we accepted uncritically the official American line that the Bomb had been dropped to shorten the war and to save American lives. We argued that 'a new war, waged by states possessing this new and terrible weapon of destruction, would mark the end of all civilisation', and we pointed to the need for the victorious nations to co-operate in building a just peace, and for social control, through socialism, of this extraordinary new source of energy.

Nuclear Fantasy and Reality

The *Daily Worker* had for years been leading the field in bringing popular science to its readers through the articles of Professor J.B.S. Haldane, and the *Worker's* scientific experts raised fantastic expectations. They predicted enormous increases in production ('hundreds of times') as man's 'mastery of nature' put the atom at his service; cheap nuclear engines would power aircraft and replace both petrol and coal. But the euphoria about unlimited energy at some future date gave way within a few days to the realisation that the A-bomb presented a new, immediate and horrifying threat to the Soviet Union. The US's Baruch Plan for controlling and 'sharing' atomic power turned out to be a scheme to perpetuate the American monopoly of weapons and of civilian know-how, through a commission in which the Soviet Union would have to accept the decisions of a hostile and American-dominated majority. The rejection of the Baruch Plan by the Soviet Union was inevitable, and the Soviet Union seemed to me to have no alternative but to protect itself by the speediest possible development of its own nuclear weapons.

Two things were missing in my reaction (and the *Daily Worker's*) to the Bomb. One, for which there was some excuse, was our total failure to anticipate the consequences for the human environment, or for life on earth, of the massive release of radioactive substances. Our ignorance seems almost unbelievable in retrospect. Several days passed before the first report came through of the mysterious sickness that was striking down people who appeared to have survived the blast at Hiroshima. Three weeks after Hiroshima we reported without comment a statement by Major General Groves, the man in charge of atomic bomb production, that Japanese claims that people were still dying of radiation were 'simply so much propaganda'. We gave an enormous amount of space both to reports of the Bomb damage and to our scientific experts, but they had no real grasp of the problems of radiation even though one of our advisers, Professor Burhop, was a distinguished nuclear physicist.

The other thing that was missing in my reaction to the atom bomb was moral outrage. We accepted, as I have said, the explanation that it was justifiable to wipe out two Japanese cities to save some American lives, but we did not see that our position was both racist and immoral. It was not until I got to know Lewis Mumford in the 1960s and began reading his books that I came round to his view, which he had published as soon as the Bombs were dropped, that by massacring civilians the British and the Americans had descended to the level of the Nazis. Mumford was the Cassandra of those days, the prophet nobody wanted to hear. The path to Hiroshima, in his view, began with the Nazi bombing of Guernica in Spain in 1937, and led through Rotterdam, the Blitz on London and other British cities, and the firestorms of Hamburg, Berlin, Leipzig and Tokyo where hundreds of thousands of men, women and children were roasted alive. In Mumford's view the British and American bombing campaign removed the last moral restraints on warfare, and paved the way to the legitimisation of the use of atomic weapons against civilian populations.

Our Opportunism

The *Daily Worker's* record (and therefore mine) on this moral issue is best described as opportunist and unprincipled. In 1937 we condemned the German bombing of Guernica. In 1940, when we opposed the war, we placed the German bombing of Coventry and the British bombing of Hamburg on a par to illustrate the scale of the 'blood and tears' that awaited the people of both countries if the war continued. When Churchill embarked on the 'saturation bombing' of Germany in 1941 as an alternative to the Second Front, we questioned (correctly) whether saturation bombing could defeat Germany, but raised no moral objections even when it was apparent that the real intention was to massacre civilians. Once the Second Front had been agreed by Churchill we urged the government to 'rain down merciless blows from the sky' by night and by day. Only at the end of 1946, when the beginning of the nuclear arms race had opened up a frightful prospect and the Labour government had given up its initial posture of calling for the atomic bomb to be 'controlled', did the *Daily Worker* write a prophetic leader:

> British policy opens the way to the establishment of the atom bomb as a completely legitimate war weapon – the number of atom bombs in one country being balanced against the number of bombs in another in interminable disarmament discussions.

Initially it was left to the individual readers whose letters we published within days of Hiroshima to raise the moral issue by protesting that 'the extermination of defenceless people' dragged us down to the level of the Nazis.

Our politicians and constitutional lawyers tell us that the British Parliament is 'sovereign', but the development of the

British atom bomb tells another story. The last thing either the Labour or the Tory parties wanted was a debate on atomic policy. In March 1946 I reported John Wilmot, the Minister of Supply, announcing an all-out effort by the government to solve the problems that stood in the way of the peaceful use of atomic energy for industry. Wilmot was at that moment a member of the Cabinet sub-committee that, unknown even to the Cabinet, was then planning to build Britain's own atom bomb at enormous expense. When Attlee informed the House in October 1946 of the decision to build the Harwell nuclear research establishment the Ministry of Supply offered the lying explanation that it would concentrate on 'the industrial potentialities of atomic energy'. The Labour government cooked the books and never asked the Commons to vote a penny for the British Bomb. Calder Hall (now part of Sellafield), opened by the Queen as the world's first nuclear power station, was designed to produce plutonium for nuclear weapons. So were the first Magnox nuclear power plants, whose plutonium was supplied to the US military in return for weapons-grade uranium. The Russians, unlike the British people, cannot have been deceived, although they might have found it hard to believe the crazy reasons that Bevin gave for wanting a British Bomb. In October 1946 he told the secret Cabinet sub-committee that:

> I don't want any other Foreign Secretary of this country to be talked at or by a Secretary of State for the United States as I have just had in my discussions with Mr Byrnes. We have got to have this thing over here whatever it costs ... We've got to have the bloody Union Jack flying on top of it.

I was right to tell the CP National Congress in November 1945 that 'the atom bomb has gone to the heads of the British and American imperialists, who hope to use it against the Soviet Union'.

12

Greek Tragedy, Yugoslav Inspiration

When Parliament went into recess in August 1945, at the end of the debate on the government's programme, Bill Rust sent me to Greece to investigate reports of a royalist reign of terror. I applied to the War Office for a civilian reporter's military permit, but three weeks later the authorities in Athens had not even acknowledged my application. The Labour government's decision to lift the ban on *Daily Worker* war correspondents (now that the war was over!) changed everything. My only real problem, as it turned out, was how to buy cap badges and shoulder flashes for my war correspondent's uniform.

The War Office told me that Hobson's in Soho was the place for badges, and I got there at 4.30 on a Friday afternoon to find a dingy door bearing the notice 'Shut at 4pm'. But the door was open. An arrow and the word 'Badges' pointed upstairs to a door which bore an inky notice saying 'no badges today'. On the far side of it fully 20 officers and civilians were trying to buy badges, but without much success. A *Daily Herald* reporter asked me 'what stage have you reached in this game', and had something like a convulsive fit when I told him that I hoped to get the badges 'today' as I was leaving on Monday. The rest of the assembled company dissolved into helpless laughter at the idea of a poor sucker expecting to get a badge the first time he called. When I reached the counter the woman replied: 'War correspondents? There's been that many notorieties coming here for them you'll have to wait. We havn't got any more today.' The telephone rang, and after a long palaver I heard her say 'Well, come at 9 o'clock, knock three times and tell the boy to say it's from the *Daily Express*.' So I came next morning before 9 o'clock, knocked three times and got my badges.

Having acquired a war correspondent's licence, a battledress uniform, visas, inoculations and a seat on an RAF Dakota I flew for the first time in my life, first to Rome and then to Athens. In Rome I spent the evening with the enthusiastic and optimistic editors of the communist daily *Unita* which had taken over the offices and plant of one of the big fascist newspapers. Next morning I found myself on a hot, sunny September day in the poshest hotel in Athens, the Grande Bretagne in Constitution Square, the scene of the police shooting the previous December. If one did not venture far beyond central Athens one could imagine that democracy was returning to Greece. I saw the Greek landscape and a few of its antiquities without the tourists, the smog and the traffic which have taken so much out of the pleasure of visiting Greece today. My interpreter Poly Kyriazis – a student who proved to be a tireless, serious, good-humoured and brilliant translator – gave me the unforgettable experience of walking over the Akropolis by moonlight, and brought me down to earth by pointing out the gun positions in the December fighting. But the realities of the terror, the poverty and the lack of food and work were inescapable. British and Americans from the United Nations Relief and Rehabilitation Agency (UNRRA) gave me grisly statistics on the appalling losses in livestock and crops, and of the malnutrition and the diversion of UNRRA supplies into royalist and black market hands.

Superficially, the Greek Communist Party and EAM (the national liberation movement) seemed to be regaining the ground they had lost in the December events – they had both opened offices in Athens and the communist daily newspaper *Rizospastis* was being published – but when I went to the Peloponnese and Macedonia I found their offices, with two exceptions, had been closed, their presses smashed, and their members arrested, beaten up and jailed. I could only visit the editor of the EAM newspaper in Kalamata by going to the prison where he was being held on a charge of 'promoting disaffection'. Before EAM's march and rally at the Athens Olympic Stadium on 27 September, celebrating the fourth anniversary of its foundation, the royalist press whipped up the gangs of the royalist 'X' organisation to violence against 'the cannibals', as one daily called EAM, and *Rizospastis* reported 100 attacks on its sellers in 24 hours. I was in the office of the liberation youth movement when it was stoned by X-ites, screaming their death slogans, without interference from the *gendarmerie* post 20 yards away. Soldiers and civil servants were forbidden to take part in the march, but some 200,000 people, headed by disabled resistance fighters in wheelchairs (not one of whom was to get a pension till the late 1980s), marched through central Athens in one of the most moving demonstrations I have ever seen. The spirit of the crowd and the range of republican speakers seemed to show that fear of a royalist coup d'etat and the daily terror were bringing together republicans who had been split by the December events.

The Secret Royalist State

In reality the resistance, which had looked to the British government to honour the terms on which ELAS had surrendered had been shamefully betrayed. The Varkiza agreement of February 1945, under which ELAS surrendered, had promised an amnesty for political prisoners, the restoration of freedom of speech, assembly and the press, free elections, free trade unions, a purge of Nazi collaborators in the civil and security services and the formation of a National Army without political discrimination. Not one of these promises was honoured. Nikos Zachariadis, the Communist leader who had recently returned from nine years in Greek prisons and Dachau, told me that Communist influence was greater than it had been before the December fighting, but he misjudged the situation. I was impressed by the courage and resilience of the Communists and EAM in the face of the defeats they had suffered and the persecution they faced, but the plain truth was that much of the ELAS army, which had controlled most of Greece when the British landed in October 1944, was now either in jail, in exile or in hiding or had taken to the mountains to save their lives. In the Peloponnese I went into the hills to meet men and women, many barefoot and some in rags, who had fled there to save their lives. I came home convinced that civil war was almost inevitable.

My status as a British war correspondent enabled me to consult politicians of nearly every tendency except the royalists. I spent two hours with the Minister of Labour. I had long discussions with Tsouderos, the republican financier and anticommunist who had been Prime Minister of the Royalist government in exile in Cairo; Sofianopoulos, the former Liberal

Foreign Minister who had negotiated the Varkiza agreement and had resigned in protest at the government's failure to carry it out; Sofoulis, a feeble republican who became Prime Minister three months later and found that he was powerless because the royalists controlled the armed and civil services; the Bishop of Kozani, who had been banished from his see on the grounds that he had 'absented himself' by taking to the mountains with ELAS; Sir Charles Wickham, the head of the British Police Mission, and General Othonaios, a republican officer of no party who had been Chief of the General Staff and was President of the Republican Clubs. Othanaios almost echoed the words of Zachariadis in telling me that 'if the King comes back a peaceful solution is impossible, and the honest people will have to take to the mountains'.

These people – the Minister of Labour excepted – were agreed that Greece was ruled by a royalist state within the state, what the Greeks call *parakratos*. Othanaios and his fellow General Bakirjis, regular officers who had been victimised for their republicanism before the war, described to me in detail how General Vendiris, a renegade republican who became Chief of the General Staff, had refused their appeals to join ELAS and had set up the Military League of officers, whose armed bands were tolerated by the Germans because they attacked ELAS. Through the League, royalist officers (many of them Nazi collaborators) had penetrated the armed forces and local and central government, whereas not a single ELAS officer had been given an active role in the armed or security forces. The League directed the ubiquitous royalist X-gangs that terrorised town and country with the toleration or even open co-operation of the *gendarmerie* which, on Wickham's admission, included many collaborators and royalists.

The Royalist Terror

It can never have occurred to the X-ite gangsters that the correspondent in British uniform they were talking to was a communist. In a working-class suburb of Piraeus they showed me how they were issuing 'nationalist-minded' citizens with the 'coupons' (which entitled electors to vote) on behalf of the *gendarmerie* whose building they shared. In the Peloponnese they showed me the passes they issued to peasants authorising them to travel from village to village, and the passes that they themselves carried authorising Greek or British forces to give them every assistance they needed. I went to a royalist rally in Salonika openly attended by officers – some wearing red staff tabs – from the allegedly non-political reorganised Army. The audience passed most of the time singing royalist songs, one of which was translated to me as

> Greater Greece will be twice as large as before;
> We'll beat ELAS and make a Communist General walk with his feet cut off;
> We're going to hunt the Greeks who like the Bulgars;
> The Bulgars will feel the Greek boot.

To the tune of 'Deep in the Heart of Texas' they sang about planting the Greek flag in Sofia. The main speaker, a vice-president of *X*, sang the praises of Anthony Eden and declared that *X*'s purpose was 'to make war on the communists and restore the King'.

The accuracy of my reports on the royalist terror in Macedonia and the Peloponnese was fully confirmed when British archives became available 30 years later. Colonel C.M. Woodhouse, a former liaison officer with the resistance who was no friend of ELAS, was sent to the Peloponnese to investigate alarming reports that ELAS was planning an armed uprising. His report to the British Embassy dated 11 August 1945 concluded (having excluded *all* testimony from the Left) that the real ground for alarm was the 'obliteration' of justice by the Right. He found, as I did, that mass arrests were being carried out without warrant, and that the victims were exclusively members of EAM and ELAS, never those who had collaborated with the Germans. The collaborators were openly protected by the authorities who would not enforce warrants for their arrest. When a member of EAM was accused of a crime all the local members were liable to be arrested on grounds of 'moral responsibility'. The National Guard that had served the Germans armed the collaborators everywhere, and the *X*-ites had set up their own state near Kalamata, maintaining a private police.

The politicians and Wickham, the British police chief, all told me that (in Wickham's words) it would be 'madness' to hold the early elections on which the British government was insisting unless the terror was repressed, the jails emptied of political prisoners, the amnesty put into effect, new electoral rolls prepared and communications restored. Zachariadis emphasised to me that the Greek Communist Party would support a government which would carry out this basic programme of democratisation, even if the CP and EAM were excluded from government for the time being, but for Bevin the only foe was 'communism', and he only believed in 'free elections' in the Soviet bloc.

The Jails

If there was one single experience that showed me the rottenness of the Labour government's foreign policy it was the visits that I paid to jails and *gendarmerie* stations where thousands of untried political prisoners were held under the eyes of the British forces that had come to 'liberate' Greece. Prison governors who would have had a *Rizospastis* reporter arrested on the spot became positively obsequious at the sight of a British officer's uniform, and allowed me to hold long discussions with the prisoners. I was, I believe, the only British reporter to investigate the Greek jails.

Under the Varkiza agreement untried political prisoners should have been released by August 1945, a month before my visit, but their number was rising every day. Two thousand prisoners had been released in the month before my arrival, but (as Wickham put it to me) pickpockets were being released to make room for more prisoners from EAM. The Greek government admitted that there were 16,500 prisoners of whom nearly 6,000 were untried members of EAM and 2,700 'collaborators'. Nearly all collaborators went scot-free. British Embassy officials admitted that the official estimates of political prisoners were far too low. EAM put the figure at 30,000 but nobody knew the real numbers.

Once I had got through the crowd of women at the gate (patiently waiting to bring scraps of scarce food to the prisoners) and persuaded a governor to let me in I would meet the prisoners' committee. They would introduce themselves and, if it was possible, offer me a cup of coffee. The prisoners' morale was marvellous, for nearly all of them faced capital charges and knew that if the King came back many of them would be executed. In the Hadjikosta jail in Athens they were putting on a play, concerts, lectures, discussions and 'keep fit' groups, nursed the sick and kept their cells clean and decorated. In a moving gesture of comradeship they gave me their 'wall newspaper' (a full-size, imitation front-page of a newspaper), every letter of which had been drawn by hand – a real work of art – and asked me to tell the British the truth about Greece. I hope that one day a secure home can be found in Greece for this part of its national heritage.

Barbaric Conditions

The conditions in most of the jails were barbaric. In the *gendarmerie* station at Kozani I found 19 men packed into a cell measuring 5 by 2.5 metres, and 21 in another the same size, where it was impossible to lie down. One of them showed me the putrid, undressed wounds on the soles of his feet where the *gendarmes* had beaten him 18 days earlier. His plea for a doctor had been ignored. Wherever I went in Macedonia EAM or the CP could produce at short notice people with recent bullet wounds, fractures, bruises, burns and other signs of beatings and torture. In Florina, Edessa, Kozani, Kalamata and other jails prisoners crowded round me to show me their injuries and to tell me their grievances, of which the greatest was not their own plight but the intolerable conditions of their families, living in burned villages, denied UNRRA relief, persecuted by the X-gangs and afraid to register for the elections.

A thousand prisoners were herded into jails in Kalamata, 700 of them penned like animals into warehouses and cellars – pitch-dark dungeons with no windows or electric light and with sewage leaking from a drain-pipe. In the town's *gendarmerie* station 178 prisoners were crammed into two rooms whose windows were permanently shuttered, separated only by open bars from the cell where eleven women from the Mutual Aid Association were detained for the crime of helping their menfolk in jail. The stock excuse for these wholesale arrests was the 'atrocities' committed by ELAS in or near Athens during the December events, but I found that ELAS members were held by the thousand in the north and south of Greece where no such atrocities were alleged to have happened.

The prison governors confirmed that the great majority of the hundreds of men I spoke to were charged with 'murders' committed during the resistance, usually the 'murder' of members of the Quisling Security Battalions or *gendarmerie* but even the 'murder' of German troops. The *Nomarch* (or Prefect) of Florina, one Zachos Xiriotis, was typical in telling me that it was a criminal act to have shot or disarmed *gendarmes* or members of the Security Battalions in Nazi-occupied Greece, or to have handed their weapons to ELAS.

The death penalty for 'murder' in Greece – as in South Africa today – extended also to 'moral responsibility' for murder. This meant that anybody who had been in EAM or ELAS could be held on a murder charge. A woman prisoner told me she was charged with 39 murders because she had been a member of an ELAS unit that attacked the collaborationist Security Battalions. At one extreme I met a prisoner charged with 2,600 murders, and at the other a group of 74 EAM men charged (as Woodhouse reported) with a single murder – accused, they said, by the very man who had ordered the burning of their homes during the occupation. Another prisoner in the same jail was charged with murdering a man who had recently visited him! The most bitter were the men who had helped British prisoners to escape or hidden them, or worked with British officers whose names they quoted to prove their good faith. Women in the workers' suburb of Tumba in Salonika told me that most of the people who had hidden nine British soldiers there were now in jail.

Churchill's Complicity

Churchill's complicity in these crimes is confirmed by the documents now available. On 19 April 1945 Sir Orme Sargent, the head of the Foreign Office Southern Department, cabled Rex Leeper (the British Ambassador) as follows:

> Your recent reports suggest that membership of EAM tends to be considered a greater crime than collaboration with the Germans. You should take every opportunity of emphasising our view that assistance to the enemy is regarded by His Majesty's Government as much worse than membership of EAM, and should be met with condign punishment.

Churchill, who happened to be in charge of the Foreign Office because Eden was ill, commented on 22 April:

> I do not agree at all with your last paragraph. It seems to me that the collaborators in Greece in many cases did the best they could to shelter the Greek population from German oppression. Anyhow, they did nothing to stop the liberating forces, nor did they give any support to the EAM designs. The Communists are the main foe, though the punishment of notorious pro-German collaborators ... should proceed in a strict and regular manner. There should be no question of increasing the severities against the collaborationists in order to win Communist approval ... Our policy is the plebiscite [on the return of the King] within three or four months, and implacable hostility to the Communists whatever their tactics may be.

This policy continued unchanged when Bevin succeeded Eden at the Foreign Office. The terror had the tacit blessing of the Labour government, and it came as no surprise to me when the royalist government decided in 1947 to 'clear the files', by executing former members of the resistance. The *Daily Worker* carried reports and even pictures of these almost daily executions (in at least one case of more than 100 victims at a time), but there was no more than a bleep of protest from the Labour government.

Churchill liked to claim when he was Leader of the Opposition after 1945 that he had 'rescued' Greece for democracy, but he made no serious effort to condemn the royalist terror in 1947, contenting himself with dropping a mild note to the Foreign Office in October suggesting that 'mass executions' were 'very unwise' and 'almost reduce us to the Communist level'. He made no public protest, although he appealed successfully to Attlee in the same year 'to do something' to prevent the execution of Field Marshal Kesselring, who had been found guilty of the most atrocious war crimes in Italy. In his view the time had come to stop killing German war criminals – or, as he preferred to call them, 'the leaders of the defeated enemy' – for this was getting in the way of the plans to revive the German Army.

What Greece Taught Me

The justification usually offered by people like Colonel Woodhouse for the repression of EAM and ELAS is that they were a communist front, and that the Greek Communist Party was plotting a revolutionary seizure of power. The contemporary records now available* show that this version grossly misrepresents both the facts and the Greek Communist Party intentions. The Greek Communist Party committed some crimes and made many errors, but as in other European countries the communists organised and inspired the main resistance movement, first to the Fascist and then to the Nazi occupation. In Greece, as in Yugoslavia, the object of the left, democratic or republican resistance movements was to liberate their country *both* from the Nazis and from the pre-war domestic tyranny. Churchill saw the resistance struggle in Greece as a civil war in which he took the monarchist-fascist side. The Right relied on the British to restore their fortunes, and the British government relied on the Right to restore Britain's position as the overlord of Greece and the master of the eastern Mediterranean. The royalist forces in exile were brought back under the wings of the British and reunited with the royalists who had run Greece for the Nazis.

It is easy to criticise the tactics of EAM and the Greek Communist Party, for whom British policy and the strength of the Greek royalists posed enormous problems. They made fundamental mistakes in accepting a minor role in the British-dominated government formed in 1944, and in putting ELAS under British command. Neither the Greek CP nor EAM ever intended to seize power, and it is arguable that their greatest error was to hand over power to the British when the Germans retreated in October 1944. The essence of their mistake was to rely on British good faith, for they failed to realise that the British were planning to out-manoeuvre them politically and, if necessary, to crush them militarily. I do not think that Bevin and the Labour government intended to create a monarcho-fascist dictatorship in Greece, but this was the inevitable result of their anti-communist phobia once they had failed to enforce the Varkiza agreement and allowed the Military League to seize power behind the screen provided by the British forces and their puppet government.

*See General Stefanos Sarafis, *ELAS, The Greek Resistance Army* (Merlin Press, 1980); P. Papastratis, *British Policy Towards Greece during the Second World War 1941–4* (Cambridge University Press, 1984); Heinz Richter, *British Intervention in Greece* (Merlin Press, 1986).

A year after my visit to Greece on the eve of the plebiscite on the return of the King on 1 September 1946 I wrote an article tracing the course of events that had led up to this 'tragic farce' for which I held Britain's Labour government responsible. The faked elections in March 1946 resulted in a monarcho-fascist government. Within a few weeks it had set up summary courts with power to pass death sentences for offences far less serious than murder or 'moral responsibility' for murder; it suspended all restrictions on arrests or searches without warrants, crushed the trade unions, purged the remaining democrats in the civil service, amnestied collaborators, made unauthorised meetings or strikes illegal and began deporting resistance fighters to the islands. The summary courts started to function on 1 July, and the first execution took place on 15 July. The plebiscite on 1 September was held in conditions of unprecedented terror, and inevitably resulted in a majority for the return of the King. Civil war was the inevitable result.

If I ask why I stayed with the *Daily Worker* until 1956 a large part of the answer lies in my experience of the British-sponsored terror in Greece. From that time onward, whenever British politicians called for 'free elections' in Eastern Europe, I took them to mean rigged elections for a terrorised electorate on the Greek model. Greece showed me the cynicism, hypocrisy and brutality of the Labour government's foreign policy, and made it impossible for me to accept at face value any of its professed objectives in the Cold War. When I visited Yugoslavia in the following two years I had an inspiring glimpse of the socialist alternative – of a nation reborn under communist leadership after inconceivable suffering, and of people tackling the daunting tasks of rehabilitation in good cheer, even when they had nothing to work with but their hands and the West was putting a hundred obstacles in their way. It was, as events were to prove, too good to last, but it was not too good to be true.

Belgrade, 1946

My first impressions of Belgrade in September 1946 were of reconstruction proceeding at a tempo that had no counterpart in Greece. The bridges over the Danube and the Sava rivers were being rebuilt, new warehouses were rising for the river port and there seemed to be a vast amount of activity in reconstructing damaged buildings and cleaning up the streets. I have no doubt that I idealised Yugoslavia, but an early experience taught me the danger of looking at the fascinating new world I saw unfolding before me through excessively red-tinted spectacles. In a letter which shows that I had been overwhelmed both by the heat (41 degrees Centigrade or 106 degrees Fahrenheit) and by the new Yugoslav *élan* I told my mother that it was grand to see the cafe of the Moskva hotel, the best in Belgrade, filled with 'honest hard-working types'. Within 24 hours one of these 'honest hard-working types' got away with my wallet, money, travellers' cheques, air ticket and British clothing coupons (perhaps the most serious loss!).

Only six months had passed since Churchill, with President Truman by his side had formally launched the Cold War against the Soviet bloc at Fulton, Missouri in March 1946. The US government, with the support of sections of the British press, was portraying Marshal Tito and the Yugoslav Communist Party as major threats to civilisation itself. In reality Yugoslavia was a threat to nobody – except, as events were to prove, to Stalin's domination. In a leading article I wrote on 28 August before leaving for Yugoslavia, I expressed astonishment and outrage at a 48-hour ultimatum delivered to Belgrade by the US government, to the accompaniment of calls from the 'yellow (gutter) press' for an atom bomb to be dropped, and from Senator Bridges for the US to be 'quick on the trigger'. The ostensible reason for these outbursts was that Yugoslavia had forced down a US warplane illegally overflying Yugoslav territory. The Yugoslavs complied with the US ultimatum demanding the return of their airmen, but not before the pilot had freely admitted that US and British military aircraft were illegally overflying Yugoslavia up to 20 times a day.

The US had organised what Yugoslav Ministers I spoke to called 'a blockade', stopping access to Trieste, blocking the credits needed for essential imports and illegally impounding Yugoslavia's Danube fleet in Austria. Britain was refusing to hand over either the freights earned by Yugoslav shipping during the war or the insurance for the vessels that were lost. US pressure led to the decision to cut off the United Nations Relief and Rehabilitation Agency's (UNRRA's) aid (on which Yugoslavia depended for food, clothing and construction equipment) by the end of 1946, when the drought caused by the hottest summer of the century had ruined the Yugoslav corn crop and forced the peasants to slaughter a large part of their remaining livestock, already devastated by wartime losses. Whereas in Greece the UNRRA personnel spent their time with me bemoaning the government's corruption and incompetence, in Yugoslavia they praised the honesty of the government and the people and bitterly attacked the American-inspired decision to terminate their work.

Unconducted Tour

The reader who suspects that the Yugoslav authorities took a credulous reporter who knew no Serbian on a carefully-conducted tour has no conception of what Yugoslavia was like. The official press office in Belgrade arranged some interviews with ministers and government departments, issued me with a permit enabling me to go where I liked (which I did) and warned the People's Committees in the places I decided to visit to expect me. The press office could not provide me with an interpreter, but I was well served everywhere through the People's Committees. The consequences of my inability to make myself understood were more comic than serious. I was arrested for a couple of hours in Sarajevo for allegedly photographing a factory (actually an old Turkish fort) from the train and for having no camera permit (the press office had told me I didn't need one). After a French-speaking traveller had explained my position the militiaman who arrested me returned the camera with a friendly grin, and when he saw that I was limping badly (for my stump had blistered in the heat), he carried my bag to the hotel!

My trip took me to Bosnia and Slovenia, to a camp of Greek ELAS fighters in the Voivodina, to a new railway being built by the Youth Movement, to some of the most devastated parts of the countryside, and to American-occupied Trieste and the Slovene parts of the Istrian Peninsula Yugoslavia had recovered from Italy. The 13-hour train journey to the terminus of the Youth Railway at Brcko – in worn-out rolling stock over a permanent way that would have been condemned as unfit for use in normal times – was itself a revelation. Practically every bridge, culvert and station building had been rebuilt, often temporarily, in two years.

When I visited the railway sites I became so infected with the enthusiasm of the work brigades who seemed to sing all day long as they worked that, despite my blistered stump, I got hold of a shovel and joined in. Every inch of the 57-mile line, which gave access to a rich supply of coal, was being built through hilly and difficult country by young people from 14 to 25, all of them unpaid. Before the war it was intended to take four years. The job was done in a year – albeit to lowish standards – with 17 bulldozers for the whole line. The youngsters seemed to have enough determination to do anything. They were sure of themselves, yet not cock-sure, proud of their work and wanting the freedom they had won for themselves to be won for everybody else. All the illiterates (40 per cent in some peasant brigades) were being taught to read and write, and the man in charge of the whole enterprise, himself a former partisan, was only 26.

The Legacies of War

Before my second visit to Yugoslavia in August and September 1947 I married Ann Wheeler (of whom more later) and the trip was really a deferred honeymoon. Bill Rust and his wife Tamara (a Georgian whom he had met at the Lenin School in Moscow) had been invited by the CP newspaper *Borba* to have a holiday in Yugoslavia, and he arranged for us to be included in the invitation. *Borba's* hospitality was, I suppose, given in recognition of my earlier reports and in payment for some articles I had written for *Borba* on British policy. We had one of the best holidays we have ever had, but we were staggered by the lavishness of *Borba's* hospitality. They gave us so much to eat and drink, in a country where food was still a problem, that I got the impression that the CP leaders were making up for the privations of war. It did not occur to me for some years that we were probably witnessing the first stage of the corruption of an elite. We flew to Dubrovnik, to which the first post-war tourists had come from Czechoslovakia, sailed up the coast to Rjeka with a stop at Split and relaxed by the seaside with Bill and Tamara in *Borba's* holiday villa. From there we flew to Zagreb the capital of Croatia, to Sarajevo to see the second leg of the Youth Railway (where we made friends with Edward Thompson, then the Commandant of the British Brigade), and back to Belgrade and home.

On this second trip I got an even stronger impression of the impact that the war had had on everybody's lives, perhaps because people saw us as friends rather than journalists. I had learned the year before to be very careful about probing into people's lives in a country where 1,700,000 out of 15 million people were killed – 'only' 300,000 of them in battle. Most were massacred, often by the Ustashi and Chetniks whose forcible return in 1945 by Britain to Yugoslavia (where some were executed) is now the occasion of some indignation in the British press. Often when we would be thinking of the lovely sunshine or the beautiful country we would be jerked back into the horrible events of the war by passing villages where the inhabitants had been massacred.

When comrade Denes, the manager of *Borba*, gave us dinner one night he puzzled us by saying, with a broad grin on his face in his best English, that their baby had been 'burnt' recently – he meant 'born'! We then discovered just what the new baby meant to them, for they had lost their first baby from dysentery in the guerrilla war in the mountains, a week after he was born. Denes had lost two brothers with the partisans, one a lad of 15. His wife became a partisan after losing their child and was parted from him for three years. Denes recalled a retreat in the winter of 1942 when a whole village had to take to the hills in deep snow, and he saw a mother and a young child walking on until the child could walk no further and had to be left, because no one could carry him. We understood why people who had been through such experiences could not accept the Marshall Plan which was intended to rebuild Germany again while Yugoslavia's aid had been cut off, and the more I learned of what they had suffered the more I marvelled at the generosity they were showing to the host of minor collaborators whose offences they ignored entirely and refused to punish.

If Greece was in the grip of a counter-revolutionary terror the Yugoslavia I saw in 1946 and 1947 was passing through one of those rare, brief periods of revolutionary energy and exaltation when anything and everything seems possible. I was left with an unforgettable impression of the capacity of ordinary people who had gone through hell to face up to the most daunting problems and to discover all kinds of unsuspected qualities in themselves. The constraints of the old power-structure had been blown to the winds and people were enjoying a heady freedom for the first time. If any revolution was a people's revolution, this was. The Yugoslavs were practising what we now call 'community politics' 30 years before we thought of it, and had more real control of their lives than we had in Britain.

The unpaid volunteers I saw were not the 'slave labour' of the capitalist press. The cheerfulness, the hard work, the spirit of co-operation and the infectious enthusiasm could not have been created by threats or orders from above. Women, having fought alongside the men, were playing roles that had been denied to them before the war, with competence and enormous energy. Many Muslim women had abandoned the veil and taken up political and social work. The government's priorities were the people's – to rebuild their lives and their devastated country. The young partisans had taken over and infected the older generations with their enthusiasm. The unity forged in the war seemed to be overcoming the ethnic and religious feuds that had led to the most appalling internecine slaughter and are tragically being revived today. The spirit of co-operation and internationalism had drawn thousands of young people from three continents into a new 'International Brigade' – not to fight a war but to build a railway.

Tito, the Cominform – and Me

The dreams of those years have not been realised, and I am not equipped to explain what went wrong on the Yugoslav road to socialism. Large elements of Stalinism must have remained in the Titoist system, and the decentralisation of industry clearly failed. What I find hard to explain is why, in tame conformity with the Cominform's decision in 1948 to break with Tito, I went along with the British Party in condemning the 'bourgeois nationalism' of the Yugoslav Communist Party and equating Tito with Trotsky as a 'counter-revolutionary' who had sold out to Anglo-American imperialism. Like most communists I felt that my place, when forced to choose was with the 'socialist camp' (to use the Cominform language) and not with the aggressive capitalist powers which seemed bent on using atomic superiority to 'roll back' the frontiers of socialism. I never lost the inspiration that Yugoslav socialism had given me, and I was shocked by the break with Tito, but I swallowed the Cominform's accusations uncritically. I could see no middle way, because the Cold War had blinded me as much (or almost as much) as the imperialists I criticised. I had been under the impression until recently that my role in the anti-Tito campaign had been a passive one, but in going through old *Daily Workers* I discovered that my guilty sub-conscious had suppressed three articles in which I venomously attacked Tito, and by implication the Yugoslav communists who had been so generous to us.

When Khrushchev and Bulganin had the painful task of trying to rebuild relations with Yugoslavia after Stalin's death in 1953 my bad conscience over Yugoslavia reasserted itself. As we will see in Chapter 15, my refusal to accept the bland explanations offered for our Party's role in the Tito affair started the process of disillusionment that ended in my breaking with the *Daily Worker* in November 1956 and being expelled from the Communist Party in 1957.

13

Do Reds Make Good Husbands?

My marriage to Anni Wheeler was not only a landmark in my personal life but one of the critical factors in my ultimate transition from Red to (socialist) Green. Although I am the more dominating or assertive character she has had more influence on my life than I have had on hers. She opened the door through which we both found our ways to an ecological view of life and politics. Anni gave me love, comradeship, a family, a secure home base, wonderful food and many other things as well. As an architect and planner with a social conscience she opened my eyes (over time) to architecture and the Arts and introduced me to new kinds of people and new aspects of life. She was the least overtly political of the women to whom I was attracted after Barbara's death, but (as I implied in Chapter 1) she had absorbed a socialist outlook from her father, Dr Maitland Radford, as he had done from his parents the poets Ernest and Dolly Radford who formed part of the circles around William Morris and Karl and Eleanor Marx. For Anni, a third-generation socialist, socialism was not so much a matter of joining 'the Party' as an attitude towards society that she had absorbed and for which, like her parents, she found expression in public service. In our marriage, socialism was not a peripheral activity but an integral part of our personal, family, professional and social lives. Most of our friends were communists or socialists or sympathisers, or politically tolerant.

Marriage, as somebody has said, is a bit of a lottery and I was very conscious of the fact that Barbara's would be a hard act to follow. It is also a fact – and Anni's experience was the same as mine – that whereas 'falling in love' with our first partners was an ecstatic, overwhelming walking-on-air experience, committing ourselves to new partners was seen by both of us as a risky, if exciting and potentially uplifting, undertaking, for we were a widower marrying a widow, or as Anni (being an architect) put it 'a designing widow', and I had had 13 months more than Anni to adjust to the idea of remarriage. I married her (she says) for her beautiful daughters, Janet and Susan. She married me (she also says) because she wanted my lustre cups (which, needless to say, got broken). We took the plunge on 22 May 1947 because we both thought (correctly) that the odds were on success.

Anni, too, had been as happy as it is possible to be in a wartime marriage, despite the fact that she and her first husband, John Wheeler, never had a home of their own. They met in the late 1930s when they were architecture students at the Architectural Association School in London, which turned out to be a school for politics as well. Anni and John were part of a group that was in revolt against the constraints of classical architecture and Chamberlain's politics of appeasement, and saw modern architecture as a socially and technologically liberating force. John was a communist and so were his sister Anne and his brother Peter. By the time Anni and John married in 1940 John was already in the RAF, and their daughters were born in 1941 and 1943. Peter was also in the RAF and won the Distinguished Flying Cross and Bar after surviving two rounds of bombing raids as a Pathfinder pilot. John, who had become a photographic reconnaisance pilot, was killed when test-piloting a new type of Spitfire on 12 September 1945.

A Cousinly Communist Community

The sudden death of somebody one loves is hard enough to take at any time, but it was trebly hard for Anni to lose John a month *after* the war had ended, and at the very moment when they were looking forward to his early demobilisation and an exciting new start to their family and professional lives. For John, who had been one of the most brilliant Architectural Association students, was needed urgently to rejoin the Architects' Co-operative Partnership (now the Architects' Co-Partnership), the firm that he and a group of avant-garde fellow-students had founded on co-operative principles at the Architectural Association in 1939. He was to have worked on the big commission for a rubber factory at Brynmawr in South Wales which set the firm on its feet and proved, ironically, to

be one of the very few buildings from those post-war years to
be listed for its architectural distinction. Towards the end of the
war Anni and John jumped at an invitation to join a com-
munal, cousinly (and communist) household in Keats Grove in
Hampstead for three young, related couples who each had two
young children and were looking for a home in London when
the husbands were demobilised.

The house, into which Anni and her daughters had moved in
the spring of 1945, was an Edwardian blot on the Georgian elegance of Keats Grove, but it had the supreme merits of being
very large, very cheap and conveniently located. It was rented
from an aunt by Sheila and Moira Lynd, whose parents Robert
and Sylvia lived next door. Sheila was women's editor of the
Daily Worker and married to John Wheeler's brother Peter, who
became accountant to the Communist Party for some years and
worked with me at the Royal Institute of British Architects
(RIBA) in the 1960s and 1970s. Moira was a publisher's reader
married to Jack Gaster, a solicitor who was one of two
Communists elected to the London County Council in 1946.
Anni had just taken a job as assistant to Judith Ledeboer, a pioneering architect in social housing.

Sheila became one of the best friends I ever had, and as a
reporter or feature writer she was one of the best journalists I
have known. As women's editor and later features editor of the
Daily Worker she broke out of the limitations imposed by most
newspapers at that time on 'women's issues'. She had the same
delicate touch as her father, Robert Lynd of the *New Statesman*,
who was one of the best writers of his day. Her friendly, bubbly
personality opened doors that would otherwise be closed to
Daily Worker reporters. She was the kind of reporter who could
turn her hand to anything and tell her story in highly readable
and accurate English – a versatile talent that made her indispensable to *The Architects' Journal* (*AJ*) in later years. As features
editor of the *Worker* she was unsurpassed in the tactful handling of prickly contributors like Professor J.B.S. Haldane, who
gave the paper the best popular science column of any newspaper at that time.

Sheila began the process of bringing Anni and me together
by asking me to supper the evening before I went to Greece, six
days after John had been killed. Anni was going through the
motions of getting the meal as if she was in a trance, unaware

of the world around her and almost completely silent. The world, as far as she was concerned, had come to an end, although she was trying hard to maintain an air of normality. Anni told me a long time later that my story about the difficulty of getting badges and shoulder flashes for my war reporter's uniform made her laugh for the first time since John's death. When I got back from Greece Sheila made a point of asking me round to Keats Grove, but it took a year for our relationship to develop and 20 months for us to decide to make the leap into the unknown. Our wedding in Hampstead Town Hall was a hilarious family affair attended by all the six Keats Grove children. The registrar was interrupted by Susie piping up with 'Is Malcolm our Daddy yet?', a question to which I was able to give an affirmative answer a few minutes later.

A Planned (and a Planning) Pregnancy

The arrival of our daughter Kathie was characteristic of Anni's belief in planning, as well as her practical skills. She had been interested in planning since she took part as an Architectural Association student in one of the earliest British studies in rural planning in the Thames Valley. Soon after I had got to know her she met Geoffrey Jellicoe (the former head of the Architectural Association School and today the Grand Old Man of landscape architecture) at the bus stop one morning. She said she was looking for another job. He exclaimed 'This must be Fate!' and engaged her on the spot to join him in the preparation of the Master Plan for the New Town of Hemel Hempstead. Her experience with Jellicoe led her to make planning her profession. So when we decided in November 1947 to have a baby she did a deal with Jacqueline Tyrrwhitt, the head of the School of Planning and Regional Reconstruction, by which she did the one-year postgraduate planning course in two terms while pregnant. Jackie asked the students if they objected to this arrangement, but they all agreed and proved to be very helpful. Anni conceived in December and astonished her fellow students by her ability to do all the work while having two children and a home to look after in the evenings. She completed the course in July, gave birth to Kathie in September and took a job in the planning division of the London County Council (LCC) a year later. She secured her professional qualification by completing her thesis on the planning of London while she was with the LCC.

Anni has always attributed her ability to have both a career and a family to the amount of paid help she got at home and to my role as a supportive husband and father who did some household chores. But when I look back on it I question whether I appreciated the burden that Anni's decision to combine a full-time job with a family thrust upon her. I do not think either of us can give an unqualified affirmative answer to the question that Anni asked me recently, 'Do Reds make good husbands?' My life on the *Daily Worker* must have made things very difficult for Anni. During the four years between 1947 and 1954 that I was in the Parliamentary Press Gallery, I was never at home for the children's bed-time or in the evenings between Monday and Thursday, eight months a year.

When I researched the *Worker's* files I was amazed (and dismayed) to discover that within a week of Kathie's birth in September 1948 I spent a fortnight in Glasgow covering Peter Kerrigan's by-election contest in the Gorbals. I spent the first ten days of January 1949 in Scotland, combining a visit to my mother with an investigation of the appalling housing conditions in Edinburgh, Stirling and Aberdeen. Having gone back to foreign affairs (in effect as a specialist on the Cold War) I spent the whole of June 1949 in Paris covering the Foreign Ministers' Conference that followed the ending of the Berlin blockade.

I also spent a lot of time in Glasgow in 1949 as the prospective Communist parliamentary candidate for Shettleston, followed by a disastrous three-week general election campaign early in 1950, in the depths both of the British winter and the Cold War. We were unable to rent any accommodation for our committee rooms, the comrades were very reluctant to canvass and although with 1,550 votes I polled better than 93 of the other 99 communist candidates it was less than half the vote the CP got in Shettleston in 1945 – which gives some measure of the CP's electoral debacle. Nevertheless I 'nursed' the constituency for another 18 months before withdrawing on the eve of the 1951 election when common sense belatedly prevailed, and the Party decided to reduce the number of its candidates to ten. Even then I went to Glasgow for the election to help Arnold Henderson (a popular shipyard shop steward and Communist councillor) who was fighting my old constituency in East Dunbartonshire. It never occurred to me to pull out of any of these Party commitments, although they must have created difficulties for Anni and the children. She thought work for the *Daily Worker* or the Party was important and she tells me that she bore no resentment.

Prejudice against Women, and Communists

Anni and I ran into what would now be called 'male chauvinism' when she worked for the London County Council from 1949. Her friend Percy Johnson-Marshall suggested that she should apply for a job with his team working on the reconstruction of London's devastated East End. Percy lived in Hampstead Garden Suburb (until he got the planning chair at Edinburgh University) with a young family in a chaotically happy household presided over by his unflappable wife April. He was (or had been) a communist and a tireless missionary for planning, a disciple of Patrick Geddes, the Scottish biologist whose view of planning as an ecological discipline and whose work in community planning and architecture inspired Lewis Mumford. The head of the planning division was Arthur Ling (who seemed to be a communist although I don't know if he ever held a Party card), who had worked with Patrick Abercrombie on the 1943 County of London Plan which saw London as an agglomeration of communities. Anni was delighted to have the chance of working at the LCC under people whose attitudes she shared, in an office that the best young architects and planners wanted to get into. It was a stimulating place to work in, full of optimism for the future and a commitment to the job of making blitzed and battered areas better places to live and to work in, and I got to number so many of Anni's colleagues among my friends that I became increasingly familiar with their work and their problems.

Initially Anni was denied pension rights and promotion beyond a very junior grade because she refused to work on Saturdays and was deemed to work 'part-time'. She found the LCC establishment officers intimidating and unsympathetic to women's needs or capabilities. While her professional superiors supported her requests for establishment and promotion, the (male) establishment officers were suspicious of women in professional jobs. Married women should, they thought, be at home, and they reacted with shock/horror to a married woman with *three* children *and* a husband on the *Daily Worker* at a time when the Labour government had instituted a witch-hunt of communists in 'sensitive' jobs. However, the obstacles placed in her way obliged her to develop a more assertive personality and the times changed. The LCC had to abandon Saturday working and Anni won both establishment and promotion to become responsible for detailed planning in North-East London.

Emotionally and politically I took part, at one remove, in the battles Anni had to fight as she progressed up the LCC ladder, both for promotion and for a humane attitude to planning and architecture. As a journalist, when writing reports on housing and related issues I gained enormously from my knowledge of the problems Anni faced in the East End. The conventional wisdom nowadays is that the post-war planners – whose plans were based on Abercrombie's analysis of London's communities – should have rehabilitated the old slums. Anni came to love the East End and the East Enders, but they were not interested in rehabilitating the slums. The cry that she encountered wherever she went was 'How soon can I get a new home?', but as the people had no idea where or when the LCC would re-house them the system made it impossible for them to play any part in the shaping of their new environment.

The savage restraints imposed on housing and other social services to pay for Labour's rearmament programmes after 1949 made it impossible to build fast enough, or to provide the parks, playing fields, schools and health centres that were integral elements in the plans. When the Tories came into power in 1951 things were no better, even when Harold Macmillan set out to build 300,000 houses a year, for the Tory Party's programme was biased towards private development, and developers were totally uninterested in the East End at that time, whether for housing, shops or anything else. Although the Stepney-Poplar area on which Anni worked for some years was a 'comprehensive development area' the LCC never created an integrated team to implement the plans. Schools, parks and health centres were only provided if the individual departments included them in their separate programmes. It was tragic for us to go back to Stepney-Poplar 20 years later, to try to explain to Joan Littlewood, the pioneering theatre director from the Theatre Royal at Stratford East, what Anni and her colleagues had tried to do, for the new housing stood in a wasteland. Sites that had been allocated for parks or nursery schools were overgrown with weeds and strewn with rubbish. Anni's experience helped me to understand the meaning of 'social architecture'.

14

Labour Digs its Own Grave

The Labour Party was more popular during the post-war years of austerity from 1945 to 1950 than before or since. Why then was it defeated in 1951? Why, if 1950 or 1951 seems to mark the peaking of Labour's fortunes, do nearly all Labour circles, from right to left, assume that Labour's record from 1945 to 1951 is well-nigh blameless? It is conceded that the nationalised corporations may now be out of date, but nobody seems keen to find any real skeletons in Labour's cupboards, or any moral blemishes that call for something comparable to *glasnost* in the Soviet Union. My purpose in this chapter is to explain the fall of the Labour government, as I saw it, and I make no excuse for devoting a lot of it to the Korean War of 1950–3, which revealed the moral depths to which anti-communism could drag a Labour leadership down. The *Daily Worker* was relentlessly smeared and persecuted. Allegations of treason (for which the only penalty is death) were made against us, not merely by the press and Tory backwoodsmen but by Labour ministers. Despite these pressures we gave our readers a more truthful account of the war and its horror than any other newspaper. I was personally involved as a member of the paper's editorial committee, as parliamentary reporter and political commentator, and I knew the people whom the Tory MPs wanted to hang. But before I tell the Korean story, from our point of view, I must put it into its historical perspective.

The Communist Party and the *Daily Worker* bent over backwards, as my parliamentary reports and sketches demonstrate, to support Labour's domestic programme in its early years. We recognized that it faced enormous problems and had some solid achievements to its credit. Labour never tried to lay the foundations of a socialist economy or to accomplish a major redistribution of power and wealth, but it carried out a very large part of the programme on which it was elected in 1945. It established a free National Health Service, raised the school leaving age, introduced a land use planning system that recouped developers' profits for the taxpayer, and provided a safety net for the poorest through the social security system. It was committed to full employment. The Communist Party backed the government's nationalisation programme despite major reservations, and Willie Gallacher led the cheering when the Coal Mines Nationalisation Act was passed in 1946. Communists did more than Labour Party members in the first two years to increase industrial productivity in the interests of post-war recovery. We accepted bread rationing and peacetime conscription in 1946.

Labour on the Slippery Slope

Labour never really recovered from the disastrous crises of 1947: the freeze-up that closed industry down in February, and the dollar crisis in August. The dollar crisis led to the first draconian cuts in capital spending. Nye Bevan's housing programme (which seemed likely to reach 300,000 houses a year) was cut to 200,000 for the next three years. Rearmament took precedence over social spending or the modernisation of industry. The government looked for financial salvation to the United States, embraced Marshall Aid, traded nuclear bases in Britain for dollars, and began to rearm. On the eve of the general election of February 1950 Bevan was muttering about resignation because the housing budget had been cut again and preference given to 'defence'. By then Labour had nothing more to offer and was living on its past. Even so, although its majority was cut to five seats, Labour retained such a strong hold on the affections of the people that it got more votes than it had in 1945. The two Communist MPs were defeated and so were the independent left-wing (or in their enemies' eyes 'fellow-travelling') group of former Labour MPs led by Dennis Pritt. When the Korean War broke out five months later the only consistent opposition to the bi-partisan Labour-Tory foreign and defence policies had been eliminated from the House of Commons.

Even before the Korean War broke out in 1950 anti-Soviet hysteria infected the most unlikely people. Bertrand Russell, the pacifist who was to sit down in Whitehall in protest against atomic weapons a few years later, declared in November 1948 that 'either we must have a war against Russia before she has the atom bomb or we will have to lie down and let them govern us'. After the Soviet Union announced that it had the A-bomb, Field Marshal Montgomery the Commander-in-Chief of the new 'Western Union' told a press conference in Washington in November 1949 that 'if anybody commits an act of aggression against Western Union we would have a real good party and kill a lot of people'. The Labour government to which he was responsible kept silent. 'Monty', I commented in the *Daily Worker*,

> thinks killing a lot of people is a 'real good party'. Hitler thought so too. So did the SS men who butchered the Jews. And so do the American Generals who want to wipe out communism with the atom bomb. But you and I are going to be the victims if we are foolish enough to let the 'party' start.

Everything seemed to point to war. The Western powers had just rejected the umpteenth Soviet offer to abolish nuclear weapons and to reduce armed forces by a third, and the US had bludgeoned Western Europe into increasing arms expenditure.

The Labour government's decision in June 1950 to back the American military intervention in Korea and give it the camouflage of the United Nations' flag can only be understood in the context of the all-pervading anti-communism. In 1988 Tony Benn called, in *Fighting Back,* for a vigorous re-examination of the virulent anti-communism that fed us for 40 years with the idea that the Soviet Union was planning to conquer Western Europe and could only be prevented by nuclear weapons. If we ask who purveyed this lie (for which there is not a scrap of evidence), or who betrayed the real interests of this country in the Korean War, the finger points (among others) to Attlee and the Labour ministers. Denis Healey, who was the toughest member of Labour's pro-nuclear and anti-Soviet lobby for many years, now says in his autobiography *The Time of My Life* that 'we were all mistaken' in believing that Stalin was out to 'conquer' Western Europe, and he concedes that their war losses explain 'the universal hatred of war among the Russian people'. In fact 'we' were not all mistaken; those whom he derides as communists or fellow-travellers were right on this fundamental point, however great their mistaken confidence in Stalin's 'socialism'.

On the other hand the Soviet Union had every reason to feel threatened by the American atom bomb, and American threats can only have intensified the Soviet nuclear programme and the Stalinist repression. By helping to foment irrational fears the Labour government became the accomplice of the US in Korea in a genocidal war that set the pattern for Vietnam and Cambodia.

The Big Korean Lie

Korea had been a Japanese colony since 1910. It was liberated in 1945 by the Red Army and arbitrarily divided into Soviet and US occupation zones at the thirty-eighth parallel. The Red Army withdrew from the North in 1948, leaving behind the communist People's Democratic Republic of Korea headed by the former resistance leader Kim Il Sung. The US withdrew from the South in 1949, having installed the dictator Syngman Rhee as President of the Republic of Korea. On 24 June 1950 North Korean forces crossed the thirty-eighth parallel and advanced into South Korea. On 26 June the US Air Force and Navy intervened without Congressional or United Nations approval. Next day the US government asked for and got the approval and assistance of the UN Security Council.

The UN decision to back the American war in Korea was justified in the Western media by the assertion that the North Korean invasion of South Korea was a threat to world peace, staged by Russia and China to extend communism in Asia or to divert attention from Russia's aggressive plans in Europe. In fact the Soviet Union had nothing to do with the initiation of the war and gave only marginal support to North Korea or China during it. China only entered the war in self-defence, when General MacArthur was advancing the US forces to the Chinese frontier on the Yalu River and had already dropped bombs on Chinese territory. The Chinese response to MacArthur's provocation led to the rout of the US and British forces and brought the world to the edge of nuclear war. Washington panicked and President Truman told a press conference on 30 November 1950 that the use of the Bomb against China was 'under active consideration'. The decision would be taken, he said, by 'the military commander in the field' – which meant the megalomanic anti-communist General MacArthur.

The Labour government bears a major responsibility for these developments. Britain never questioned the dubious second-hand evidence on which North Korea was condemned by the United Nations without a hearing. Britain obligingly moved the UN resolution approving the advance into North Korea that provoked China's entry into the war – which MacArthur had already begun without consulting Britain or even the UN in whose name the war was being waged. British troops participated in the advance towards China. With typical sycophancy the Labour government voted for the US-inspired resolution at the UN, branding China (yes, China!) as the aggressor. It was only when President Truman made threatening noises about the A-bomb that Attlee, faced with a split in the Labour Party, belatedly discovered that he was being taken for a ride on the back of the American nuclear tiger. His flight to Washington failed to secure any undertaking that Britain would be consulted before the Bomb was used. Truman's denial that the US had any intention of using the atomic bomb was a half-truth, for the US had been considering its use for six months and continued to do so. Four months after his meeting with Attlee, on 6 April 1951, Truman signed an order to the Joint Chiefs of Staff (without consulting Britain) approving immediate atomic retaliation against China in certain circumstances.

A month later the Labour Foreign Secretary, Herbert Morrison, gave his consent in principle to the bombing of bases inside China by the US. Five months later the US carried out a number of dummy atomic bomb runs over North Korea, and later used the threat of atomic bombing to exert pressure on China during the truce talks. I mention these facts because, although we lacked the specific information at the time, they show how near to the truth we were on the *Daily Worker* when we accused the US of planning nuclear war. In my own contributions I implied that the Joint Allied Chiefs of Staff were planning for war against the Soviet Union, but I suspect that if I had known what we now know about what was being discussed I would have been even more alarmist.

The Truth About Korea

In *Korea: the Unknown War* John Halliday (an East Asia specialist) and Bruce Cummings (the Professor of East Asian

History at the University of Chicago) have brought together a mass of information from contemporary reports and previously confidential documents that totally demolish the idea that the 'invasion' of South Korea was a threat to world peace. It was, they say, the continuation of a civil war that had been going on for some years, with guerrilla war in South Korea and numerous clashes (many of them provoked by South Korea) at the thirty-eighth parallel. They confirm the *Daily Worker's* reports that Syngman Rhee was planning to seize North Korea. The question 'who started the war?' strikes them as irrelevant, for the Korean War, like the wars in China and Vietnam (and I would add Afghanistan) was in essence 'a civil war fought between two domestic forces, a revolutionary nationalist movement which had its roots in tough anti-colonial struggle, and a conservative movement tied to the status quo, especially to an unequal land system'. The reality, they say, was not a United Nations 'police action' against Soviet-sponsored aggression but 'a people's war ... guerrillas fighting well before and after June 1950, people working in caves and underground factories to sustain a peasant society against the greatest power on earth'. Alan Winnington's reports in the *Daily Worker* portrayed the Korean War in much the same light.

Labour backed the terrorist, gangster regime of Syngman Rhee in South Korea which, according to an article by James Cameron which we published after *Picture Post* had suppressed it, was 'about as democratic and high-principled as Caligula's Rome'. Its barbarities took place under the flag of the United Nations, but the UN delegation in Korea told Cameron that it was powerless to protest, for in reality 'the United Nations here means the US Army, and that means General MacArthur'. The Labour government turned a blind eye to Cameron's plea that the United Nations should stop the atrocities being committed in its name and failed to investigate them. It preferred to give unconditional support to a war that laid North Korea waste, burning countless women and children alive and killing around 4 million Koreans and Chinese – a veritable holocaust, or should I say 'a real good party'?

The *Daily Worker* was the only newspaper to have access to both sides of the story. We used Reuters' coverage and picked up the damning facts reported by the few investigative reporters on the US side. Alan Winnington covered the entire war and two years of peace talks from the North Korean side, and earned the hatred of the US command because he provided the Western press with accurate information (which the Americans tried to distort or suppress) about the talks themselves and about American bombing of the neutral zone where the talks were taking place. For three years he experienced daily bombing, napalming of civilians and the laying waste of an entire country.

It was Alan's gruesome report in August 1950 of mass graves at Rangwul, 'a US Belsen' where, he said, thousands of political prisoners had been massacred by Syngman Rhee's police under American supervision, that led to one of the first suggestions (probably prompted by the US) that he was guilty of 'treasonable' activity. The Americans later alleged that it was the North Koreans who had perpetrated the massacres, but Alan interviewed more than 20 villagers who had been forced at rifle point to dig the pits and saw the victims being executed under the supervision of American officers. He took photographs and collected the American bullets and cigarette packs that littered the scene. Similar massacres were witnessed by British troops and confirmed by James Cameron's suppressed report to *Picture Post*.

Alan did not, it is true, report any atrocities committed by the North Koreans or Chinese although it is undeniable that, as in all civil wars, there were atrocities and brutalities on both sides, but he reported what he saw, and nobody who reads Halliday's and Cummings's review, *Korea: the Unknown War*, can doubt that the atrocities committed by the communist side were small in comparison to those committed by the American side. The greatest atrocity of all was the American bombing on a genocidal scale which was intended, in the words of MacArthur's orders of November 1950, quoted by Halliday and Cummings, to turn North Korea into a 'wasteland' by destroying 'every installation, factory, city and village'. If these orders were not a war crime I do not know what is. The Americans silenced their consciences by de-humanising the Koreans into sub-human 'gooks' and the Chinese became 'hordes'. The Labour government looked the other way.

'Treason!'

Within days of Alan Winnington's arrival in North Korea in July 1950 the Foreign Office announced that it was 'investi-

gating the legal situation', that is, whether it was treasonable
for Alan to report the war from the 'enemy' side. But it was
Alan's visits to the British prisoners of war (PoWs) from 1951 to
1953, and the publication in the *Daily Worker* of their messages
to relatives and reassuring reports about their treatment (at a
time when the US media were regaling the American public
with horrific stories about the treatment of prisoners) that got
under the Establishment's skin. Sir Hartley Shawcross, Labour's
Attorney-General, expressed the view that the activities of the
Daily Worker 'have every appearance of coming within the definition of treasonable offences'. On the strength of this opinion
Shinwell, the Minister of Defence, said that 'the state of hostili-
ties between China and ourselves is sufficient to bring the act
of "giving aid and comfort" to the Chinese within the definition of treason'. He added that although it was 'difficult' to
prosecute 'because the only penalty for treason is death ... the
position will be closely watched'.

Our lawyers told us that legally Shinwell did not have a leg to
stand on. Britain was not at war with China. Passing on messages from PoWs and reporting on their condition gave aid and
comfort to their relatives, not to China. The law knew of no
such offence as treason against the United Nations, but we did
not know how far the Labour government would go, and my
former colleague Peter Fryer reminded me recently that at the
height of the treason uproar I thought the Party might be
forced to go underground. It certainly suited Labour's book to
smear anyone who visited North Korea and told the truth
about conditions there. Hugh Dalton, the Minister of Town
and Country Planning, sacked Monica Felton, the Chairman of
Stevenage New Town Development Corporation, on her return
from a women's mission to Korea. Monica, whom I interviewed
on her return, was smeared as a 'traitor', but her story should
have moved every member of the Labour Cabinet to think
again about the shameful war it was waging.

Alan always believed that his reports of germ warfare in 1951–
2 were the principal reason for the 'treason' allegations made
against him. His factual reports of the evidence and of the
massive counter-measures taken by the Chinese and Koreans
were ridiculed by the American and the British authorities. But
the Western governments made no attempt to refute the evidence scientifically, relying mainly on bland assertions that it

was 'unthinkable' for the US government (which later drenched Vietnam with Agent Orange) to commit a war crime. An international commission of scientists (which included experts in all the relevant sciences) upheld the charge that the US forces were using germ warfare. The two captured American pilots who gave Alan the story of the operation did not withdraw their statements when they got home, and the US government abandoned the investigation of one of them, Colonel Schwable. The British government never attempted to smear the commission's chairman, the Cambridge scientist Professor Joseph Needham, with 'treason', for Needham had experience of Japanese experiments in germ warfare when he was the scientific counsellor at the British Embassy in Peking. He spoke Chinese and was one of the West's foremost authorities on Chinese science. The British government preferred not to take him on.

'Torture' – but no Victims

In 1954, following a hostile campaign in the American press, the Foreign Office confiscated Alan's passport when he applied for its renewal to enable him to represent the *Daily Worker* at the post-war Geneva conference. However, the storm did not finally burst over Alan's head until March 1955, more than a year after the Korean War had ended, when Harold Macmillan, the Minister of Defence, published a White Paper on 'The Treatment of British Prisoners in Korea' – a concoction of disinformation that deserves to rank with the Foreign Office's 'Zinoviev letter' forgery that brought the Labour government down in 1924. A year before the White Paper, the 530 British PoWs were examined on their return and found, according to a Major-General in the Royal Army Medical Corps, to be 'all in very good form ... very cheerful and not a grouse of any kind', and the Ministry of Defence said that there was 'no evidence' to support allegations of torture or mistreatment.

The White Paper implied that Alan Winnington had interrogated and 'brainwashed' them, and it made the most grotesque allegations of systematic torture. It said that prisoners had been marched barefoot onto the frozen Yalu River where water was poured over their feet in temperatures well below 20 degrees of frost, and left for hours with their feet frozen into the ice, yet there were no cases of frostbite or gangrene. No checkable dates

or places were given. Ministers refused to name even one prisoner who was allegedly tortured, frozen to the Yalu River,
interrogated or 'brainwashed' by Alan. Not a single prisoner
ever came forward to support the charges, although many came
to Alan's defence.

The report was debated in the Commons in what my successor in the Press Gallery, Peter Fryer, called 'an atmosphere of
blood lust'. The Attorney-General conceded that there was no
evidence on which Jack Gaster (who had gone to North Korea
with an international legal commission) or Monica Felton
could be convicted of treason, but he kept the charge of treason
hanging over the heads of Winnington and Michael Shapiro
(an employee of the New China News Agency) by saying that if
either of them returned to this country he would carefully consider whether proceedings for treason should be instituted.
Alan had no doubt that in taking this line the British government was yielding to American pressure. He was exiled for 20
years before he could return to Britain without fear of prosecution. He had to leave China because, with his usual integrity,
he stood out against the pressure and persecutions of 'The
Great Leap Forward'. He settled in East Germany where he died
in 1983, and I hope that one day this country will recognise the
services he rendered in exposing the truth about Korea.

The British White Paper was shown to be pure invention
when the US Army investigated the reasons why 38 per cent of
the 7,190 US prisoners (who were held under the same conditions as the British) died in captivity. The report of the enquiry
showed that the atrocity stories extracted from US prisoners on
their return and blazoned across the US press and TV screens
were inventions. GI prisoners had collaborated with the
Chinese and North Koreans, precisely as Alan had reported,
because they had been indoctrinated to expect torture at the
hands of the 'gooks', and were astonished to find themselves
greeted 'with a smile, a cigarette and a handshake'. Their
morale collapsed. They abandoned badly-wounded prisoners.
The strong stole food from the weak. Helpless dysentery cases
were rolled outside the huts by their comrades and left to die.
But most of them died from what Alan called 'give-up-itis' – a
diagnosis confirmed by the US Army report which said that
'you could actually predict how long it would take such a man
to die' once despondency had set in.

The US government used the Korean War and the fear of world war it generated to push the Labour government into a gigantic £4.7 billion rearmament programme at the end of 1950, and into accepting the rearmament of Western Germany. In so doing the Labour government dug its own grave. This was not so much because the Korean War was desperately unpopular (with minor exceptions the electorate only got the official version of events) but because the cost of rearmament brought Labour's reforming programme virtually to a halt. One-time left-wing Labour politicians salvaged their careers by taking on the dirty work of waging the Cold and Colonial wars – John Strachey, the one-time guru of the Left Book Club, as Minister for the Colonies and then for War, and Shinwell as Minister for War and then for Defence. Shinwell, who had used George Sinfield our industrial reporter to leak stories favourable to himself when he was Minister of Fuel and Power, gave credence to the charges of 'treason' against his old friends on the *Daily Worker*. Even the £4.7 billion rearmament programme was not big enough for Shinwell, although it was so far beyond the capability of British industry that Churchill's first action on winning the general election in 1951 was to cut it back.

Playing the Parliamentary Game

When I returned to the Press Gallery after Churchill's victory in October 1951 I saw a Labour Opposition hopelessly divided by its commitment to Tory foreign policy, the A-bomb and rearmament. Nye Bevan and Harold Wilson had resigned from the government in March 1951 in protest against Gaitskell's budget, which imposed charges for teeth and spectacles to help pay for rearmament. Bevan alone had the fire and talent to lead an effective Opposition, for he was in a class by himself in the House of Commons. He was loathed by the Tories, for they could never find effective retorts to the wounding phrases that exploded from his lips. But Bevan was hopelessly compromised. He had gone along with NATO, rearmament and the Korean War. A month before he resigned as Minister of Labour he had backed the £4.7 billion rearmament programme, although he also said that the Soviet Union had neither the intention nor the industrial capacity to attack the West. As Minister of Health he had backed the order that introduced the principle of charges in the National Health Service. He launched devastating onslaughts on the Tories to divert attention from his own failures (in housing, for example) while ignoring the friendly critics on his own side.

Attlee tried to keep up the pretence of 'opposition' by playing parliamentary games in which Shinwell was one of the star performers. In 1952 Shinwell put on what I called 'The Punch and Manny Show', offering 'all-night variety, slapstick comedy, superb illusionism, juggling (with statistics), tightrope walking, promise-swallowing, verbal acrobatics and even the occasional punching bout', and kept the House sitting for over 24 hours 'opposing' a Home Guard Bill that he himself had originated as Minister of Defence and to which, at the end of the debate, he pledged support. A debate in July 1952 on the American bombing of the Chinese-Korean dams and power stations on the Yalu River ended (to quote my report) 'in the rout and humiliation of the official Labour opposition'. Mr Attlee and his friends refused to challenge the Yalu bombings, American policy in Korea or the cringing servility of the Tories. Mr Noel-Baker's speech, as Churchill said, was primarily an attack on the left wing of the Labour Party and attempted to justify everything that America had done in Korea.

Why Labour Lost

Attlee's censure motion in the debate of February 1952 on the Tory government's Defence White Paper was a classic example of his use of what I called the 'blank shot' technique – firing off blank ammunition to create a loud noise and the illusion of a tough fight while doing no damage to the Tory government. His amendment expressing 'no confidence' in the Tories' ability to carry out the rearmament programme actually endorsed it. Its practical effect was to force 55 Labour MPs to vote against it.

For a time in 1953 Churchill seemed to have grasped the enormity of the danger to which Britain, with its American nuclear bases, was exposed by the development of the more powerful hydrogen bomb by the US. I was amazed (although pleased) when he made a speech in the House urging the West to take advantage of the death of Stalin in March 1953 to hold a summit – himself, President Eisenhower and Malenkov the new Soviet leader – to explore the possibility of calling a halt to the Cold War. He was frustrated by Eisenhower, by his own Cabinet (which couldn't wait for him to retire) and by a stroke which he concealed from the world. His attack of sanity was short-lived. In February 1955 he announced his government's decision to make the H-bomb, and when, two weeks later, the Commons debated the government's Defence White Paper (which based Britain's strategy on the first use of nuclear weapons), he plumbed the depths in a blood-curdling speech in which he called for a showdown with the Russians in the three years that remained of Western nuclear supremacy.

That debate could have been a triumph for the Labour Party, for Bevan winkled out of Churchill the admission that Eisenhower had vetoed his notion of a post-Stalin summit, but Attlee had put down another of his 'blank shot' censure motions, 'censuring' the government's defence policy but supporting its decision to make the H-bomb. Bevan, who got an evasive reply when he challenged Attlee to say whether his amendment committed Labour to first use of nuclear weapons, abstained from voting, along with 57 other Labour MPs. His expulsion from the party was only defeated on the National Executive by one vote, but the damage had been done. Attlee's nuclear policy had split the Labour Party from top to bottom on the eve of the 1955 general election. Ironically, Bevan ended his career as Labour's foreign policy spokesman with his famous (or infamous) refusal to go 'naked into the conference chamber' without the H-bomb.

The Tory Party was a sitting duck in the 1955 election. Churchill was a spent force. Eden, who had succeeded him, was obviously unwell and already obsessed with the Suez Canal, but it came as no surprise to me when the Labour Party lost it. If Churchill was prevented by his own party from seizing the opportunity for detente presented by the changes in the Soviet Union the Labour Party was inhibited from doing so by the anti-Soviet paranoia of its leaders and their love affair with the H-bomb. They offered no real alternative to the Tories, who polled 412,000 fewer votes than they did in 1951, but won because the Labour vote slumped by more than 1.5 million below its all-time high of nearly 14 million in 1951.

The sham battles over Korea and defence policy seemed to me to reflect a basic flaw in Labour's approach to politics. The

Labour Party is an electoral machine and it fights its main battles in Parliament, but in my time, from 1945 to 1956, Labour made no serious reappraisal of the parliamentary system. Both in government and in opposition the Labour leaders used their control over parliamentary time to stifle debate and to reduce MPs to mindless lobby-fodder, like the Labour MP who stopped me one night to ask 'What are we voting on?' My reply, 'page three line 13 of The Agriculture Bill leave out "as nearly as may be"', left him none the wiser. When Bevan tried to secure a debate on the explosion of the American H-bomb at Bikini, Harry Crookshank the Tory Leader of the House refused to offer a debate in government time but mischievously pointed out that a debate could be held in Opposition time – knowing that the last thing Attlee wanted was a debate on the nuclear policies that he had introduced. No debate was held.

I have always believed that Parliament should have a central role in any democratic system, but it can never acquire the status and character it needs unless Labour sheds its slavish attachment to the stifling procedures and traditions that (as Tony Benn has recently shown) turn Parliament into a travesty of democracy. In constitutional theory the Commons control the government; in reality the Prime Minister controls both the government and the Commons, and takes major decisions without informing or consulting Parliament. When Attlee's government ran into the inevitable obstruction from the House of Lords, it ran away both from its commitment to abolish the Lords and from any serious attempt to reform the creaking machinery of Parliament. It was left to Tory governments to introduce Life Peers and to improve MPs' pay and conditions. When Labour lost the 1951 election despite having won more votes than the Tories I recalled Herbert Morrison's scornful denunciation of Willie Gallacher's attempt in 1949 to intro-duce proportional representation into the Parliament Bill. Morrison, like all Labour's leaders before and since, preferred 'strong' government to representative government. The first-past-the-post electoral system, which seemed in the 1940s to give Labour turn-and-turn-about in office without having to win a majority of votes, has given us, as I write, more than ten years of 'strong', minority Thatcherite government.

I have to confess that I enjoyed my years in the Press Gallery.

At its best the House of Commons with Churchill, Bevan, Dalton, Shinwell and Macmillan was splendid theatre, very unlike today's dismal shouting matches. The most boring debates almost invariably taught me something, sometimes serious but more often farcical – as in the case of Labour's Mr Follick who brushed his teeth in the House with the revolving toothbrush he had invented, and demanded measures to deal with people who licked the icing off buns but would not buy them. I became the nearest thing the *Daily Worker* had to a constitutional expert and acquired a good working knowledge of the bizarre rituals, rules and customs that are mastered only by a handful of MPs.

Daily exposure to professional politicians produces a high level of cynicism in parliamentary reporters and ensured that even at the worst moments in the Cold War neither Peter Zinkin, our lobby correspondent, nor I were made to feel unwelcome in the Press Gallery. When I entered for the Gallery golf championship the committee charitably gave me a duffer's handicap of 22 strokes, presumably because I was 'disabled'. I savoured defeating a diehard but gentlemanly Tory in the final; I could hardly have lost. The silver cup stood on our mantelpiece for a year and once, when I climbed on my soapbox in Hampstead, the communist chairman introduced me as the Parliamentary Press Gallery Golf Champion. It still gives me pleasure to think that whoever holds the cup today can see the name of the *Daily Worker* permanently engraved on its plinth alongside the names of *The Times*, the *Daily Telegraph* and Reuters.

15

The Day the Party had to Stop

I can date the beginning of my disenchantment with Stalinism and the Soviet regime from 16 May 1955, the day on which Bulganin and Khrushchev stood on the tarmac at Belgrade airport and read their grovelling apology to the Yugoslav government and Communist Party. Bulganin and Khrushchev tried to shuffle off their responsibility onto Beria, the evil genius of the KGB, but the British Communist Party or the *Daily Worker* could not. The *Worker* had played a major part in spreading the lies about the Titoite conspiracy that had now been withdrawn. Our foreign editor, Derek Kartun, had reported (albeit in good faith) the staged trials in Prague of Slansky and his comrades (including Ludwig Freund, who had worked with me on the *Worker* in 1944–5) and of Rajk in Budapest. I had to face up to the fact that all the trials based on the 'Titoite conspiracy' must have been frame-ups, and that we had made ourselves accomplices in the judicial murders of our own comrades. It seemed to me essential for the Party not only to make its own apology and retraction but also to recognise the devastating implications of Bulganin and Khrushchev's admissions, both for the Soviet Union and for ourselves.

I took the matter up immediately with Pollitt and others, but got nowhere. As late as February 1956, just before Khrushchev's secret speech on Stalin's crimes to the Twentieth Congress of the Communist Party of the Soviet Union (CPSU), I raised the matter again at a meeting of my Party branch in Hampstead, where Emile Burns, who was still a member of the Political Committee, blandly denied that the Party had made any mistake. In a subsequent letter to me he argued with his usual air of sweet reasonableness that the Soviet attitude had changed because Tito had 'drawn back from the imperialist path' on which he set out, and he suppressed a long letter I sent to the Party weekly, *World News and Views*.

179

By the middle of March 1956 my confidence both in the Soviet Union and in our own Party leaders was being further undermined by Khrushchev's revelations and by the ineptitude and dishonesty with which they were handled by the Soviet Party and by our own leaders. Harry Pollitt and George Matthews attended the Twentieth Congress of the CPSU where Khrushchev condemned Stalin's 'cult of the individual' and Stalin's 'mistakes' in the open session, and gave assurances that the necessary measures had been taken to prevent its recurrence. Gorbachev's *glasnost* or openness was not Khrushchev's or Pollitt's way. The *gulags*, or labour camps, were closed and their prisoners released by stealth. Khrushchev made the real revelations on 25 February in a closed session from which the fraternal delegates from other countries were excluded. His speech was not published in the Soviet Union but was circulated only to leading Party cadres, who read it to closed Party meetings. The fraternal delegates were allowed to return home without being given an inkling of the shock that was in store for them when the substance of the speech was leaked in Bonn in March by US Intelligence, and then published in full from the same source in July.

The Truth About Stalin

On their return, Pollitt and Matthews insisted that the Soviet leader's public utterances had 'frankly and courageously' laid bare 'the cult of the individual' and taken all the necessary steps to restore collective leadership. They presented the Stalin cult as a side issue that must not detract from the real significance of the Twentieth Congress – the CPSU's peace policy, the new Soviet Five Year Plan and the rising standard of living in the Soviet Union. Khrushchev had indeed extrapolated the rising curve of Soviet production into the future and prophesied that the Soviet Union would overtake the US in per capita production, or as he put it, would 'bury' the US economically. Anything more inept than Pollitt's and Matthews' interpretation of the Twentieth Congress could hardly be conceived. When the text of the secret speech was splashed all over the world press it was obvious that the truth was infinitely worse than anything that had so far been admitted, for Khrushchev accused Stalin not merely of personal dictatorship and of departing from the Leninist system of collective leadership, but of decimating the Party, murdering more than half the members of the Central Committee, personally authorising torture and behaving with an inhumanity that Hitler himself could not have surpassed.

This touched a sensitive nerve, for I had written a number of articles in 1949–50 rebutting 'lies and slanders' about the Soviet Union. Some of them were indeed malicious inventions but others were now admitted to be true. To pass off Stalinism as 'the cult of the individual' when Stalin's death three years earlier had been treated by the *Daily Worker* as the departure of the greatest man of our time was more than I and many other Party members could stomach.

Even before his secret speech was leaked, Khrushchev's guarded public criticism of the Stalin cult provoked a flood of letters to the *Daily Worker*. The British Party leaders' responses, like those of the German Democratic Republic 33 years later, were too little and too late. I had become the features editor, and I proposed to publish the letters. Johnny Campbell referred the matter to the Party's Political Committee which agreed to publication even of the most critical in the hope that the storm would blow itself out. Two weeks later, on 12 March, Johnny declared the discussion closed, and congratulated the correspondents on not having indulged in 'exaggerated denigration of Stalin', but within days the leaking of the secret speech provoked an even bigger flood of letters. I published them, but from then onwards there was a continuous struggle over the readers' letters. No sooner had Johnny told me (on instructions from the Political Committee) that 'enough is enough' than some fresh revelation from Eastern Europe would enable me to publish another batch of letters revealing the profound split that was developing in the Party.

Judicial Murder

When I read today about the torrent of discussion in the Soviet Union resulting from *glasnost* and *perestroika* I am reminded of the endless and often heated discussions we had on the *Daily Worker* in 1956. Those who felt as I did found themselves in perpetual conflict with Johnny Campbell, who was profoundly shaken by the revelations. He must have known the truth for many years, but his loyalty to the Soviet Union and the Political Committee overrode his conscience. The issue that began to tear the staff apart was 'judicial murder', which was brought to a head by some odd coincidences. On the very day that the Khrushchev speech was leaked I published a moving interview by Sheila Lynd with Rose Sobell, whose son Morton Sobell had been framed and given 30 years for his alleged part in the 'conspiracy' for which Ethel and Julius Rosenberg had been electrocuted in June 1953. The charges against the Rosenbergs, although widely believed at the time, were absurd for they were said to have passed the 'secret' of the atomic bomb to the Soviet Union. The depth of the lynching mood of which they were the victims can be gauged by the statement of the judge at their trial that 'your conduct ... has already caused ... the communist aggression in Korea, with the resultant casualties exceeding 50,000'. The *Daily Worker* led the British campaign to save the Rosenbergs, and huge crowds protested in London on the night of their judicial murder, after President Eisenhower had refused to exercise clemency.

One day after Sheila's article appeared, Rakosi, the Hungarian Premier, announced the rehabilitation of Rajk, the former Party Secretary who had been shot as a traitor after the show trial in Budapest that Derek Kartun and Peter Fryer had reported for the *Worker*. I felt that while we had been opposing judicial murder in the US with one side of our mouths we had been condoning and even justifying judicial murder in the Soviet bloc with the other. Walter Holmes, a veteran socialist and spicy columnist who had worked on George Lansbury's *Daily Herald*, was 'copy-tasting' when the news of Rajk's rehabilitation came through on the tape. He would have spiked the story had Peter Fryer not spotted it, and when he reported it to the daily news conference I proposed that we should publish a leading article on the judicial murder of Rajk and the Rosenbergs. Walter asked 'Who the hell cares about Rajk?' and Johnny Campbell rejected my idea, but the arguments continued and the split in the staff widened.

... In the Best of All Possible Worlds

Even after Khrushchev's secret speech had been leaked, and the flood of letters became a torrent, the position of the British

Party leadership hardly changed. In an article on 24 March on 'The Role of Stalin' Pollitt insisted that 'if wrongs were to be righted the truth about the past must be publicly stated', yet he never referred to Stalin's 'crimes'; the Party leaders would only use the weasel word 'mistakes'. They said that it was 'the enemies of the working class', and the security services, not Stalin or the Party leaders, who had brought false charges against innocent people. Pollitt expressed total satisfaction with the 'frank and honest' procedure by which the Soviet Party had supposedly ensured that 'past mistakes' could not be repeated. I had always had a great affection for Pollitt, but when I went to see him he astonished me by saying 'you hate my guts, don't you?' – as if my disagreement with the line he was taking had caused me to hate him. He was incapable of abandoning the uncritical solidarity with the Soviet leadership on which he had built his political life, and, like Khrushchev, he and his closest colleagues on the Political Committee still preferred secrecy to openness. Pollitt made his report on Yugoslavia and the Twentieth Congress to the British Communist Party Congress on 30 March to a private session.

I went to the Congress as a delegate, determined to raise the roof, but my speech remained in my pocket. Johnny Campbell, who chaired the closed session, called Peter Fryer but not me, perhaps on the principle that one dissident *Daily Worker* journalist was enough. Pollitt made the most extraordinary statement (all too typical of his emotional approach to politics) that he respected revolutionaries who confessed to crimes they did not commit rather than 'give in to the class enemy'! I wrote a letter to Pollitt the next day:

People who swallow this will swallow anything. It is the duty of a communist to expose torture, murder and other abominations even more under socialism than under capitalism, if only because no communist can possibly stoop to such methods to settle political differences. A false confession only perpetuates the evil, sends more comrades to their deaths, and hinders the advance to communism. It was the mistaken loyalty of this kind that led to Stalin's excesses in the USSR, and yet you hold up this kind of thing as a model for us all to admire. Presumably, Tito should have 'confessed' and knuckled under to Stalin. Apparently, whatever happens, all is for the best in the best of all possible worlds. Rakosi was right to put Rajk on trial, being deceived by Beria; Rajk was right to confess, because had he not done so he would have exposed Beria and shaken our confidence in the Soviet Union; Rakosi is right now to 'rehabilitate' Rajk.

When Pollitt made his speech he was in possession of a confidential report from Sam Russell, our Moscow correspondent, which specifically confirmed Khrushchev's admissions that torture had been used in the Soviet Union; that Stalin had justified its use in a message to Party leaders in the 1930s, and that Stalin had specified the tortures to be used on the doctors who had been arrested shortly before his death. 'This information' I wrote to Pollitt, 'had you given it, would probably have explained Rajk's confession'.

Inner Party Democracy

As further revelations were made the leadership's head-in-sand attitude inevitably caused the situation to get out of hand. On 9 May 1956 our correspondent in Warsaw, Gordon Cruickshank, reported the sacking of the Polish Minister of Justice and the release of 30,000 prisoners from jail. On 16 May Pollitt resigned on the grounds of age (he was 65) and ill-health and was succeeded by Johnny Gollan. The Executive Committee (EC) issued a long statement which contained the apology and complete retraction on Yugoslavia that it should have made a year earlier and expressed 'shock' at the number of those *arrested* in the Soviet Union. Again it was too little and too late. It was not so much the arrests as the murders and tortures that had shocked the Party, but these were passed over with a mealy-mouthed reference to 'victims of deliberate provocations and fabricated evidence'. The statement promised that *future* policies would be more critically examined 'from whatever quarter they come', but promised no further probing into what had gone wrong in the Soviet Union or the 'people's democracies'.

The leadership's only real concession to the critics within the Party was to announce that a special commission had already been established to examine methods of discussion, election, criticism and self-criticism and the improvement of 'inner party democracy'. Yet even this concession was misleading, for no steps were taken to establish the commission for another two months. In July I accepted an invitation to join the commission, but by the time we met in September Poland was already on the verge of eruption, there were mass demonstrations in Hungary and sinister signs of the coming Franco-British attempt to seize the Suez Canal.

The issue of inner-party democracy had been brought to a head by Edward Thompson and John Saville, two of the best known members of the CP's Historians' Group. When the Political Committee refused to publish their criticisms of Soviet and British Party policies in the Party press after the Khrushchev speech they published them in a cyclostyled journal called *The Reasoner*, which achieved a circulation of 1,500 copies by its third issue. In an attempt to prevent its circulation among Party members the Political Committee forbade any discussion of it in the Party press and instructed Edward and John to stop publication. It also accused them of two of the worst crimes in the Party calendar: producing a political journal without the Party's consent and creating a 'faction' within the Party. By issuing this Canute-like edict on 13 September, the day after the commission on inner-party democracy had its first meeting, the Executive Committee made it crudely obvious that it had no intention of allowing the commission to challenge the way in which it operated democratic centralism. It laid down as principles the very practices that we were supposed to investigate – in particular the absurd principle that even, in a country with a free press, communists were only to have access to the non-Party press with the consent of the Party's bosses and had no right to publish 'a political journal dealing with the Party' without the Party's formal approval. When John and Edward refused to stop publication they were threatened with expulsion from the Party, and resigned.

Two letters I sent for publication in *World News and Views* (the CP's weekly) in September, presenting an argued case against the Executive Committee statement on *The Reasoner*, were rejected. John Gollan (who had been assistant editor of the *Worker* and a close friend) never spoke to me but informed me by letter that 'we [presumably the Political Committee] would decide in due course whether or not any discussion should be opened'. In short, the power to allow or to forbid discussion was to remain with the Party leaders. Johnny's reply and the treatment of *The Reasoner* underlined the point I had been making since February – that all the seeds of degeneration which had brought about the Stalin terror were to be seen in our own Party.

In its statement on *The Reasoner* the EC said that all members had the right to express their views within the Party under 'a democratic procedure which no other political organisation in Britain can equal'. I tested this claim by accepting an invitation from the secretary of the Uxbridge Communist Party to speak against the EC's policy on Hungary at a special 'aggregate' meeting of Uxbridge members, but when I got to the meeting Frank Foster, the West Middlesex District Secretary, ruled, on instructions from Gollan, that the branch must not hear me. 'It would set an entirely new precedent' he said 'if all comrades who disagreed with the Party's policy were entitled to fight against it in Party organisations other than their own'. The meeting accepted his ruling by a majority. As Frank Foster was more or less my brother-in-law, having married the sister of Anni's first husband, John Wheeler, this carried the split into the family – and we were not the only family to be split by the events of 1956. It took years for the scar to heal.

Seven Years' Solitary

It was the turmoil in the autumn of 1956, first in Poland (where the Soviet Union backed down from military intervention at the last minute) and then in Hungary, that brought the crisis in the Party to a head and pushed me out of the *Daily Worker*. I was delighted by the replacement of Gero, the hardline Stalinist Premier of Hungary, by Imre Nagy and by the popular uprising that freed the political prisoners. I was shocked by the first Soviet invasion, but what really brought the terror home to me was the release of Edith Bone, who had been jailed in Budapest, in solitary confinement without trial, for seven years. I did not know her and was unaware of the fact that she had gone to Hungary accredited by the *Worker* to enable her to contribute occasional pieces, nor did I know that she had 'disappeared' not long after her arrival in Budapest. Some members of the staff *had* known, including Allen Hutt whose comment when the news of her release came through on the tape was 'So old woman Bone's turned up again!' When I discovered the facts I was almost as appalled by Allen's cynical

comment as I was by the fact that we had allowed our correspondent to be jailed without lifting a finger to help her. I
drafted a statement to the Executive Committee of the Party,
which was due to have an emergency meeting to which Allen
Hutt and I had been invited. Sixteen of the *Daily Worker's* journalists – about half the total – signed it:

> The imprisonment of Edith Bone in solitary confinement without
> trial for seven years, without any public inquiry or protest from
> our Party even after the exposure of the Rajk trial had shown that
> such injustices were taking place, not only exposes the character of
> the regime but involves us in its crimes. It is now clear that what
> took place was a national uprising against an infamous police dic-
> tatorship which disgraced the good name of Communism. The
> danger that fascist elements will attempt to gain control in the
> present state of disorder cannot affect our judgment that the
> people of Hungary had had enough, and resorted to arms to obtain
> freedom. The Government and the Soviet Union were wrong to
> attempt to crush the uprising. No Government which has forfeited
> the support of its people has the right to crush the people with
> foreign arms.

The statement went on to ask for an immediate admission of
the mistakes the Party had made before and after the
Hungarian uprising, the opening of the *Daily Worker* to discussion, an end to the repeated bans on correspondence and the
publication of a series of articles by Peter Fryer and Charlie
Coutts, our men in Budapest, on the causes of the uprising.

The emergency meeting of the CP Executive Committee on 3
November gave the leadership its last chance to face the moral
and political issues posed by the events of 1956. They threw it
away with the same misplaced loyalty to the Soviet Union that
had characterised their earlier responses to events. I read the
Daily Worker journalists' statement, and drew the admission
from Pollitt and Campbell that they had made abortive
enquiries about Edith Bone but had neither protested not complained. The EC ignored our statement.

Soviet – and British – Culpability

I also read to the meeting a message I had received the previous
day from Gordon Cruickshank in Warsaw, conveying the confi-

dential views of the new Polish Party leadership in Warsaw on the Soviet Union's responsibility for the crisis:

> The Polish Party considers that the major inflammatory factor in the Hungarian situation was the intervention by Soviet troops. Such an intervention in Poland, where the stage was all set and where even the call was given, was stopped at the 11th hour by the Polish Party. Although the Party here is restrained and cautious in its public declaration, and is genuinely concerned to avoid a break with the Soviet Union, privately leading members express their point of view about the Soviet Party leadership with considerable feeling. They clearly have little confidence in that leadership. They contend that their viewpoint is based on 10 years of almost entirely bad experiences.
>
> To understand Hungarian events, they maintain that they have only to study Soviet methods in the Eastern democracies over the past years: their insistence that there is only one way to build socialism – their way. Their insistence on the transference of their pattern to all departments of life, large and small; their insistence on the organisation of the Stalinist type of security police and the use of Stalin type methods. The Polish and Hungarian events therefore must be seen not only as caused by economic adversity and misery but also as an eruption of accumulated resentment against what was felt to be the overbearing domination of the Soviet leadership – resentment which became hatred in some cases, and which has affected a number if not a majority of the best socialist and communist workers, making them a prey even to reactionary influences. Which is a tragedy indeed.

I can imagine Gorbachev and today's Solidarity leaders saying 'ditto' to that. But the extended EC decided that its first duty was to stand by the Soviet Union and to endorse the second invasion by the Soviet Army, which overthrew Imre Nagy on the day the EC met.

Nagy and his colleagues took refuge in the Yugoslav Embassy, but left after receiving assurances from Janos Kadar, the Premier installed by the Soviet Army, that no action would be taken against them. Treacherously, they were seized in the buses taking them to their homes, abducted to Romania, charged with treason, and tried secretly a year later. Those who expressed contrition were jailed. Those who would not, including Nagy, were shot. Nagy's real offence (as his articles that constituted much of the evidence against him make clear) was his desire, like Dubcek's in Czechoslovakia in 1968, to restore communist democracy and to give socialism a human face. There can be little doubt that if the foreign communist parties had spoken up in his defence his life would have been spared, but the majority of the EC failed to provide any rational explanations for the Hungarian disaster, and our Party's despicable silence on the judicial murder of Nagy betrayed their failure to understand the political and moral challenge they faced. Nagy was 'rehabilitated' in Hungary in 1989, by the oblique process of giving him an honourable reburial, but even then the Hungarian communists did not make a full admission of their crimes.

The Anglo-French invasion of Egypt on 30 October almost drove Hungary out of my mind, and signalled the all-clear for the second Soviet invasion of Hungary. Two days earlier I had interviewed some disgruntled reservists on Salisbury Plain who had been recalled for the Suez invasion but exhibited no signs of patriotic enthusiasm. I went back to Parliament to report the Suez debates and in my last parliamentary report, on 7 November, I recorded the Tories' discomfiture over Eden's announcement of the cease-fire. I also expressed concern that Hugh Gaitskell's priority as the Labour spokesman was to re-form the Tory-Labour consensus and the UK-US international front against the Soviet Union which Eden's invasion of Egypt had broken. In the last feature article I wrote for the *Daily Worker*, the next day, I endorsed Bulganin's warning that the world could be on the verge of a third world war and backed the Swiss Government's call for an emergency meeting of the 'Big Four' and India:

> The Soviet Union [I wrote] is not free from blame and has contributed to the present situation in Hungary, which is still a danger in the present international situation. Whatever we think of the Hungarian tragedy, there is one thing on which we can all agree: Hungary must not become the excuse for a third world war. To line up Tory and Labour, and all the countries of the Anglo-American alliance, to press for armed intervention in Hungary can only provoke a third world war. The more that intervention is pressed, the more will the Soviet Union be convinced that all the western powers are interested in is pulling Hungary into the anti-Soviet camp, and using it as a platform for further adventures.

The Last Straw

Suez proved to be no more than a temporary distraction as far as I was concerned. The last straw proved to be Johnny Campbell's decision to suppress Peter Fryer's despatches from Budapest and Gabriel's cartoon comparing Khrushchev's invasion of Hungary with Eden's invasion of Suez. I had no intention of quitting the *Daily Worker* when I went to the weekly editorial conference on Wednesday 14 November. I expected Johnny Campbell to make a rational reply to what were becoming my customary criticisms of Party policy and editorial decisions over Hungary, but Johnny had just come back from Moscow where talks with the Soviet Party had reinforced his habitual belief that it was the supreme duty of every communist to stand by the Soviet Union regardless of his personal misgivings. He charged me not so much with opposition as with an anti-Party conspiracy. He placed the most sinister interpretation on my actions in getting half the editorial staff to sign the statement I submitted to the EC and in having telephone conversations with Cruickshank in Warsaw. I suddenly realised that argument was pointless. I walked out of the meeting, collected my papers, left the office and never went back.

When I got home, still bubbling with anger and incredulity at the way in which Johnny Campbell had accused me of treachery, I told Anni that I had understood for the first time how Stalin's victims must have felt when their old comrades and friends suddenly turned into their accusers. Many former communists have had similar thoughts. What shocked me was the realisation that Johnny Campbell, whom I loved and admired despite increasing difficulties in our working relations, might well have been one of my accusers and executioners in a British 'people's democracy'.

These events precipitated an exodus from the editorial staff. Peter Fryer resigned while he was in Hungary and splashed his story in the *Daily Express* on his return. Although the hard journalist core – Allen Hutt, Walter Holmes, Peter Zinkin and George Sinfield in particular – stuck with the paper, it never recovered from the haemorrhage of much of its best and newest talent – Jimmy Friel, otherwise 'Gabriel' its cartoonist for over

"GENTLEMEN. THE BUDGET HAS BEEN BALANCED."

Neville Chamberlain balanced his 1936 budget at the expense of the poor; these clippings from a single week expose the reality of the 1930s – the effects of unemployment, the Means Test and near starvation.

Daily Worker, 21 April 1936

MUSTN'T WAKE THE BABIES!

A prophetic cartoon: published four months before the Nazi invasion of Austria in March 1938, and ten months before Chamberlain's betrayal at Munich handed Czechoslovakia to Hitler.

Daily Worker, 22 November 1937

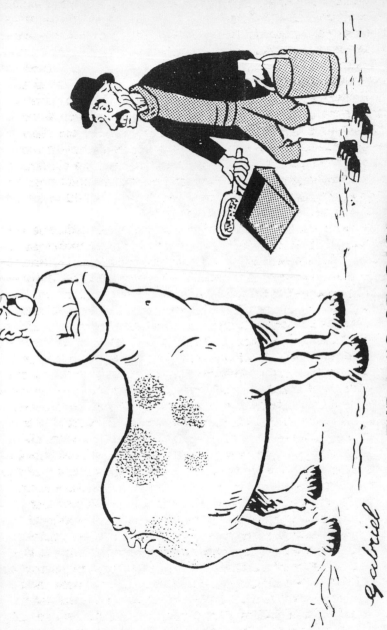

THE AXIS STABLEBOY

Hitler and Mussolini formed an alliance, the self-styled Rome–Berlin Axis, symbolised by Gabriel's Axis horse, emitting stench from both ends as it cavorted through the last months of a bitter decade.

Daily Worker, 16 December 1938

"Wouldn't it be better to abolish this little bomb now?"

Daily Worker, 24 June 1946

The USA's Baruch Plan, presented as a scheme for 'sharing' nuclear power, would have given a monopoly of atomic weapons and nuclear know-how to a world agency in which the USA and its clients could out-vote the USSR.

MR TSALDARIS, Greek Foreign Minister,
April 16th: "We must act in a Christian
spirit based on idealism and charity...."

CHRISTIAN ACTION, FIRST INSTALMENT

Greek republicans, democrats, socialists and communists paid with their lives for Churchill's and Bevin's policy of restoring the Greek monarchy and crushing the Greek resistance movement at the end of the war.　　　　*Daily Worker*, 8 May 1948

TAKING THE WEIGHT

The British worker bore the weight of and generated the profits for Labour's rearmament programme – so far beyond Britain's capability that Churchill cut it back when the Tories won the 1951 general election.

Daily Worker, 13 October 1950

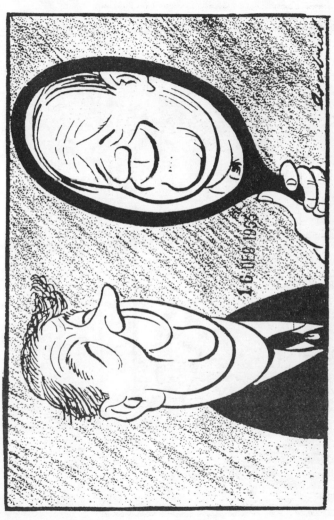

REFLECTIONS ON NEW LABOUR LEADER

'Butskellism' describes where Labour and Tory policies virtually coincide. The newly elected Labour leader Hugh Gaitskell sees the Tory Rab Butler as his mirror image.
Daily Worker, 16 December 1955

"YAH! YOU'RE AN AGGRESSOR!"

Johnny Campbell, editor of the *Daily Worker*, refused to publish Peter Fryer's despatches from Hungary and (on 5 November 1956) Gabriel's cartoon treating both the Soviet invasion of Hungary and the British–French invasion of Suez as aggression. Gabriel and half the journalists left the paper.

20 years, Phil Bolsover its star reporter, Sheila Lynd and Rose Grant, and two of our best young journalists: Leon Griffiths who became one of TV's most gifted dramatic writers and the creator of 'Minder', and Llew Gardner who made his name as a TV interviewer. I refused to make any statements to the press. All I did was to write a short letter to the *Daily Worker* (which it published) saying that I had resigned from the *Worker*

> because I consider that the uncritical endorsement of Soviet policy in the name of 'international solidarity' is helpful neither to the Soviet Union nor to ourselves ... It is necessary for those who think as I do to obtain freedom of action within the Communist Party to fight for a change in policy, and not to acquiesce in wrong policies or the suppression of truth, both of which can lead the Party to disaster.

The Achievement of the *Daily Worker*

I have never had any regrets about my years with the *Daily Worker*. The real tragedy was its failure to realise the dream that inspired Bill Rust from the moment when the ban was lifted in 1942 – the idea of a left-wing socialist newspaper with a mass circulation, democratically owned by its readers, that would break the monopoly of the millionaire press barons. Technically and journalistically we succeeded. We raised £250,000 (£7–8 million in 1989 money) to transform an old warehouse in Farringdon Road into a modern newspaper plant with a high-speed rotary press and room for expansion, from which the new, redesigned, larger paper was launched on 1 November 1948. We had an army of collectors and worker-correspondents in factories, mines, rail depots and offices. We had 33,000 shareholders in our co-operative, The People's Press Printing Society, including many hundreds of trade unions and co-operatives. Each shareholder had one vote and was limited to 200 shares. Many Labour Party branches would have sub-scribed had the Labour Party not proscribed The People's Press Printing Society. Five thousand members used to attend the annual general meetings held at several centres from London to Glasgow.

We filled the Albert Hall for our annual birthday rally, until we were banned from using it. When Bill Rust died of a heart attack in 1949 at the age of 45, only four months after the new paper had been launched, 5,000 people marched behind his coffin to Golders Green crematorium. We won the newspaper design prize twice, and although the tone of the paper became more sectarian and shrill as the Cold War intensified, the *Daily Worker* was a good newspaper with a breadth and depth of news and features in a confined space that often put its richer and larger contemporaries to shame. The print unions held us to ransom but, the printers apart, we were an egalitarian collective of unselfish idealists, all paid the same basic rate, working for a cause, not for money. Our shareholders were socialists too: the one thing they did *not* want was a dividend or interest on their shares. Whenever I gave shareholders an assurance at an annual meeting that the Society would never pay a dividend there was thunderous applause.

In reality, however, the Party leaders did not want the readers to control the paper, which was their main tool for propaganda and for leading and mobilising the Party. When Bill Rust first proposed to transfer the ownership of the *Daily Worker* to a co-operative Harry Pollitt demanded and got an assurance that it would remain the organ of the Communist Party. Bill could not conceive, any more than I could at the time, that the CP might split one day and that a majority of the shareholders might deprive the Party of control, but democracy proved to be the Party's undoing in 1986: a rebel group led by the editor of the *Morning Star* (as the *Daily Worker* had become) won a majority at the annual meeting of the People's Press Printing Society.

It was already obvious when Bill Rust died in 1949 that the *Daily Worker* would not become a mass circulation paper. Arthur Christiansen, the editor of Lord Beaverbrook's *Daily Express*, paid tribute to Bill as 'a successful editor and a two-fisted writer in his own cause', but it was not enough to have a great editor, a good staff, and an enthusiastic corps of supporters. Not only was the *Worker* too political for most tastes, but our commitment to Soviet policies and the Soviet system tied us politically and morally to Stalinism at the height of the Cold War. Johnny Campbell put his finger unwittingly on our split political personalities at Bill's funeral, when he said that 'Bill knew that communism was freedom, not forced labour or a vast soulless bureaucracy'. We did indeed see ourselves as democrats, but others had good reason to identify us with 'forced labour and soulless bureaucracy'. By refusing to repudiate Stalinism the *Daily Worker* threw away whatever chance it had of restoring its credibility.

16

Expelled and 'Rehabilitated'

It did not take me very long to realise that my departure from the *Daily Worker*, which seemed like a second amputation at the time, was a blessing in disguise. It cut me off for a long time from half the people who had been my friends and associates for the past 13 years, but I did not suffer from the traumas of a political amputation, for three reasons. One was that I remained a member of the commission on inner-Party democracy, which gave me new insights into the difficulties of introducing what would now be called *glasnost* or *perestroika* into the communist system. This became a full-time preoccupation for the next few weeks and completed the process of disillusionment. Another was that I was plunged into the politics of what came to be called the New Left, and the third was my good luck in getting a fascinating new job with *The Architects' Journal*, which began to open up a much wider world than the one I had left, and got me interested in resource conservation.

I had been forced out of the political habitat that had both nurtured and confined me for some 20 years, but it had taken nearly 18 months of agonising rethinking to sever the cord that had bound me to the *Daily Worker* for so long, or to make a cool appraisal of the Communist Party's real weight in British politics. It never occurred to me to become a professional anti-communist. Nor had I any thought initially of helping to form a New Left movement. I was still a Party member and my priority in November 1956 was to let the fresh air of free discussion and access to information into the CP, and to scrap the rigid centralisation and control of information and debate misnamed 'democratic centralism' that seemed to me to hold the key to the degeneration of the Soviet Union and of the CP itself.

We had been living in a self-created Party ghetto. Anni's job at the London County Council (LCC) had widened my circle of friends, but even so most of the architects and planners we knew were Party members or sympathisers and the heated arguments of recent months had taken place within our closed circle. I was so accustomed to working and thinking within the Party framework that I still cherished the illusion that the battle for democracy within the Party could be won through the commission on inner-Party democracy. It proved to be a classic example of the techniques by which the Party frustrated inner-Party democracy.

At its first meeting the five rank-and-file members objected to the blatant packing of the commission. Ten of its 15 members were full-time salaried Party officials, of whom five were members of the executive committee. There was only one industrial worker and two teachers. Three members were known critics of the Party's line on recent events – myself, Christopher Hill and Peter Cadogan, a maverick teacher from Cambridge who later became one of the Committee of 100 which led the non-violent protests against atomic weapons. The Party officials included Emile Burns and James Klugmann, the Party's in-house 'experts' on Marxism who between them controlled its propaganda, education and periodicals, and Betty Reid from the central organisation department. Betty, who has since mellowed, was a hardliner if ever there was one, but equipped with a keen brain as well as a strong will. She had helped to run The Left Book Club for Victor Gollancz in the 1930s with Sheila Lynd and John Lewis, the Marxist philosopher she married. She was adept at producing arguments to provide an intellectual cover for the stupidity, inflexibility and dogmatism of our chairman, Johnny Mahon, the leader of the Party in London, and the type of Party 'apparatchik' who is now obstructing Gorbachev's reforms in the Soviet Union.

Comedy Scripts

Johnny Mahon saw his job as securing the defeat of the 'revisionists', but it was more difficult for Emile and James, the two intellectuals whose knowledge of the weakness of their position made them unyielding in argument. I had known Emile since my student days, but I had seen little of James until the commission brought us face to face for three months. I could not help liking him, for he was the most charming man one could meet, kind, considerate and patient. As a contemporary of Guy Burgess and Anthony Blunt at Cambridge he has, of course, been listed as a Soviet spy – most unconvincingly for he never concealed his political views. He played a part in British Intelligence in Cairo during the war in securing British support for Tito and the Yugoslav partisans. When he returned to civil life he sacrificed what might well have been a brilliant academic career to work for the Party. He stood both for all that was best in the Party – unselfishness, disregard for making money, lack of personal ambition, devotion to the cause and a keen intelligence – and for one of its most fatal defects: carrying loyalty to the point where it silenced his conscience and blunted his good sense. He accepted an instruction (against his better judgment, as I later discovered) to write the notorious book *From Trotsky to Tito* showing that both Tito and Trotsky were fascists.

In the early meetings of the commission all five rank-and-filers supported my proposal that the commission should hear witnesses and call for documents on specific cases, such as the British Party's response to the expulsion of Yugoslavia from the Cominform, the control of the Party press since the Twentieth Congress, the 'recommended list' system of elections at Party congresses and the working of inner-Party democracy in the Soviet Union and Eastern Europe. All ten Party officials opposed it because the last thing the Party leadership wanted was an investigation of the way in which the Party leaders manipulated information and controlled debate either in Britain or in the Soviet bloc. Instead of investigating what actually happened the commission held a series of academic debates on papers drafted by its members which could have provided some useful scripts for comedies by Dario Fo. When Christopher Hill tried to draft a paper on 'Party discussion' jointly with James Klugmann he could only amend James's draft by inserting negatives into James's sentences.

Johnny Mahon told us times without number that discussion was intended to lead to action, but he refused to see that discussion had many other purposes, such as changing minds, getting at the facts, deepening understanding, changing policies or even changing the leadership. He insisted, as did all the

Party officials, that once 'the line' had been decided by the leadership discussion must stop – although in many cases 'the line' was decided by the Political Bureau or the Central Committee without any discussion in the Party. Klugmann conceded that after 'the line' had been decided Party members might be allowed to go on discussing 'problems of art and literature', but to imply, as this did, that once the leadership had decided to back the Soviet intervention in Hungary the Party should have discussed Hungarian art and literature struck me as black comedy. Emile, James and Betty refused to understand Christopher's most fundamental argument, that the really difficult problem in the communist movement was not how to rewrite the Party rules but how to recreate the democratic spirit and method of working that it had lost.

The 'Traitor'

The outcome of the commission's work was a foregone conclusion, but I thought that we were going to win the backing of the two uncommitted rank-and-filers until Peter Cadogan wrote a letter to the *News Chronicle* criticising the Soviet invasion of Hungary. There was nothing wrong with the letter, but the Party leadership made it the excuse to suspend Peter's membership. At the next meeting Christopher and I defended Peter's right to express his opinions and objected to his suspension, but Betty Reid gave a fine exhibition of the leadership's emotional need for loyalty at all costs by refusing to sit down with him because he was 'a traitor'. As I was out of work and Christopher was far too busy I wrote a minority report in collaboration with Christopher which took me a couple of weeks. Peter's suspension was lifted in time for him to sign the minority report, but his letter proved to be a tactical blunder, for once the cries of 'loyalty' and 'traitor' had been raised the other two rank-and-filers could not be persuaded to make common cause with us. They signed the majority report, albeit with reservations so fundamental as virtually to endorse the minority report. But it was the signatures not the small print that mattered to the Party leadership.

The majority report endorsed without reservation the Stalinist concept of the monolithic party speaking with a single voice, conceding only that too much emphasis had been laid on centralism and not enough on democracy. We extracted two practical concessions. One was the publication of the minority report in full. The other was a recommendation to publish 'a theoretical journal', *Marxism Today*, now the vehicle of reformism, which Christopher and I can legitimately claim to have brought into existence.

In writing the minority report I had in mind Lenin's draft programme of 1902 for the Russian Social Democratic Party, which called for 'inviolability of persons and homes, unrestricted liberty of conscience, freedom of speech, of the press, of meetings, of strikes and combinations, self-determination for all nationalities, the right of every citizen to prosecute any official'. By the time the commission's two reports were published in January 1957, I had lost my stomach for continuing the fight inside the CP. I was in a minority in my own Party branch, which would not send me as its delegate to the Party Congress. I had also contributed an article to the first issue of *The New Reasoner* which had been launched by Edward Thompson and John Saville in the spring of 1957 as 'a quarterly journal of socialist humanism', and joined its editorial board. In this article I pleaded

for the restoration of real Marxism, the end of all the myths and shibboleths, an end to doctored history and the presentation of half-truths as the whole, a victory for honesty and frankness in the Communist Party and throughout the socialist movement.

On the whole the Party's working-class membership, drawn mainly from the skilled trade unions, stood by the Party during the crisis, but its middle-class and intellectual members deserted it in thousands. The result was that when the Party Congress met in the spring of 1957 it endorsed the commission's report by an overwhelming majority, which included a young miner by the name of Arthur Scargill. Christopher Hill made a spirited defence of the minority report but Johnny Mahon attacked it in language that would not have seemed out of place at a Stalinist trial of 'wreckers' or an 'anti-Party group': 'The minority report gives some lip service to democratic centralism, and then assembles a number of proposals into a sort of platform from which to wreck democratic centralism.' The *Daily Worker* did not even report Christopher's speech and he resigned from the Party immediately afterwards. I took Bernard Shaw's advice ('never resign') but was duly expelled two months later for refusing to resign from the editorial board of *The New Reasoner*, which had been placed on the Party's index of forbidden publications. The chairman of the panel that heard my case at a perfunctory but perfectly friendly hearing was Johnny Mahon. Had we been in a 'people's democracy' I think he would have shaken my hand before firmly despatching me to the gallows.

Postscript

Early in 1989, as I was curious to know how far the Communist Party of Great Britain (as it is once more called) had gone in *perestroika*, I asked its Executive Committee to rescind my expulsion and to 'rehabilitate' me. The response was friendly but it seemed to me to be characteristic of the confusion in which Communist Parties now find themselves that the answer was both 'no' and 'yes'. The EC refused to rescind the expulsion on the ground that I had been expelled not for my views but for advocating them in a manner that was inconsistent with the Party's rules at the time. Gordon Maclennan, the Party Secretary, explained that the Party had not rescinded a conference decision made a few years earlier to reaffirm the place of democratic centralism in its constitution, and I had seen how the Party had invoked the principles of democratic centralism to expel its opponents in the split with the Stalinists who took control of the *Morning Star*. However, the EC said 'yes' to 'what you describe as your rehabilitation', because 'the Party made mistakes', and 'some of the criticisms you made were justified'. In short, I was right to become an editor of *The New Reasoner* in 1956–7 and the Party was right to expel me for doing so. I feel no inclination to rejoin the Party, despite the fact that I am once more on good terms with several of its members.

Part 3
After The Party

17

'Motropolis'

Expulsion from the Party, my enthusiastic involvement with *The New Reasoner* and my new job with the *Architects' Journal* combined to expand the circle of our friends and to expose us to new and stimulating ideas. And this happened in the aftermath of Suez and Hungary, when the explosion of the British H-bomb tore the Left in the Labour Party apart and gave birth to the Campaign for Nuclear Disarmament (CND), one of the greatest and most inspiring mass movements ever seen in Britain. 'Bevanism', the Left movement in the Labour Party, was destroyed by Aneurin Bevan himself. His response as shadow Foreign Secretary to the British H-bomb at the 1957 Labour Party Conference was to ridicule the unilateralist policy of the Left as 'an emotional spasm' and to declare that renunciation of the H-bomb would send a future Labour Foreign Secretary 'naked into the conference chamber'. Bevan's apostasy and Labour's confusion led to Labour's third successive electoral defeat in 1959. The time was ripe for an analysis of the failures of both the Communist and the Labour Parties, and for new initiatives to find a way forward at a time of apparently permanent Tory domination.

The New Reasoner was a major force in creating the New Left. Its editors, Edward Thompson and John Saville, were political workaholics. Although both were teachers and pioneering historians deeply involved in writing and research they seemed to find unlimited time and energy to lead the 1956 revolt of the communist democrats. Edward even typed the copy for the original *Reasoner*, 40,000 words, in four days. *The New Reasoner* ran to well over 100 pages every quarter, and was produced without any full-time staff or professional help by a dedicated band of unpaid volunteers in Yorkshire around Edward and Dorothy Thompson and John Saville.

I was involved in planning future issues but only to a small extent in writing them. The board usually met at Tanza Road. Edward Thompson, with his extraordinary gift for polemical writing, was the most inspiring figure in *The New Reasoner*, which drew heavily on the immense resources of the old CP Historians' Group and CP economists – Eric Hobsbawm, Michael Barratt-Browne, Peter Worsley, Ralph Milliband, Kenneth Alexander, John Rex, John Hughes and Ronald Meek. I contributed regularly, but my pieces reflected my continuing preoccupation in 1957–60 with the changes in the Soviet Union, which had failed to carry through the Khrushchev reformation, and China which seemed to hold out far more hope for a new kind of communism. I wrote a detailed exposure of the secret 'trial' and judicial murder of Imre Nagy and Pal Maleter.

In ten issues our lack of interest in women's interests (let alone feminism) and environmental or ecological issues stands out a mile. We took too little interest in the Third World. But with those exceptions I am still agreeably impressed by the breadth and the width of the fields we were able to cover; a short story by Doris Lessing (who was a member of the board) on 'The Day that Stalin died'; two poems by Berthold Brecht; a piece by Arthur Miller on the freedom of the writer; a review of Boris Pasternak's *Dr Zhivago* by Iris Murdoch; a report on Kenya by Tom Mboya the young Kenyan socialist who was President of the People's Convention Party and was later assassinated; Paul Hogarth's account of 'A Visit to Strydom's South Africa' poignantly illustrated by his drawings of the victims of apartheid; an art supplement on Diego Rivera, whose murals in Mexico City proved to be a political as well as an artistic inspiration when Anni and I saw them some years later; articles on the arts by John Berger, and contributions on French politics from Claude Bourdet the editor of *La Nouvelle Observateur*.

The *New Left Review*

At the same time as the CP had given birth to its illegitimate child *The New Reasoner*, a group of four Marxist students at Oxford had responded to the events of 1956 by producing the *Universities and Left Review (ULR)*, which they saw not so much as the voice of a militant student movement as an attempt to break down the mood of political apathy which gripped their generation of students at a time of world crisis. The *Universities and Left Review* people were a generation younger than us and not hung up by long cohabitation with Stalinism as we were, although one of the four, Raphael Samuel, came from a communist family. The *ULR* was even more academic than *The New Reasoner* and its range was, if anything, wider both in politics and the arts. By 1959 each journal was developing an embryonic social and political movement. The *ULR* had ten Left Clubs. In Fife Lawrence Daly (a member of the *Reasoner* Board and later Secretary of the National Union of Mineworkers) had established the Fife Socialist League and won a seat as an independent communist on Fife County Council. The *ULR* established a club in Soho that blossomed into the Left Book Centre, a *ULR* coffee house and the Partisan Café, and attracted fairly large audiences to meetings addressed by such speakers as Isaac Deutscher, the author of the classic biographies, *Trotsky* and *Stalin*, Richard Hoggart, John Berger and Peter Shore, who was then regarded as a left-winger in the Labour Party.

Despite their different origins the political overlap between the two journals, and the problems of producing two journals by volunteers on shoestrings, forced them together. By the middle of 1959 neither could carry on alone, and the two editorial boards met at Tanza Road to thrash out the details of a merger. There were no serious political differences, and in Stuart Hall the *ULR* provided a first-class editor. The *New Left Review (NLR)* was launched in November 1959 at a meeting in St Pancras Town Hall, with a formidably intellectual platform including Edward Thompson, Raymond Williams, Stuart Hall, Iris Murdoch and the philosopher Freddie Ayer. The first issue focused on the decline of Labour and the sickness of Labourism.

By 1961 the *NLR* was teetering on the brink of a fatal crisis. Much of the steam had gone out of the people who had launched the two magazines six years before. The *NLR* was plagued by financial problems and the inevitable inefficiency of a voluntary outfit. A gap was opening up between Edward Thompson and the younger academics of *NLR*. Stuart Hall had to give up the editorial chair at the end of 1961, bi-monthly publication faltered and the stop-gap editorial team that was set

up made an unholy financial mess of the first issue they produced because Raphael insisted 'for editorial reasons' on
printing more pages than there was either money or paper for.
Attendance at board meetings declined, so that the *NLR* ceased
to be a genuine collective of like-minded people working
together. I played an active part, for a time as vice-chair, but
my enthusiasm was waning and I only contributed one piece to
the *NLR*. In April 1962 Edward protested, characteristically in a
vehement circular, that members had tendered fatuous excuses
for absence from board meetings such as their presence in
Chicago, Moscow, the Orkneys and Stockholm (the last being
me). He told us that for the next meeting the academics had to
cancel their meetings, while Ken Alexander and Raymond
Williams 'are going to be brought in chains'!

In fact, the crisis was already over. An unexpected donation
had enabled us to pay the most pressing debts. At an emergency meeting with the editorial team in January 1962 Edward
and I agreed as chair and vice-chair that the *NLR* could not be
produced as a bi-monthly by a spare-time team, and appointed
Perry Anderson as a provisional editor. The decision was confirmed by the editorial board at its next meeting.

There were serious differences between Edward and his
friends (among whom I numbered myself) and Perry and the
new editorial board from which all the old *NLR* people withdrew, or were excluded in 1963. Before resigning Edward
penned a blistering 10,000-word critique of the theoretical and
political faults of the 'new guard', written more in sorrow than
in anger. Socialist humanism, he suggested, should be deeply
suspicious of the rhetoric in some *NLR* articles about a revolutionary struggle in which the 'proletarian Third World' would
overthrow the 'West' by violence. He saw no reason why such a
victory should produce a socialist solution, and warned perci-
piently that 'a really nasty indigenous bourgeoisie or military
elite' might take power in the newly liberated African or Asian
countries. Edward viewed the scenario of a violent struggle
between the Third World and the West (for which he placed
much of the blame on Sartre) as both horrifying and unrealistic,
and argued from history that a common interest involved the
working class of the West and the impoverished peoples of the
Third World in a common struggle against common oppressors.
He viewed the scenario of violence with horror and preferred to

believe that British socialism, 'insular, moralistic, empirical, affluent and compromised' as it might be, might still provide the key that would open the way to a world socialist society.

Perry remained as editor for the best part of 20 years, during which he put the *NLR* on its feet as a journal and publishing house with a world-wide circulation. He had the money to keep the *NLR* afloat, but his academic approach to Marxism had little in common with Edward's polemical and crusading spirit. At times I found the *NLR* unreadable, even with a dictionary. However, in recent years under Robin Blackburn's editorship the *NLR* has got rid of most of its incomprehensible philosophical jargon, and has become far more relevant to contemporary Marxism. It gave its readers the first real insight into the relationship between socialism and the Green Party in Western Germany.

The Architects' Journal

If the *New Left Review* marked the end of one stage in my development my new job at *The Architects' Journal (AJ)* marked the beginning of another, which led me, almost by accident, to take the first step towards an ecological approach to politics. As my departure from the *Worker* was unpremeditated I hadn't a clue about the kind of job I wanted, or how to find it. As I had not denounced communism my record ruled out most jobs in journalism, even on liberal papers such as the *Manchester Guardian* and the *News Chronicle*. I applied for some public relations jobs, but found no PR firm whose wares I wanted to push and no PR firm took to me. Anni and I explained my problem to Leo de Syllas, one of several architect friends who had just left the Party. He phoned Colin Boyne, the editor of the *AJ*, and although Colin knew nothing about me, apart from Leo's paeans of praise for my journalistic talents, he was so annoyed by the incompetence of two of his editorial assistants that he immediately created an ill-defined editorial job for me. Some weeks later he brought in Sheila Lynd.

Colin was, in theory, subordinate to Jim (now Sir James) Richards, a leftist who was the architectural critic of *The Times* and responsible as 'house editor' for overseeing the entire editorial output of the Architectural Press. Jim had to refer my appointment to the real editorial boss, Hubert de Cronin Hastings ('H de C'), an eccentric and autocratic genius who was co-proprietor of the Architectural Press and 'editorial director' of the *AJ* and the monthly *Architectural Review (AR)*. He was highly amused by the rumour, conveyed to Colin by Ian Leslie, the 'high Tory' editor of the rival magazine *The Builder*, that communists controlled the Architectural Press, and warmed to Colin's proposal that the *AJ* should take on two real (if ex-) communists. It might have been nearer the truth to have said that the Architectural Press was controlled by Roman Catholics – H de C's co-proprietor Maurice Regan and several others were Roman Catholics. So H de C clinched the decision by remarking that 'we have so many Catholics we may as well have some communists'.

I found it hard to see what contribution I could make to an architectural magazine, and H de C did nothing to enlighten me at a brief interview. I was ushered into a large room, crowded with bric-a-brac but shrouded in semi-darkness because the blinds were drawn, in which I could dimly see a stout man wearing such dark spectacles that he can only have seen me in outline. This was odd, for as he'd already agreed to take me on I could see no point in the interview except to satisfy his curiosity to see a communist in the flesh. I only saw him three times more, for H de C was a hermit who erected an almost impenetrable wall between himself and his staff and contributors. The prosperity of the firm allowed him to combine a lavish lifestyle with freedom to indulge his artistic and architectural fancies.

The Architectural Review was H de C's flagship, a superbly designed, glossy magazine of architectural fashion and aesthetics, published almost regardless of expense, which achieved world leadership in its field. A yearly handbook called *Specification* barely paid its way. The book department kept many contributors happy by publishing beautiful, trend-setting but not very profitable books. All this was paid for out of the profits of the *AJ*, the bread-and-butter weekly magazine that no architect could do without – well-informed, newsy, gossipy, entertaining but packed with pictures, plans, sections, working details and technical data about new buildings, materials and techniques.

Modern architecture had been one of H de C's driving passions in the 1930s, but his avant-garde enthusiasm was waning by 1957 and his tastes were far too eclectic for him to make the mistake of nailing the Architectural Press flag irrevocably to any one architectural mast. The *AR* published scholarly and well-illustrated articles on Georgian and Regency architecture and landscape. It pioneered a taste for Victoriana but it also supported the building conservation movement created by William Morris, whose 'anti-scrape' campaign saved many medieval buildings from 'restoration' in Victorian Gothic. The *AR* had such a wide range that it commissioned my first article on national parks in 1972. The Architectural Press occupied three houses in Queen Anne's Gate, a fine Queen Anne terrace just off Birdcage Walk and St James's Park. The last thing H de C wanted for a home or an office was a rectangular glass box, and the last thing that H de C and his editors wanted was conformity or dogmatism; what they wanted was originality, style and skill, and they created one of the happiest and most stimulating places to work – in spite of the fact that Regan used its attractions to secure the talent they wanted at very low rates of pay.

Engaged to 'The Bride of Denmark'

It would be hard to imagine anything more different from the austerity of William Rust House and its down-at-heel surroundings than the elegance of Queen Anne's Gate. But the Architectural Press and the *Daily Worker* had several things in common. Both were unorthodox by conventional standards. Both attracted talented people who were more interested in the cause for which they were working than in the money they were paid. Both were schools of journalism, for young people who were drawn to the Architectural Press by their interest in art or architecture picked up the journalist's trade. Hugh Casson, a kindly wit and a backer of Architects for Peace, who brought modern architecture to life in the 1951 Festival of Britain, contributed to the *AJ's* mischievous gossip column by 'Astragal'. John Betjeman, who began his ascent to the Poet Laureateship on the *AR*, loved working there although he detested modern architecture. Osbert Lancaster, whom I used to observe working on his *Daily Express* cartoons during wartime press briefings at the Foreign Office, was for a time one of the editors of the *AR*. In the *AR* Ian Nairn made blistering attacks on 'Subtopia', the cancerous growth of ill-designed buildings and artefacts creeping over the countryside.

This appealed to H de C who encouraged alternative ideas on design and landscape. The word 'townscape' originated in the *AR*, where two brilliant artists, Gordon Cullen and Kenneth Browne, illustrated their ideas for uplifting urban areas and breathed life into the ideas suggested by Nairn and others. Reyner (otherwise Peter) Banham was sharpening his outstanding skills as a journalist and author at the *AR* and establishing his reputation as the apostle of 'the new brutalism'. His best-seller *Los Angeles* reflected his belief that the LA freeways had liberated people and created an 'ecology' in which architecture could flourish – in contrast to my view that LA was built on the profits of the war industries, was socially and racially divisive and epitomised capitalism's tendency to squander space and natural resources. Sheila Lynd quickly found a niche for herself on the *AJ*, running the 'publication' of buildings – a highly skilled job calling for the highest quality of photography, technical drawing, costings and a critical text – and later became news editor. She charmed innumerable architects into giving the *AJ* the chance of publishing their work or their ideas, and in Colin Boyne's words, not only did she bring 'compassion' into her work but she also 'made all us men feel ashamed of our laziness' so gladly did she do all the boring chores. Tragically she died of cancer in 1975 after years of deteriorating health.

In contrast to the *Daily Worker* the pace at the Architectural Press was relaxed. All work stopped for half an hour or so while the staff gathered in the basement for the morning coffee break, which enabled me to get to know a group of friendly and stimulating people in a surrealist atmosphere. For the basement was H de C's fantasy. Using mirrors, bar fittings, tables, seats, a huge but friendly-looking stuffed lion, light fittings and bric-a-brac of every kind scoured from the Blitzed sites of the East End, he had turned the basement of 9–13 Queen Anne's Gate into a traditional pub (and a museum of Victoriana and Edwardiana) which he christened 'The Bride of Denmark'. As it had no licence all the drinks had to be free, but it cost the Architectural Press far less to entertain contributors and advertisers in 'The Bride' than to take them out to expense-account lunches. Anybody who aspired to be anybody in the architectural world was to be seen there sooner or later, including government ministers and their Opposition 'shadows', and when I became assistant editor in 1958 I and my guests had the run of the bar. Joining the *AJ* was the beginning of a three-year engagement with 'The Bride of Denmark'.

Architecture as a Social Art

One might imagine from this description that the appeal of the Architectural Press was directed almost exclusively at a readership of self-indulgent aesthetes, but that would be to forget the *AJ*. In Colin Boyne it had a young editor, educated as an architect in the spirit of the modern architectural movement, who combined a social conscience with a talent for enlisting collaborators and a fierce intolerance of incompetence in journalism or architecture. Colin was a good friend and a great editor who tried to save the architectural profession from the calamities that it brought on its own head. He tells me that I was welcome to him 'because for the first time we had professional standards of journalism in the paper'.

I had no pretensions to be an architectural critic, and I had nothing to do with the technical side for I was an architectural ignoramus, despite an architect wife and many architect friends. It has even been alleged in what I claim to be an apocryphal story that when the name of Mies van der Rohe, the supreme architect of steel, glass and concrete, came up at one of my first editorial meetings on the *AJ* I queried 'Miss van der Who?' However, I could edit the writings of architects, some of whom I found to be barely literate and few of whom had been taught to write the good, simple English that would have helped them to clarify their ideas and to present them to clients, contractors or users. Nobody else on the staff had shorthand and there were plenty of events for me to cover as a reporter. As I got to know more about architecture and architects I began to feel the political pulse of the profession and the industry. After six months I was given the title of chief assistant editor. But I got far more out of the *AJ* than I put in. What the *AJ* really gave me was a crash course in architecture, architectural politics and architectural journalism and a visual education.

The *AJ* focused on designing and building for human needs, on value for money and technical and managerial know-how and, in the spirit of the modern movement, on the transition of building from a craft to an industrialised process. 'Modern architecture' was already degenerating into a style, stripped of its social content and exploited by developers and bureaucrats to maximise profits or the utilisation of space. 'The Bride of Denmark' was the centre of a lobby nicknamed 'the chain gang', centred in the public service, which promoted the alternative trend of architecture as a social art through a web of contacts and informants. The chain gang was led, almost surreptitiously, by Stirratt Johnson-Marshall who had been the Chief Architect to the Ministry of Education and the driving force behind the post-war school-building programme. His colleagues included Robert Matthew, Chief Architect to the London County Council, Donald Gibson, Coventry City Architect, and Robert Gardner-Medwin, Chief Architect to the Scottish Office. The chain gang helped to make the *AJ* the best place in London for me as an architectural novitiate to get 'into the know', and it was the success of members of the chain gang and their sympathisers in the 1959 RIBA Council elections that opened the way for me to take a job with the RIBA early in 1960.

The Problem of the Car

The scope on the *AJ* for a journalist who had neither architectural nor any other technical or artistic qualification was obviously limited. I had to develop some expertise of my own, but of what kind? I can't remember any particular incident that led me to take up the impact of motor traffic on the city, and thereby eventually to enter the field of resource conservation, but what Colin Buchanan was to call the conflict between traffic and 'environment' was already becoming a political issue. Anni's experience at the London County Council of the conflicts between planners and highway or traffic engineers suggested to me that there was an opening for a journalist who would challenge the mindless clamour from the road construction lobby for a huge urban motorway-building programme and point the way to an integrated or planned solution. It seemed to me that, in the process of trying to solve the problem of traffic congestion by providing more road space, the blinkered engineering approach would create even worse problems and inflict untold damage on our cities and their inhabitants in the process. In 1958 700,000 new vehicles were poured into a road system that was virtually unchanged since 1939, and the government saw votes in road construction. The M1 between London and Birmingham was rushed through (by skimping its construction) in time for its opening before the 1959 general election.

I was astonished to find, when I familiarised myself with the British and American literature on the subject, that hardly any research had been done into the consequences of building a new highway system to cater for the predicted vast increases in traffic, and above all of private cars. No attention was being paid to the profound effects such a programme would have on the vitality of railways and public transport, on the location of employment and homes, and on the structure, growth and life of towns and cities. Early in 1959 I outlined my ideas for a special issue of the *AJ* to be called 'Motropolis' to Colin Boyne, and once I had got his backing and that of H de C I set about collecting material, consulting experts and clarifying my ideas. When published in October it proved to be one of the turning points of my life, for within a couple of years it had led both Anni and me to change our jobs and to strike out professionally in new directions.

'Motropolis' is still a lively and readable indictment of the 'fantastic degree of waste and inefficiency' with which society was (and still is) using the motor vehicle. I did not discuss lead poisoning, acid rain, the ozone layer or the 'greenhouse effect' because little or nothing was known about them at the time. But I quoted from Harrison Salisbury who had written in the *New York Times* about 'Gasopolis, the rubber-wheeled living region of the future ... nestled under its blanket of smog, girdled by bands of freeways, its core eviscerated by concrete strips and asphalt fields'. The waste that worried me was not the squandering of finite oil resources but the deaths (7,000 a year), the injuries, the waste of money and the devastating impact on daily life of danger, din, fumes, congestion and pointless road building. My approach was essentially techno-logical rather than humanistic or ecological. I was looking for a top-down professional solution rather than a bottom-up demo-cratic one. I claimed to offer no cut-and-dried remedies, but in fact I came out strongly for massive investment both in public transport and in the large-scale reconstruction of city centres, except where redevelopment was excluded by the quality of the existing environment or by cost. Above all I attacked the naive belief that building more roads could solve these problems. Thirty years later, as I was writing these lines, I heard on the radio of a 35-mile hold up on the M25, and of Mrs Thatcher's government's plans for another vast road-building programme. The penny has still to drop.

Colin Buchanan

'Motropolis' marked the beginning of our friendship with Colin Buchanan, who was then a planning inspector in the Ministry of Housing and Local Government. I got in touch with him because he had recently written a controversial book on the motor car called *Mixed Blessing*, and 'Motropolis' was substantially influenced by his ideas. It is very unusual for civil servants to publish controversial books, but Colin proved to be a very unusual person. His unique triple qualification as a civil engineer, planner and architect enabled him to see the social, spatial and aesthetic implications of construction projects that are invisible to those engineers whose values can only be expressed in numbers. He dressed at that time as a civil servant, complete with bowler hat, black overcoat, umbrella and briefcase. His craggy face made him look as inscrutable as a judge, and his job as a planning inspector made him behave like one. But behind this formal, even forbidding exterior there lurked a wit, a skilled manual craftsman and a man who combined a passionate love of the countryside with a mastery of his profession as a planner. Whereas the majority of the members of the Royal Commission on London's Third Airport were content to survey the key sites from a helicopter and to reach their conclusions on the basis of cost–benefit analyses, Colin made up his mind when writing his minority report by getting to know the sites on foot.

Colin has no time for politics, but we found common ground in our approach to planning as the key discipline for reconciling competing demands on land. He has a ruthlessly logical mind and an unrivalled talent for the lucid exposition of complex issues. He also has a subtle sense of humour, his jokes, as often as not, being told against himself. When he was holding the inquiry (around this time) into the proposal to build a nuclear reactor at Trawsfynydd, in the heart of the Snowdonia National Park, evidence was given in support of the project by Professor Allen, a professor of landscape architecture retained by the National Park Committee. The Professor showered such lyrical praise on the architectural trimmings provided by Basil Spence, and on the magnificence of the immense structure in the rugged landscape, that Colin summed up his evidence by asking him: 'am I to understand that in your considered opinion no national park is really complete *without* a nuclear power station?' Colin advised against the project (how right he was!) but the Minister overruled him.

Colin's gritty integrity made him unpopular with the senior administrators in the Ministry of Housing and Local Government, whose Permanent Secretary, Sheepshank by name, punished him for objecting to the promotion of unqualified civil servants to professional posts by exiling him to the backwater of the planning inspectorate. This was intended to bring his career to a stop, but characteristically Colin turned the appointment to his advantage. He used the time between hearing planning appeals not only to rebuild his house and to design and build a highly original (and beautifully-finished) motor caravan, but also to write *Mixed Blessing*, his book about the motor car. It was written with such robust common sense that when Ernest Marples, the Minister of Transport, read it on a plane returning from the US in 1960 he told his officials to find the author and engaged him to make a study of urban traffic problems. By this time Anni had got to know Colin, and joined his team at the Ministry of Transport, whose work culminated in the famous 'Buchanan Report', 'Traffic in Towns'. Its central message that unrestricted motor traffic destroys the city has been ignored by successive British governments.

A 'Communist' in the RIBA

The reception given to 'Motropolis' by radio and TV gave me an instant reputation, however spurious, at a time when the RIBA was on the lookout for new people to carry through the quiet revolution, largely inspired by the chain gang and their friends, that had been proceeding under its new Secretary Gordon Ricketts since 1957. It was also known in architectural circles that I had played a leading part with Peter Rawsthorne of the *News Chronicle* in creating a public scandal over Jack Cotton's crude proposal to develop a site at Piccadilly Circus as a vast illuminated advertisement hoarding – a scheme that was rejected by the government after a public inquiry conducted by Colin Buchanan, who condemned it in a masterly report. I persuaded Richard Sheppard, the Honorary Secretary of the RIBA, that it needed an effective public relations and information arm if it was going to give the public some understanding of the benefits to be gained by 'modern' or (as I saw it) social architecture. Dick persuaded the RIBA Council to put up the money for a new Chief Information Officer, and the job was advertised towards the end of 1959.

The idea that the job would suit me had not occurred to me, but when I was urged to apply for it I did so, albeit with considerable misgivings. Colin Boyne told Stirratt Johnson-Marshall that I would be a good man for the job and, despite my insistence that I must be free to publish freelance articles under my own name – provided they did not conflict with RIBA policy – I was offered the job subject to formal endorsement by the RIBA Council.

When my appointment came before the Council, Kenneth Cross the immediate-past president and one of the old guard, took objection to the appointment of a 'communist', and asked ironically which newspaper was published by my previous employer, The People's Press Printing Society. Basil Spence, the President, took the sting out of the question, by replying 'The *Daily Worker*, of course; everybody knows that'. My appointment was confirmed virtually unanimously after half an hour's debate. It says a great deal for the RIBA that it was willing to appoint somebody who had so recently been an active communist, and had never denounced communism. I know of no other professional institute that would have done so, and the RIBA kept its promise to give me the freedom I had asked for.

18

'Excludable Trove'

When I look back at the 1960s I am struck by the contradiction between our happiness and the background of war, violence and the threat of nuclear annihilation. At a personal level we had never, to use Harold Macmillan's phrase, 'had it so good'. We had more money than ever before. Our daughters were growing up, and by 1962 both Janet and Susan had left home. As 31 Tanza Road had become too big for us we converted it into three dwellings, added a storey and moved into an open-plan penthouse overlooking Parliament Hill Fields with a sun-facing terrace in the treetops. The conversion had the incidental advantage of giving me, as the official spokesperson for the RIBA, firsthand experience of a successful client–architect relationship (in which Anni played the major part on the client side) which was the beginning of a long association between us and our architect, John Winter.

Good as life was, one never knew from one moment to the next whether some crisis, like the Cuban missile crisis of 1962, would bring on the nuclear holocaust. In 1964 President Johnson made a trumped-up naval incident the pretext for launching the war of extermination in Vietnam that split the US in two and led ultimately to its defeat. In 1968, the year of the Paris uprising, the Soviet Union suppressed 'socialism with a human face' in Czechoslovakia and thereby destroyed what was left of the internal cohesion of the Soviet world and the Communist Parties. The Arab–Israeli war of 1973 and the world oil crisis of 1973–4 not only emphasised the instability of the world economy but also signalled the alarming fact that our consumer society was wholly dependent on a finite supply of the fossil fuels it was squandering recklessly. There were connections between the anti-war movements generated by the H-bomb and Vietnam, the anti-authoritarian inner city movements, and the movement inspired by Rachel Carson's *Silent Spring* in 1962 for conserving resources and stopping the rape of the living world. It was not until I got to know the American philosopher and polymath Lewis Mumford and his works (to whom I'll return in Chapter 19) that I began to understand these connections.

Traffic and Environment

The dramatic change in Anni's life that began with two exciting years in the Ministry of Transport exploring new ideas and new situations profoundly affected both our relationship and our thinking. The 'Traffic in Towns' report, which was published in 1963, had its faults both of diagnosis and of remedy, but it was the first major study of urban traffic to put people and their living and working environment first. Anni and I had, in effect, become specialists in the same field, she as a professional and I, far more superficially, as a journalist. Our marriage extended into our work, and I accompanied Anni on the trips she made to study traffic, planning and environment in Denmark and Sweden.

From the time of 'Motropolis' we were engaged in a continual and mutually enriching dialogue on all kinds of planning, traffic and environmental issues, including the studies on which Anni was engaged and my own involvement in local issues through my chairmanship of the South End Green Association, which was formed to resist a proposal to build a dual carriageway along the west side of Hampstead Heath. For a couple of years I was a member of the action group formed to oppose the London 'Motorway Box', but dropped out because I thought that many of its members were primarily interested in keeping the motorway out of the posher areas where they lived, and did not share my view that some new roads were desirable – provided they formed part of a comprehensive social, environmental and public transport package.

Anni's insistence on treating cities as living, social organisms in her studies of such historic cities as Bath, Edinburgh and Greenwich often brought her into conflict with the traffic engineers, whose computer programmes and cost–benefit analyses took account only of information that could be quantified and of values that could be expressed in time and money. They seemed never to have encountered anybody who took environmental issues seriously or had the dogged persistence with which Anni wears opponents down. Just as Anni gave me helpful advice and moral support in my local work, I was able to give her moral support, and occasionally some help as a journalist, in her most difficult studies. She did not often win, but the citizens of Edinburgh have Anni to thank for stopping the City Engineer's motorway-scale road on the edge of the city's historic centre, bridging the valley that separates Edinburgh's old and new towns. The engineering consultants in the Edinburgh study, Freeman, Fox and Partners, had no objections but Anni, as Buchanan's partner-in-charge, refused to consent to it. The City Engineer rushed down to London in a fury to urge Colin to overrule or to sack the maddening woman who was frustrating his life's ambition, but Colin said 'no', and the bridge was never built.

The RIBA's 'liberal' Phase

Within months of my appointment as Chief Information Officer at the RIBA Gordon Ricketts made me the head of a new department with responsibility, in addition to public relations, for the *RIBA Journal*, relations with RIBA members at home and abroad, and relations with the Commonwealth Association of Architects and the International Union of Architects. I became a member of the management team of six senior staff who ran the RIBA, and developed policies and programmes for the RIBA Council and its boards or committees to consider. My youthful experience as a solicitor and my training as a communist organiser helped me to find my way through the RIBA's cumbersome decision-making and bureaucratic systems. The institutional resemblances between the RIBA and the Communist Party were uncanny, and the techniques for managing the two remarkably similar. At the same time the scope of my responsibilities took me to every part of the country, and until 1968 it was literally world-wide.

The prevailing atmosphere was liberalism with a small 'l'. I doubt if any of the nine RIBA presidents for whom I worked were voting Tory at that time, and each of them in his own way reflected the new kind of architect that had taken over the RIBA. Basil Spence, for whom art was everything, endeared himself to me by delivering a tough attack on Conservative housing policies that I drafted for him. Peter Shepheard, landscape architect and Dean of the architectural faculty at Pennsylvania University, was the only one to call himself a socialist. He was also a naturalist with an attractive if disconcerting habit of turning out endless, superb drawings of animals (mainly birds but sometimes girls) throughout RIBA Council or committee meetings. It was equally characteristic of the time that six of the nine presidents had worked in central or local government. Lord Holford, one of the authors of the post-war planning system, was above all a gifted diplomat. Lord Esher was an articulate aesthete, but he was not particularly interested in the RIBA, which he hardly mentions in his autobiography. Sir Donald Gibson was a technocrat who let the staff run the show. Sir Hugh Wilson, whose presidency was plunged into confusion by the tragic death of Gordon Ricketts in 1968, had been the chief architect of Cumbernauld New Town which pioneered the separation of vehicles from pedestrians and cyclists, but is marred by one of the most brutal concrete town centres in Europe, and Alex Gordon tried, well ahead of his time, to focus the efforts of the RIBA on resource conservation.

The president with whom I worked most closely was Sir Robert Matthew, for he was the only president who fully understood how to make use of my skills. I drafted nearly all his RIBA papers and speeches, not only while he was President of the RIBA from 1962 to 1964 but also for the much longer period that he was President of the International Union of Architects (in which he was the real driving force for several years) and Chairman of the Commonwealth Association of Architects. Our outlook on architecture and professional issues was sufficiently close for him to like most of my ideas, but the final draft was always a 'Matthew' speech or article – if not the one he would have written by himself.

It was largely because Robert Matthew came to rely on me to draft his speeches that I widened my experience by taking part in international or Commonwealth conferences in Cuba and Mexico, in Paris (where the 'Traffic in Towns' team received the Patrick Abercrombie award of the International Union of Architects (UIA) in 1964), in Malta and in India. The Cuban architects had invited the UIA, before the Castro revolution, to hold its congress there in 1963. After Castro's victory the

American Institute of Architects, under pressure from the US government, declared a boycott of the Cuba UIA Congress and tried to get the venue moved to Mexico. Robert attached enormous importance to the fact that the UIA had the almost unique quality, when the US's paranoia over China was at its height, of bridging the gulf by having 'Red' China in membership. He persuaded his executive to stand by its decision to go to Havana although, as a sop to the United States, the UIA held a conference in Mexico City the following week.

The Cuba UIA Congress was an enormous success and we were, I think, the first international gathering with 'Western' participants to come to Cuba since the revolution 18 months earlier. Castro's speech proved to be a tour de force because he spoke so much good sense. Officials at the British Embassy had warned me and others not to be taken in by Castro propagandists who would boast to us about the excellence of their new housing estate, New Havana, which had been designed in pre-Castro days. The warnings backfired, for Castro took New Havana as an example of the kind of housing that should *not* be built in future. He objected, for example, to its tall blocks, mainly because Cuba could not manufacture lifts and should waste neither scarce hard currency buying them nor scarce electricity operating them.

Cuba at that time exuded a heady air of friendliness and optimism. There was none of the stuffy, puritanical formality of the Soviet bloc and hopeful signs that Cuba would establish standards for education, nutrition and a health service that were entirely new in the Third World – as has, indeed, proved to be the case.

Gordon Ricketts

If I owe the freedom I enjoyed at the RIBA to any one person it is to Gordon Ricketts, who had come to the RIBA in 1957 as a high-flyer from the Confederation of British Industries. Gordon had been opposed to my appointment but we became good colleagues although never close friends. He was the least bureaucratic administrator I have ever known and infected everybody who worked alongside him with his own enthusiasm. Gordon was exceptional in recruiting two women to the management team: Joan Milne, who was in charge of administration, and Elizabeth Layton who came to us from *The Economist* to take charge of education. Gordon saw his job as equipping the RIBA with a skilled, professional administrative staff and devising policy initiatives that would help the profession to make its mark in the post-war world. He identified managerial and technical inefficiency as the architects' main weakness, and in 1961 he set up a survey of architects' offices to establish the facts and to devise appropriate remedies.

The result was devastating: only 11 per cent of a large sample biased towards the more efficient offices achieved all-round excellence in management, technical efficiency and quality of design. Architects were also found to be rapidly losing their grip on technical and cost services to other professions. As designers they were being reduced more and more to a cosmetic role, and they were near the bottom of the league table for professional earnings. While the survey pointed to the practical shortcomings in architects' offices, and set the course for some years for the RIBA's expanding programme of work, it was so organised that it could not spot the more fundamental weaknesses that were to shatter the profession's reputation in the late 1960s – the sheer ugliness, inefficiency, wastefulness and inhumanity of far too many public and private developments and the destruction of familiar places.

Under Gordon's leadership we all worked hard: in my case much too hard. I allowed myself to be persuaded at the end of 1964 to take on the editorship of the *RIBA Journal* (an architectural magazine with a circulation of more than 20,000) while remaining head of my department. Editing the *Journal* with an executive editor to do most of the work might have been feasible, but the idea was to relaunch the magazine in colour with a new format and content, so as to extract far more money from advertisers and to make it more appealing to the RIBA members for whom it was the one free perk they got in return for their subscriptions. I made the (almost) fatal mistake of choosing a new and supposedly cheap colour printing technology that had to be abandoned when it proved to be unreliable, expensive and of indifferent quality. I gave myself endless worries by giving my two assistants more responsibility than they were capable of handling. It all came right in the end, but the strain was enormous, although I did not realise it at the time. I thought it important to have more exercise and took up swimming in a big way. Anni taught me the crawl, I took lessons in the back stroke and even came third in the 1,000-metre race at the Club Mediterranée in Corfu! I prided myself on my fitness, only to feel a strange pain in my chest one morning. I slipped out, after telling my secretary that I was going to see Hugh Faulkner, my doctor and he drove me immediately to University College Hospital where to my amazement a coronary thrombosis was diagnosed and I found myself flat on my back in hospital, where I spent two months from January to March 1966.

Ward 33

My heart attack was profoundly upsetting for Anni, not least when I had a second one two weeks after the first and the registrar took her into a laundry cupboard (the only space, it seemed, for private chats with relatives) to tell her that I might not survive a third. But I recovered and, from my (entirely selfish) point of view my attack proved, rather like my leg amputation, to be one of the best things that ever happened to me.

Once the crisis of the first two weeks was over, life in Ward 33 proved to be vastly more interesting than life in the private room where I'd passed six months in 1933. It was a medical ward with 25 patients, nearly every one of whom had an interesting story to tell. Many of them were depressed by the consequences of illness and the inability of the social system to support them. The long-distance lorry driver was going to lose his job after his coronary. The Polish travel agent couldn't see how he could keep his business going if he were to act on the advice he had been given to work no more than four hours a day. The doctors told him not to worry but his wife rang up to say that his staff (one girl) had failed to turn up, and what was she to do? A skilled craftsman had just lost his wife in a car crash, and had been offered £300 in compensation – which he called 'an insult'. Another patient would have to give up his rented room because he would be unable to manage six flights of steps and did not know where he could find another room on the ground floor. The dirtiest man in the ward was called Jones. He worked in Ghana but could not stand 'coloured' people and insisted on lying on the bed with all his clothes on

– socks included – watching TV. In contrast, the only black man, whom we all addressed as Mr Joseph, was the gentlest and most considerate man in the ward. We also had the occasional drunks, an overdose of sleeping pills and the drama of total heart failure or 'cardiac arrest'.

In the next bed to me was Andy Bishop, an overweight and badly-paid hospital porter whose constant worry was how he was going to keep his car if, as he was advised, he had to give up his second job as a tote clerk when he came out. Andy was on a starvation diet to get his weight down, and I could see the curve on his weight chart going downwards day by day. One morning I got one of the patients to hand me the chart and extrapolated the curve with a dotted line to the bottom of the sheet. I then added a statement to the effect that, as Mr Bishop would cease to exist on the twenty-fifth of June if the trend continued, it would be advisable to take some corrective action before that date. The chart was duly handed to the consultant next morning when he came on his round with his retinue of registrar, sister and students. I was agreeably surprised when he laughed, turned round to me, asked me if I'd done it and, when I pleaded guilty, told me that I should have charged a fee.

My admiration for the nurses' good humour, tireless work and skill was unlimited, but as I talked with them I learned, of course, that they had the same human problems and frailties as the patients – not to mention boy friends, husbands, parents and a chronic shortage of money as their commitment was exploited by underpaying them. Despite a number of deaths the ward seemed almost to exude gaiety, even laughter. Bernard Shaw was right to say that 'life does not cease to be funny when people die any more than it ceases to be serious when people laugh'. Cheerfulness was an essential antidote or anaesthetic to the suffering, anxiety and deaths which were as commonplace as the endless routines that broke the monotony of the day. The comradely support that I got in the ward confirmed me in the decision I made after losing my leg never to go to a private hospital or a private room again.

Deported

When I got back to work after an absence of six months Gordon relieved me of the overwork that had brought on the stress. I was to remain a member of the senior management team, but with only two responsibilities: to edit the *Journal* and to be the RIBA's 'ambassador-at-large'. He suggested that I should make a round-the-world trip in the spring of 1967, beginning with the Commonwealth Architects' Conference in Delhi and then go on to visit the local societies of architects allied to the RIBA in Singapore, Australia, New Zealand, Fiji and Jamaica.

The whole trip took two months, and was in many ways an eye-opener. India, although poverty was everywhere, seemed to be a much happier place than the US which I had visited in 1963 for the first time since 1936. Le Corbusier's new capital for the Punjab at Chandigarh contained two works of genius, the law courts and the parliament building, but seemed to have been designed without regard to the climate to which traditional Indian architecture is so well adapted. I was entertained hospitably everywhere, and gave the keynote address on professionalism to the New Zealand architects' conference. My communist 'past' seemed to have receded into history, until it returned to hit me over the head in Los Angeles where I had planned to change planes en route to Jamaica, where I was to spend a week with my old ex-Party architect comrade Bill Hodges and his doctor wife Margaret. The US Consul had told me that transit passengers do not need visas, and I duly arrived at LA on an Air France plane having made friends en route with an Australian ICI chemist, Dr Schloss, who was carrying more bottles of whisky than he could get through the US customs. I agreed to take one through for him, but when I followed him past the immigration desk the officer looked at my passport, lifted the phone and uttered the unforgettable sentence: 'I've got a trove here, from Papeete to Kingston, and he's excludable. I'm sending him downstairs.'

I never discovered what a 'trove' was though my guess is that it's an acronym – TR for 'Transit', V for 'Visa' and E for 'Excludable'. I was taken down to some nicely-furnished dungeons, where Officer F.J. Gross courteously offered me a coffee, and explained why I was 'excludable'. The number on the US visas issued to me in 1963 revealed that as an ex-communist I was ineligible for a US visa unless my ineligibility had been waived by the Department of Justice, while the Mexican stamp 'entrada de Cuba' on my passport told them that I had committed the un-American act of visiting Castro. Officer Gross conceded that transit passengers needed no visas – unless, of course, they were ineligible for visas, in which case they did – 'Catch 22'. As I had no visa, he had no option but to deport me as an ex-communist 'whence I came' – 4,000 miles back to our last stop at Tahiti. This struck me as crazy. 'If you want to get rid of me,' I asked, 'why not put me on the plane to Mexico City?' Officer Gross thumbed his way through what was, I suppose, the 'Indexed and Annotated Regulations of the US Immigration Department', but the sighs he uttered as he reached the foot of each of the pages he consulted told me that they all said the same thing: to deport me 'whence I came'.

It might help, he suggested, if I would answer some questions; had I, for example, joined the CP voluntarily? I should, of course, have said 'no', but unwisely I explained that in the UK, as in the United States, membership of the CP was not compulsory. He then tried a more promising tack: had I opposed the CP actively since leaving it? Had I made speeches against it? Alas, no, but as evidence of my reformed character I told Officer Gross that I had been a member of two committees of the Labour Party that had advised Harold Wilson on traffic and building before the election in 1964. His reply was not hostile so much as bewildered: 'Harold Who?' – and then 'Is he a member of your government?'

Once I had persuaded him that Harold Wilson was indeed the British Premier, things looked up for a moment. But my answers to his next question 'Do you know any other members of the government?' got us badly ensnared in the doctrine of the separation of powers. He flatly refused to believe my assertion that R.J.S. Crossman, Tony Benn or Peter Shore, with all of whom I claimed (a slight) acquaintance, could be members both of the government *and* of the House of Commons – which for the sake of clarity I had compared to the House of Representatives. He then took alarm at the fact that I was taking notes, and wanted to know why – to which I replied that I was a journalist, and that my deportation would be a good story. This persuaded him to have me put secretly onto the Mexican plane on which I was booked, without formally admitting me, but by the time he had thought up this wheeze the plane had left. The prospect was now overnight detention – 'and that means' he said 'the FBI, the CIA, guard dogs – the lot!'

He left the room and came back with authority from someone in Washington to let me stay in LA for the night in the custody of Air France, who promptly signed a bond and transferred me to the custody of Air Mexico, who signed a receipt for me and immediately set me free. They gave me a taxi and free bed and board at a nearby motel and I spent an agreeable day looking around LA before I came back to be deported the following evening.

When I got back I wrote an article about the 'Excludable Trove' in *The New Statesman*, in which I said that if Dr Schloss would get in touch with me I would let him have his bottle of whisky back. Some weeks later Dr Schloss phoned, and when we had lunch together I gave him a somewhat better bottle of whisky than the one I'd consumed with the Hodges in Jamaica.

The Bubble Bursts

My world tour proved to be the last as well as the first of my big expenses-paid trips as the RIBA's ambassador-at-large, for the RIBA was overtaken before long by an acute financial crisis and an even more acute loss of professional confidence. When I was convalescing in Corsica in 1966 Ian Nairn, who had been the scourge of the 'spec builder' in the *Architectural Review*, had found a new enemy – the architect himself. In a series of blistering articles in *The Observer* headed 'Stop The Architects Now!' Ian fastened virtually all the blame for the failures of city centre redevelopment, tower blocks, speculative office blocks and the destruction of familiar places on the architectural profession. I thought then, and still do, that it was a highly emotive attack that reflected a very superficial view of the social, economic and political forces that caused the failures of which he legitimately complained. I hastened my recovery by writing an equally blistering reply, which I published in the *RIBA Journal* as 'MacEwen's Guide to Nairn'. However, although I was right to expose the flaws in Ian's indictment, it took me a year or more to realise that Ian had felt the public pulse more accurately than I had done.

His articles helped to set in motion the public reaction against architects that exploded in 1968 with the collapse of Ronan Point, a concrete panel, system-built tower block in West Ham. Architects and planners were made the scapegoats for failures for which politicians, businessmen and many others were at least equally to blame, and the baby of 'modern architecture' was thrown out with the bathwater as if it were merely an outmoded style. My job could no longer be the promotion of modern or social architecture. While doing my best to prevent architects being made the scapegoats for failures for which others were often more responsible I had to discover to my own satisfaction where architecture had gone wrong.

19

Crisis in Architecture – and in Energy

By 1968 architecture, architects and the RIBA began to face a multiple crisis. The profession's reputation was collapsing; 'modern architecture' was being discredited; the RIBA's scale of fees and other 'restrictive practices' (notably the ban on touting or advertising for work) were under attack by the Labour government, and its salaried members – the majority of the profession – were in revolt against increased subscriptions which did not seem to benefit them. The accidental death in 1968 of Gordon Ricketts robbed the RIBA of leadership at a most difficult time. My main job as editor of the *RIBA Journal* left me with far more time to think, to travel and to investigate these problems than is usually granted to senior executives. I began to exercise my right to publish articles as a freelance journalist, and from 1968 the BBC radio producer Leonie Cohn invited me to research, write and present programmes in her environmental series 'This Island Now'. These programmes, which focused initially on architecture and planning, did pioneering work on the conservation of natural resources and the threats to the environment posed by nuclear power. In pursuing these themes I found the greatest inspiration in the American philosopher and polymath Lewis Mumford.

I had read very little of Mumford's work until he came to the RIBA in 1961 to receive the Royal Gold Medal for Architecture for his work as a journalist, historian and thinker on planning, architecture and the environment. Characteristically, he disregarded the conventions surrounding this formal occasion and delivered a trenchant paper on the threat posed to humanity by the nuclear arms race and the abuse of technology. I asked Lewis and his wife Sophie to Tanza Road and, much to my surprise, they accepted. We felt an immediate sense of comradeship and their visit laid the foundations for a lasting friendship. Over the next few years I read virtually all Mumford's works, and discovered the connections he had been making since 1934, when his *Technics and Civilization* appeared, between the apparently disconnected phenomena of wars of mass extermination, the rape of the cities, the lifestyles and revolts of the rising generation, the misuse of technology and the destruction of the biosphere on which life depends. Until 1961 our knowledge of Mumford had been confined to his *City in History* and the earlier *Culture of Cities* that had appealed to the radical left when Anni was an architectural student in the 1930s. I did not know that Mumford had said everything that I had said in 'Motropolis', and a great deal more, in an article reprinted six years earlier in *The Highway and the City*.

Mumford's Message

In 1971 Leonie Cohn and I arranged for me to have two radio interviews with Lewis, on what proved to be his last major work, the profound but tragically neglected *The Pentagon of Power*. It conveyed what would now be called the 'green' message in its starkest form, by demonstrating that no solution to the problems of war, social disorder and environmental degradation could be found without abandoning the high-energy, high-mobility, intensely individual style of life developed by the advanced industrial nations and applying science and technology in an ecologically sound manner to the real needs of mankind. In Mumford's view a false concept of 'progress' obliged society to follow technology or science wherever they showed a profit, or could be used for military purposes, while the scientists and the professionals on whose skills the ruling elite depend had allowed themselves to be neutered, morally and politically. As a philosopher 'generalist' he warned against the dangers of narrow specialisation and took the entire human experience for his field.

In *The Pentagon of Power* his ultimate criterion for mankind's biological and cultural success is to live in harmony with nature, not to conquer it, and he measured success by the quality of life and human creativity and not by the maximisation of production or consumption, which are the goals of a power-complex driven by a lust for power, profit, property, publicity and 'progress' – the 'pentagon of power'. Mumford forced me to recognise the criminality of the Allies' bombing of German and Japanese cities which, in his view, copied Hitler's methods and, by removing all moral restraints on the extermination of civilians, paved the way for the atomic bombing of Hiroshima and Nagasaki and the genocidal wars in Korea and Vietnam. Mumford was the first distinguished American to protest against the war in Vietnam in an open letter to President Johnson, sent to all the principal US newspapers – which all but two refused to publish.

Leonie Cohn and I were able to record Mumford's thoughts in much greater depth and breadth in 1976, in a series of nine programmes (two of which the BBC lost!) at his home in Amenia, a rural backwater in up-state New York, in celebration of his eightieth birthday. These programmes enabled us to convey something of the scope of Mumford's work as the critic of architecture and science, the historian of technology and of American culture, the essayist on the role of personality in history, the diagnostician of the 'diseases of civilization', the interpreter of Freud and Jung and, above all the passionate but rational believer in the full life and the inveterate enemy of the anti-humanist trends in our time. My own pleasure was enhanced by the fact that Lewis told me some years later how much he enjoyed these programmes, partly because we had caught him while he still retained his full mental and physical powers.

Human and Hi-Tech Architecture

Thirty years before the vogue for 'community architecture' Mumford was insisting that architecture must express the purposes and values of people, not machines, and satisfy the aspirations of the human spirit as well as the needs of body and mind:

> So closely are aesthetic form, moral character and practical function united in my philosophy that the absence of any one of these qualities in any work of architecture turns it into a hollow shell: a mere piece of scene-painting or technological exhibitionism ... not a fully-dimensioned building that does justice to the varied demands of life.

He saw the ideal city not as a mass of disposable containers to be swept away to feed an expanding economy as soon as the maximum profit had been extracted from them, but as an organism, changing at a pace that can be assimilated by human beings and retaining its function as an organ of collective memory.

By the 1960s, however, architectural students had no time for Mumford. Their guru was Buckminster Fuller, the engineer, inventor and high priest of 'hi-tech' architecture who held student audiences spellbound all over the world throughout the decade by talking non-stop for hours about 'anticipatory design science'. When 'Bucky' came to the RIBA in 1968 to receive the Royal Gold Medal for Architecture for his contribution to architectural philosophy and engineering he poured out thousands of words in less than two hours and left me as editor of the *RIBA Journal* with the problem of making sense of the unintelligible transcript. I sent it to him with a request to reduce it to 3,000 words, and received a delightful cable in BuckyFullerese of which the following is an extract:

MY SPONTANEOUS COMMITMENT TO COMMUNICATE SO INTENSE AND TIME SO SHORT I ACCELERATED TWOFOLD MY USUAL SEVEN THOUSAND WORDS PER HOUR OUTLOUD THINKING RATE STOP WITH TRANSCRIPTION OMISSIONS AND SIMULTANEOUSLY GESTURED COMMUNICATIONS RESTORED AND INCLUDED CONVEY ADEQUATELY IN PRINT WHAT I COMMUNICATED TO AUDIENCE WITHOUT RISKING FATAL MISUNDERSTANDINGS WILL REQUIRE FIFTEEN THOUSAND WORDS TOTAL COSTING ME NUMEROUS SECRETARIAL RETYPING OFFICE OVERHEADS AND TIME AGGREGATING TWO THOUSAND DOLLARS AND THIRTY DAYS OVERALL STOP SUGGEST YOU RUN ONLY PRESENTATION STATEMENTS TOGETHER WITH THIS CABLEGRAM MY ETERNAL THANKS AND YOUR OWN STATEMENT WHY SPACE TIME FORBIDS TOTAL DISCOURSE AND SUBJECT IMPORT DOES NOT PERMIT CONTRACTION AND FACT STOP CORDIALLY GRATEFULLY BUCKMINSTER FULLER

My reply, also in BuckyFullerese, ran (in part)

GRATEFULLY RECEIVED YOUR TELEGRAPHED SUGGESTION FOR SOLUTION OTHERWISE EMBARRASSING IMPASSE ON EDITORIALISING TRANSCRIPT WHICH REFLECTS YOUR ADDRESS AS DELIVERED STOP WOULD NOT DREAM IMPOSE FURTHER COSTS ON YOU BUT ... HAD ASSUMED YOUR GREAT PRINCIPLE MORE WITH LESS APPLIED NOT ONLY PHYSICAL STRUCTURES

BUT ALSO ORAL AND WRITTEN COMMUNICATIONS UNDER
EXCESS WEIGHT WHEREOF SUFFERING HUMANITY BEING
SUBMERGED AS WITNESS PROLIFERATING TELEVISION
PROGRAMMES AND SUNDAY SUPPLEMENTS NOW CONSUMING
MANY ACRES SOFTWOOD FORESTS OTHERWISE AVAILABLE TO
PROVIDE HUMAN SHELTER AND OTHER USEFUL PURPOSES STOP
HUMBLY SUGGEST IMPROMPTU EXTEMPORARE AD LIB AD HOC
OUTLOUD THINKING RATE OF TWICE SEVEN THOUSAND
WORDS PER HOUR COULD AT TIMES RESULT IN WORDS
PHRASES SENTENCES PARAGRAPHS SUPERFLUOUS REDUNDANT
IRRELEVANT OR PERIPHERAL YOUR MAIN THEME WHICH WITH
CRISPLY EXPRESSED LANGUAGE ECONOMY AND MEANINGFUL
BREVITY COULD SAVE TIME AND PAPER STOP YOUR MESSAGE
DISTILLED THREE THOUSAND WORDS WILL DO MORE WITH
LESS THAN FIFTEEN THOUSAND ... WILL THEREFORE WITH
THANKS AND BEST WISHES DO AS YOU SUGGEST

Bucky's 'philosophy' was the narrow technological approach
that Mumford had been exposing for the past 40 years, and the
Bucky Fuller cult was incompatible with Mumford's ecological
and resource conscious view of the world. When *Architectural
Design* published an issue reviewing Bucky's life work, which I
read on the day that Nixon resumed the bombing of North
Vietnam in 1972, I commented that 'his design science is
neither anticipatory nor comprehensive, but suffers from
funnel vision so acute as to amount to blindness'.

Bucky was an engineering genius, as his geodesic domes
testify, but he could only see political or social problems in
technological terms. His solution to every problem was to
increase 'performance per pound weight'. He believed that

> wealth is now without practical limits ... science has hooked up to
> the everyday economic plumbing of the cosmic reservoir. You can
> now have your cake and eat it. The more you eat, the more and the
> better quality of the cakes to be had by further production.

Without realising it he provided a whole generation of architects and engineers with an amoral, value-free technological
justification for the ethos of greed and growth, and propagated
the concept of so-called hi-tech architectural solutions for the
consumer society divorced from human need. He was not
himself an amoral man, and he objected to the massive waste

of wealth and technology on 'weaponry'. His solution to the poverty of a black community in Mississipi was to provide it with a dome-covered 'moon-crater-shaped living facility'. He stood, in effect, for the obliteration of the world's diverse cultures by a single, value-free culture based on the most advanced technologies. He could not explain why the US, with all its wealth and technological know-how, had massive and growing poverty. The students' craze for Bucky and their indifference to Mumford foreshadowed the way in which architecture (and capitalist society) was going.

Ronan Point and After

The collapse in 1968 of Ronan Point, a 20-storey block of flats in West Ham in London's East End, released a wave of pent-up indignation over much post-war housing – tower blocks and technical failures such as leaking flat roofs and condensation – and the destruction wrought by clean-sweep redevelopment. Ronan Point signalled the end of the fashion for 'modern architecture', which had degenerated into a number of styles, and the end of the movement for social architecture for which the post-war impetus had been exhausted. It was not difficult for me to point out, as I did, that Ronan Point was not so much a failure by the architect as the structural failure of an imported concrete panel system, designed by engineers and sold to local authorities by building firms as a package. Macmillan's Tory government had introduced subsidies for high blocks, and the Labour councillors built them to stop the exodus of Labour voters from the borough.

Ronan Point was a social and environmental as well as a structural failure. If, as the RIBA claimed, architecture was 'essentially a service to the community' why had so many architects fallen hook, line and sinker for inhumane and technically defective systems? The RIBA could not dodge the fact that public dissatisfaction with much recent building was solidly grounded in experience, and it had made matters worse by claiming for architects a far bigger role in environmental design than they were actually playing – as Ronan Point showed.

Ronan Point was also a watershed in my attitude to the RIBA. Ian Nairn's onslaught in 'Stop The Architects Now' had forced me to take a more critical look both at the gap between the facts of architectural life and the claims made by the RIBA for itself and the architectural profession. I had been arguing, for the RIBA, since 1962 that architects were rendering a public service by enhancing the environment, a role for which they were uniquely qualified. The RIBA justified its privileged status as a charitable body (which was exempt from paying rates or taxes) by asserting that it was committed by its Royal Charter to the 'advancement of architecture', and argued that by controlling architectural education and upholding its ethical code of behaviour it ensured the integrity and the competence of its members.

The concept of 'professionalism' rests on the assumption that the buyer of professional services – of a doctor, an architect or an engineer – lacks the knowledge to evaluate the quality of the service being offered. He has to rely on the theory that a professional body has certified the professional's competence and will punish him for any misconduct. When I looked more closely into the RIBA and other professional institutions I had to face the fact that the claims made for professionalism were largely bogus. Neither solicitors, engineers, surveyors, doctors, accountants nor architects regarded even technical incompetence as professional misconduct for which a member should be disciplined, unless it was criminal or mere petty managerial inefficiency.

I was convinced that, while the public had a right to expect a competent technical service, it was not enough for the architect to deliver technical skills, however professionally. I agreed with the theory being developed by Bill Hillier, my colleague at the RIBA, that architecture should be concerned not only with design, aesthetics and three-dimensional space but above all with the architects' ability to see and comprehend the building, its environment and its impact on people as a whole. For buildings are not just art objects or containers for activities: they modify climate, behaviour and culture; they consume resources and have symbolic as well as practical effects. They profoundly affect relationships between people, and between people and nature. Also, Mumford had convinced me of the folly of rejecting the past. All this seemed to me to point to the need for a new professionalism (one might call it 'green') based on a far broader interpretation of competence, which reflected a duty owed by the architect to the whole community, and to those who use buildings as well as to those who pay for them or profit from them.

The Professional Dilemma

I had begun to explore these themes when I addressed the New Zealand architects on 'professionalism' in 1967. By 1968 it was obvious to me that it was not so much architects' managerial incompetence as their design skill and technical competence, the fitness of their products and the social and environmental consequences of their decisions that were being questioned. Yet not only was the RIBA unable to give the public any guarantees of the quality of its members' services: it took no action over numerous complaints about the behaviour of John Poulson, the architect who was later convicted on corruption charges, until *Private Eye* and Poulson's bankruptcy proceedings forced the scandal into the open in 1972.

In 1970 I went to the US to see whether I could learn anything useful from the effort being made by the American Institute of Architects (AIA) to involve architects in the inner cities in the aftermath of the ghetto riots. My report to the RIBA, 'Service to the People, the Environment or Mammon?', described the growth of the new 'poverty industry' and the split personality of the American Institute, pulled one way by the younger generation's concerns about race, war, pollution and the environment, and the other way by big business practitioners. I advised the RIBA to initiate what would now be called a 'community architecture programme', by encouraging architects to offer free or cheap services to poor communities, but I also argued that 'the community' could not control its environment without access to land, money and political power.

I need hardly say that the idealists lost in the US, and I am struck by the similarities between the American scene in 1970 and the British scene in the late 1980s. The 'community architecture' movement fostered briefly by the Prince of Wales and Rod Hackney, the President of the RIBA from 1987 to 1989, has an uncanny resemblance to the AIA's cosmetic programmes. Architects should serve communities, but 'community architecture' as practised in Thatcher's Britain can at best only have a marginal effect on the massive and growing problems of homelessness, sub-standard homes and poverty. The resources going into it and the scale of the effort are trifling when contrasted to the billions poured into the development bonanza in London's docklands, where the architects have exacerbated the problems of the local communities and of London itself.

Small Is Beautiful

It was my good fortune that Alex Gordon, a Cardiff architect who was President of the RIBA from 1971 to 1973, shared my increasingly ecological and resource-conscious approach. We organised the RIBA's 1972 conference around the theme 'designing for survival', and I secured the participation of the (socialist) American biologist Barry Commoner and the (capitalist) Aurelio Peccei, a director of Fiat and Chairman of the Club of Rome whose report 'Limits to Growth' had caused a world-wide sensation. Although their politics were poles apart they were agreed that the world was on the brink of an ecological disaster. The radio programme in the series 'This Island Now' on 'the world environmental crisis' in October 1972, during which Leonie Cohn and I staged an argument between Commoner and Peccei on the reasons for the crisis and the best ways of dealing with it, was the first in which we tackled the fundamental ecological issues.

The publication of *Only One Earth* by Barbara Ward and René Dubois in 1972, of Fritz Schumacher's *Small is Beautiful* in 1973, the emergence of Friends of the Earth as a major force in the US, the oil crisis of 1974 caused by the war between Israel and Egypt and the miners' strike and the three-day week that followed, created for the first time an atmosphere in which the media took an interest (which expired as soon as the crisis was over) in the limits to growth and the dangers threatening the world's natural resources. Jonathan Porritt has argued that although 'small is beautiful' is the one green slogan that has penetrated the mind of mass industrial society, it actually misrepresents Schumacher's views. For Schumacher did not say that everything big is bad or everything small is good; nor did he say that all growth is bad. What mattered to Schumacher was retaining the human scale. Sharing a platform with Schumacher at a Design and Industry Association conference in Rome in November 1973 gave me a better understanding of his distinction between cancerous growth (such as the further enrichment of the rich nations), superfluous growth (which fattens them) and beneficial growth in which industry operates at the human scale, lives on renewable energy rather than non-renewable capital (such as fossil fuel) and does no violence to the natural or the human environment.

There was a strange irony about the series of five programmes on the energy crisis presented by Jeremy Bugler and myself during the miners' strike in February and March 1974. While urgent messages were being flashed from Broadcasting House telling the nation to 'switch off' we were being slowly cooked in the BBC offices at a temperature of 80 degrees Fahrenheit by the combination of solar gain from the windows and an inefficient heating system. As I remarked when introducing the first programme on 'The Conservation of Energy', as soon as the miners went back to work seven out of every ten tons of the coal they produced would be wasted, for the main product of the Central Electricity Generating Board (CEGB) was not electricity but waste heat – hence my suggestion to re-name it the Central Waste Heat Generating Board. As I might have guessed, the campaign urging us all not to waste electricity was dropped immediately by the new Labour government. When I interviewed Eric Varley, the new Energy Minister, he told me that high-priced fuel would persuade people to use energy more efficiently – almost the same message as the nation got from Cecil Parkinson 14 years later when he successfully resisted an amendment to the Electricity Bill that would have required the privatised companies to promote energy conservation because (he argued) market forces would promote 'efficiency' – which can be very far from being the same thing as conserving resources from the point of view of companies whose objective is profit.

Long Life, Low Energy

I like to think that our modest programmes and our articles in *The Listener* helped to sink the CEGB's megalomaniac plan to squander billions on trebling electricity generating capacity by the year 2000 by building 36 nuclear reactors so that by the year 2010 the average person would be consuming four and a half times as much electricity as in 1974. The CEGB, it seemed to me, was behaving like a man who runs his bath with the plug out, complains that there is not enough hot water, and rushes off to buy a bigger boiler instead of looking for the plug. For 60–70 per cent of the primary energy used to generate electricity was being wasted at the power station (it still is), and a great deal of the electricity was being wasted through poor insulation, inefficient appliances and other causes (it still is). Yet the CEGB boss Walter (now Lord) Marshall, who took part in our programme on 'The Energy Trap', was so besotted with the technology of nuclear power that he pinned his faith to the Fast-Breeder Reactor (FBR), which breeds plutonium for military as well as civil use. The CEGB hoped to have ten FBRs in operation by 1986; in 1988 the government all but abandoned the British FBR programme, and in 1989 it had to abandon the privatisation of nuclear power because the CEGB's fairy tales about 'cheap' nuclear power had been exposed as untrue propaganda which some people must have known to be lies.

The people we brought into our programmes on energy conservation in 1974 and 1975 were years ahead of governments or the electricity industry. Engineers from Scandinavia told us how cities like Stockholm and Copenhagen heated homes and factories by Combined Heat and Power (CHP) which uses the heat that the CEGB (now National Power) still discharges into the sea or wastes in its huge cooling towers. Amory Lovins, the American Friends of the Earth physicist, pointed out that increasing energy supply by building nuclear power stations is slow, risky, costly and short-lived, whereas decreasing demand by saving energy is fast, cheap, safe and of lasting benefit. Sir Kingsley Dunham, Britain's leading geologist, told of his worries (since amply justified) over the disposal underground of nuclear wastes that would stay radioactive for 30,000 years and lay up trouble for future generations. Carrol Wilson, the former manager of the US Atomic Energy Commission, warned of 'the possibility of a catastrophic failure of a light water reactor system', as was to happen five years later at Three Mile Island. He saw a crash programme of energy conservation as the only way of making a safe transition to alternative sources of power as oil and gas ran out. Mrs Thatcher, who took alarm at the 'greenhouse effect' in 1988, should have listened to Gerald Leach in 1974 when he said that 'in the long term you've got nasty problems of global limits to energy consumption, and of large regions using so much energy that they actually alter the climate' – an early reference to the 'greenhouse effect'.

While the BBC gave us air time to discuss the waste of energy in all its forms the RIBA was utterly indifferent to the massive waste of energy and other resources in the area that was the architects' main responsibility – the construction and use of buildings, which accounts for nearly half the waste of primary energy. Alex Gordon made the conservation of resources in buildings a priority for his presidency. In 1972 he initiated the 'Long Life, Loose Fit, Low Energy' (LL/LF/LE) programme, a study of buildings that would be durable, adaptable and above all economical in the use of resources both in use and in construction. But in 1973, when the membership voted down a foolish proposal to increase subscriptions far beyond the level that members were willing to pay, the RIBA Council refused to put any money into the LL/LF/LE study.

At the same time the RIBA refused to fund an idea I had floated in 1971, when I had resumed my old job running public relations with the fancy title of Director of Public Affairs. I got committee approval to investigate the transformation of the RIBA into an 'architecture centre', but the RIBA turned it down. This was the last straw as far as I was concerned. I applied to the Leverhulme Trust for a £5,000 research fellowship to enable me to pursue the study myself, and asked for – and got – 14 months' leave of absence from the RIBA to enable me to do it. That was, for all practical purposes, the end of my career with the RIBA.

Crisis in Architecture

It says a lot for the RIBA as a liberal institute that in 1984 it published the book, *Crisis in Architecture*, that was the outcome of my Leverhulme study. It was, as its critics pointed out, an oddly contradictory work, for while it argued that the RIBA had immense potential for furthering the cause of architecture if it could confront some unpalatable truths it was also a damning criticism of the institute itself and of the failures both of contemporary architecture and of professionalism. I attributed the architectural failures not to 'modern architecture' as such but to the ways in which it was practised. The social content that originally inspired it had been drained out of it, allowing its methodology and styles to be exploited and abused by developers and public authorities alike. Failures were often caused by architects' blind worship of new technologies and untried materials which they did not understand, and by their indifference to the need for historic continuity. The result was that architects were seen by the public to be part of the problem rather than part of the solution.

The root of the 'professional dilemma' as I saw it was that that architects were caught up in a social system that rewarded their most selfish and destructive impulses while repelling their most generous and creative ones – the basic issue that is obscured by arid controversies about the stylistic merits of 'modernism', 'neo-modernism', 'post-modernism' and 'classicism'. Style is not the issue. Good architecture of any period has its roots in history while employing contemporary technology. Architects in private practice were (and still are) often no more than agents hired to enable the developer to make money or to advertise. Although the public offices had done more good work than they were credited with, all the pressures were to cut costs and standards. Architects working for the public sector were usually separated by the bureaucratic nature of public authorities from the people who needed their services, and with whom they should be closely involved.

The RIBA found it easier to accept my analysis of the disenchantment with architecture than to face up to the need to give the public effective guarantees of the competence, integrity and social responsibility of its members. It could not accept (except in theory) my notion that professionalism should imply a duty to the public to be socially and environmentally responsible that overrides the duty to the client. I suggested ways in which the RIBA could enforce a revised code of ethics, but I was very conscious of the fact that it was going to be increasingly difficult to introduce or to enforce such a code when political and economic pressures were forcing the profession down the commercial road – a trend that accelerated under the Thatcher government.

My advice to the RIBA was to resolve the conflict between its contradictory roles by hiving off the job of 'advancing architecture' to an architecture centre, at the heart of which would be the RIBA's scandalously neglected library which, with its Drawings Collection, is one of the two greatest architectural collections in the world. I wanted the RIBA to house the centre in its building at Portland Place, and I asked the RIBA to accept the fact that it could neither afford to maintain a great international collection nor cling to the old idea that architecture was in some way the private preserve of architects. On the contrary, I wanted the RIBA to invite all those bodies and individuals who were involved or interested in architecture to get together under its leadership to manage and to finance the centre, and so to give a new impetus to the public's understanding of architecture in all its complexity. The financial responsibility for the collection now lies mainly with the independent British Architectural Library Trust, but it took the RIBA 15 years to decide to bring the library and Drawings Collection together as 'an architecture centre' at Portland Place. Unfortunately, by failing to involve people or institutions outside the profession in its decision the RIBA has made it very difficult to raise the tens of millions that this project demands.

Crisis in Architecture got the mixed reception it probably deserved. The *AJ* caught its flavour rather well by saying it would arouse both admiration and fury:

> admiration, because MacEwen throws up suggestions and ideas by the score in a very entertaining way; fury because what he says may not accord with what many architects assume to be the role of the RIBA ... or their own professional lives and problems.

I was called a 'Jekyll and Hyde' because I both staunchly defended the RIBA and was its harshest critic. Two teachers at the Architectural Association tested their vocabulary of abuse to the limit: 'dishonesty, hypocrisy, shallow, sham, laughable, paternalistic, emotionally written, institutional propaganda'. Two reviewers, John McKean and John Carter, feared that the RIBA was inherently too conservative to play the disinterested role that I suggested for it, and most of the architects who welcomed the 'architecture centre' idea saw it primarily as a device by which the RIBA could market the services of architects. In 1987 the RIBA put 'marketing' at the centre of its strategy, and flattered though I am by its proposal to transform its building into an 'architecture centre' I fear that 'marketing' is the real purpose.

The Break-up

My affair with the RIBA proved, like my affair with the Communist Party, to combine elements of love and hate. I have both affection and admiration for architects, whose skills are all too often underrated, misunderstood and misdirected. They work in a profoundly frustrating political, economic and cultural context, but the profession and its work reflect the society in which it operates, and by 1974 the old conservatism and a new commercialism were asserting themselves. There was no point in staying on and I took early retirement at the end of March 1974 when *Crisis in Architecture* was published.

I was agreeably surprised when the RIBA Council decided to elect me to membership as an Honorary Fellow

as a mark of the profession's appreciation of the work you have done in comunicating an enthusiasm for architecture to the public, while not fearing to draw the attention of architects and the institutions with which they are concerned to the problems which face the profession.

I left the RIBA on a high note rather than on a low one. I began work as a government-appointed member of the newly formed Exmoor National Park Authority on the day after I left the RIBA.

20

The Man from *The Times*

By an odd coincidence buying a house in Exmoor in 1968 ultimately led to a new career in conservation for Anni and me. We knew that Exmoor was a national park, but we were almost totally ignorant of the national park system of England and Wales. What attracted us was the house and the landscape, and what brought us there was my passionate desire to have direct access to open country that had some resemblance to the wildness of the Highlands. What we did not foresee was that buying the house would lead to my appointment to the Exmoor National Park Committee by a Tory government in 1973.

Such knowledge as I had of the countryside of England and Wales had been gained by 18 years of caravanning. In the early years of our marriage our two modest incomes would not run to weekends in the country or to family holidays in hotels or guest houses, so in 1950 we bought a small caravan for £300. This proved to be one of the best investments we ever made, giving us holidays in Wales, Cornwall and France in the days when it was still possible to put up for a night or a week on almost any farm. Thanks to the generosity of a series of left-wing friends we found bases for weekends or holidays in the countryside.

In 1968, when my mother was 91 and was no longer able to live on the Black Isle, we had to decide whether to keep the cottage there as a holiday retreat and, ultimately, as a retirement home. Our caravan was succumbing to old age and we wanted something more permanent and comfortable as a country home. Much as I loved the Highlands my roots there had withered, the cost of getting there frequently was prohibitive and, to cap everything, it was planned to drive the main highway from Inverness to the North over a new bridge at Kessock and through the garden at Braehead. We decided to sell Braehead, and the proceeds together with our earnings from my job at the RIBA and Anni's partnership with Colin Buchanan gave us the means to realise one of the characteristic ambitions of the professional, two-income family – a second home in the country within reach of London, for holidays and weekends, and perhaps for retirement.

Discovering Exmoor

After scouring the southern countryside for a year we had found nothing to our liking that we could afford. But in the end our search for open country and my insistence that we must be able to see heather from the window led us to focus on Exmoor and finally to buy Manor House in Wootton Courtenay. Manor House is a grand but misleading name for a simple house built of stone and cob (mud and straw) some 350 to 400 years ago, with three rooms below, three rooms above and an old hayloft and stable at the back. At one corner the cob wall has been worn away and rounded off by centuries of horses and carts coming and going in the yard. It is not listed as a building of architectural or historic interest, but it retains the original stud-and-panel oak partitions downstairs. It has a south-sloping garden with wonderful views over the Avill Valley, the Brendon Hills and the heather-clad slopes of Dunkery Beacon. It is above all a marvellously friendly, quirky building in which not a single surface is flat or a single space exactly rectangular. It is full of surprises and a delight for children, and makes us conscious when living there of our affinity with the people who went before us.

By this time we had been enjoying the countryside of England, Scotland and Wales for over a quarter of a century, but we had been passive observers. Much as I loved gardens and the countryside I had inherited or acquired none of my mother's, my grandfather's or Barbara's interest in botany, natural history or even gardening. Despite two years of zoology and botany at Aberdeen I have the utmost difficulty in remembering the names of flowers, shrubs and even trees, and have to be reminded of their names when they surprise me by their reappearance every year. I failed to observe most of the damage that was being done by new farming technologies in those years. We felt no urge to join any of the amenity or conservation bodies, or to take any part in countryside politics. It took us a couple of years after we had bought Manor House even to make contact with The Exmoor Society, the local conservationist group that had been formed in 1959 in a successful attempt to stop the afforestation of Exmoor's remotest moorland, The Chains, by the Fortescue Estate.

Our priority from the start was essentially selfish – to get to know Exmoor, to relax there and to enjoy it. For the next few years we explored the moor on foot and on horseback in every weather, a trip to Ireland having convinced us that despite having only two good legs between us we were neither too old nor too disabled to take up riding again. Riding opened up an entirely new world by extending our range far beyond the eight miles or so that was our walking limit. By the time I was appointed to the Exmoor National Park Committee in August 1973 I knew Exmoor very much better than some of the county or district councillors on the committee. Few of the local farmers walk, and many of them I found to be very ignorant of the countryside beyond the range of their regular movements, unless they hunted.

When we joined the Exmoor Society in 1971 and went for the first time to its annual general meeting at Porlock we had no serious intention of becoming involved in national park issues. But we rapidly became very close friends of Tim Burton, the outgoing Chairman of the Exmoor Society, and his partner Anne, in whom we found fellow spirits. Tim was in love with Exmoor, but saddened by the pace of its degradation by moorland 'reclamation' and afforestation and the exodus of the small farmers and farm workers. To Tim, as a socialist, Exmoor meant the people as much as the landscape, which he saw as the product of interaction between the land and the people who worked it. He was already the author of *Exmoor* which is still the best book on the subject and he had served on the first, ineffective, national park committees. He was an invaluable guide to the weaknesses of the national park system and the job of the independent conservation movement, and it was a sad loss both for us and for Exmoor when Tim and Anne returned some years ago to his native Staffordshire.

National Park Politics

Christopher Hall got me involved politically in national parks at the national level. I had got to know him as a neighbour in

Hampstead when I was Chairman of the South End Green Association and he was running a successful campaign to save the North London Railway from closure by British Rail. Chris was a socialist and an articulate campaigner and a journalist who laced his most aggressive passages with such biting wit that even his victims had to laugh. He had left the Labour *Daily Herald* to become Barbara Castle's press officer at the Ministry of Transport in 1964. By 1971 he had become Secretary of the Ramblers' Association, and soon afterwards he became the Director of the Council for the Protection of Rural England (CPRE) – a staid, very middle-class and in places conservative body strongly based in the shires and suburbia – which he jolted into a more vigorous life and a broader vision. Chris and the CPRE were uneasy bedfellows and he made a timely move to the editorial chair of *The Countryman* when his aggressive radicalism had probably become too much for the CPRE.

Chris was the moving spirit behind the campaign by the Standing Committee for National Parks (at that time a satellite of the CPRE and today the Council for National Parks) to strengthen the national park provisions of the Tory government's 1972 Local Government Bill. The national park system established by the Labour government in 1949 was almost farcical, except in the Peak District and to some extent in the Lake District, where the parks were run by semi-autonomous planning boards. Elsewhere they were run by county council committees and, in parks located in more than one county, by a multiplicity of committees – three in Exmoor and five in Snowdonia – which had no staff of their own, little money and few powers.

The Bill incorporated a compromise reform agreed by the Association of County Councils (which wanted to keep the status quo) and the Countryside Commission (which wanted every park to be run by a board on the Peak District model). Each park was to be run by a single authority (a planning board in the Lake District and Peak District and a county council committee elsewhere); each authority had to appoint a national park officer and to prepare a management plan for the whole park, and the government promised to pay 'the lion's share' (which turned out to be 75 per cent) of the park authorities' costs. However, as events subsequently proved and our books on national parks demonstrated, the national park lobby was right to argue that county council committees would still lack the independence, the powers and the resources they needed.

My modest contribution to the campaign was to speak at a few meetings, but that was enough to give Chris the idea that I might be the articulate and determined person that the Ramblers' Association was looking for, to propose as a government appointee to the new Exmoor National Park Committee of Somerset County Council. A majority of the 21 members would be Somerset and Devon county councillors, but a third of them would be appointed by the Secretary of State for the Environment to look after the 'national interest'. I did not rate my chances of being appointed by a Tory minister very high. My knowledge of Exmoor was limited and of the other national parks or the national park system even less. At 61 (in 1973) I was liable to be ruled out as too old. If I was known at all it was as an ex-communist and a socialist. I was undeniably the archetypical, middle-class, professional incomer and second-homer who had no roots in the community. Paradoxically, when the Exmoor crisis came to a head the strength of my position on the park committee lay in the fact that I did *not* have to worry, as other members did, about keeping their local supporters happy.

I felt that my chances of being appointed would be greatly increased if within the next year or 18 months I could establish myself as an 'authority' on national park issues. I could also see that I had no chance of achieving anything if I was appointed to the new authority, in which I would inevitably be in a minority, unless I could turn myself into its best-informed member and forge strong links with the national conservation movement and the media at local and national levels. The government's appointment in July 1971 of the National Park Policies Review Committee, chaired by the Reverend Lord Sandford, the undersecretary responsible for countryside matters at the Department of the Environment, had opened up an opportunity for articles and radio programmes on national parks. The Sandford committee was touring the parks in 1971 and 1972, and stimulating the demand for more radical reforms.

Man, God and Snowdonia

The range of my contributions to Leonie Cohn's Radio 3 series 'This Island Now' was extending beyond architecture, planning and resource conservation to embrace countryside matters. When I took up my Leverhulme Fellowship in 1972 I used my free time to research and to write articles and radio programmes not only on nuclear power and North Sea oil but also on national parks, farming and other countryside issues. The piece that hit the bull's eye was a radio programme on copper mining in Snowdonia, which *The Listener* published in October 1972 as its front page article under the title 'Man, God and Snowdonia'. The broadcast and the article delighted most conservationists and the national parks lobby, but outraged those at whom it was aimed. For weeks after the broadcast the air was buzzing with threats of writs and demands for apologies from distinguished people in the conservation world. They had made a foolish error, in most conservationists' eyes, by accepting membership of the Commission on Mining and the Environment set up by the multinational, mining company Rio Tinto Zinc (RTZ). Having been caught red-handed by Friends of the Earth, drilling secretly for copper in Snowdonia without planning permission, RTZ had set up and paid for this 'independent' commission with ambiguous terms of reference.

Land Use Consultants, the consultancy set up by the distinguished naturalist Max Nicholson when he retired from directing the Nature Conservancy Council, was paid by the RTZ-funded commission to design new landscapes to replace those that would be removed by copper mining. These designs figured prominently in the report of the commission, of which Max himself was a member. Another member of the commission, the chemical engineer Sir Frederick Warner, had also worked for RTZ in the past. I did not question the motives of the members of the commission but they did not seem to understand that their business relations with RTZ could not fail to aggravate the misgivings of people who distrusted RTZ's intentions in financing the commission's work. The commission's report was published by RTZ in what seemed to many conservationists a transparent attempt to burnish its tarnished image and, if possible, to obtain the green light to mine in national parks.

The chairman, Lord Zuckerman, subsequently won my respect by his forthright exposure, with all the authority of a former Chief Scientific Adviser to the government, of the folly of the nuclear arms race. But I regarded his performance as

Chairman of the Commission on Mining and the Environment as a disservice to the national parks, and I was astonished, when I interviewed him, by his naiveté, for he observed, with more innocence than I could have believed possible from an old Whitehall mandarin, that he could see no difference between a mining company looking for ore and a naturalist looking for birds – although birds, as I remarked, are not exploited like minerals to make profits by devastating the landscape.

The Charmed Circle

It was one thing for my name to be put forward by the Ramblers' Association and quite another for the Countryside Commission and the government to admit me to the charmed circle of the Great and the Good who are fit to serve as government appointees on quangos (quasi-autonomous non-governmental organisations). However, the Chairman of the Countryside Commission, Sir John Cripps (the son of Sir Stafford Cripps the one time Popular Fronter and Labour Chancellor), had been appointed by the Labour government and was an extraordinarily conscientious man. He interviewed me and everybody else whose name had come up through the Countryside Commission's grapevine as a possible candidate for appointment to any of the new national park authorities. I got the impression from my interview that I would get his backing.

I also got to know the Tory minister responsible for national parks, Lord Sandford, by reporting the national park conference in Dartmoor in the spring of 1973 for *The Times*. *The Times* had never bothered to report national park conferences but it accepted my offer to do the job as a freelance. I covered three conferences for *The Times* and wrote a couple of articles for it, and thereby acquired a somewhat spurious status which proved to be highly advantageous to me. My metamorphosis from a *Daily Worker* man to a *Times* man surprised many of those who had known me in my previous incarnations.

I soon found that I was in friendly company in the national park world. Reg Hookway, the Director of the Countryside Commission, was the architect of the reform of national parks that had been put through by Peter Walker in 1972, but he was also a lifelong middle-of-the-road socialist. John Sandford turned out to be an unusual type of upper-class Church of

England clergyman whose main political interest was in local government. As the under-secretary he was drawing up the lists of government nominees to the new national park authorities that had to be appointed by the summer of 1973. I had by then declared my Exmoor hand in an article in *Country Life* (whose editor, Michael Wright, had been my assistant editor on the *RIBA Journal*) on 'Ploughing up the National Parks: the threat to Exmoor'. My line was anathema to the farming lobby but it could not have put Lord Sandford off. He was moved to another job a few weeks before my appointment was formally notified to me in August 1973 by his successor, Lady Young, but I have never doubted that he was responsible for my appointment by a government to which I was strongly opposed. It was my good fortune that a 'wet' (in Thatcherite terms) was responsible for national parks at that time, and it did not surprise me that John Sandford was thought to be too 'wet' to get another job in government after Mrs Thatcher's victory in 1979.

21

Meeting the Exmoor 'Mafia'

I had no idea what I was in for when the new Exmoor National Park Committee of Somerset County Council met for the first time in November 1973. I only knew one of the 21 members, Douglas Juckes, who was at that time the Head of the Dulverton Middle School and Chairman of the Exmoor Society. Ten of the other 19 were landowners (including farmers who owned their land) and another two were personally or professionally associated with the landowning interest. Of the seven members appointed by the Secretary of State for the Environment to look after the national interest in conservation and recreation three were farmers and landowners. Two of them, Ben Halliday and Squadron Leader Whinney, were active members of the Country Landowners' Association (CLA), while the third, John Edwards, represented Exmoor hill farmers at the conference of the National Farmers' Union (NFU).

The committee's first decision was to appoint a subcommittee of seven members, who had been hand-picked in advance, to interview candidates for the key post of National Park Officer. It consisted of six landowners and Douglas Juckes, whom the majority regarded (rightly as it turned out) as a pliable conservationist. This proved to be the normal pattern. Every subcommittee, panel or working group that affected the landowning-farming interest was dominated by an overwhelming majority of farmers and landowners.

The subcommittee recommended the appointment of R. Dare Wilson, a retired Major-General. Wilson must have thought he was going to be very much at home with his new command in Exmoor. So many of the members were retired officers that a report in the *West Somerset Free Press* compared the committee to a meeting of the United Services Club. 'The General', as he was called, was not only a crack tobogganist and parachutist but a member of the pheasant-shooting circuit, with a farm on the outskirts of Exmoor as well, but as a local government officer he was a fish out of water.

The dominant figure in the Tory caucus was Mrs Phillips, the Tory leader on Somerset County Council. She was a powerful politician and she played an increasingly prominent role as the crisis developed. She would sign her letters to me in the friendliest way as 'Penny', while urging the Secretary of State for the Environment to kick me off the committee. The chairman had to be elected from the eight Somerset county councillors, seven of whom were Tories. The ministerial appointees and the Devon county and district councillors were ineligible for the chair, so that in this and in other ways they were second- or third-class members.

I liked our first chairman, George Wyndham, a former Chairman of Somerset County Council and a landowner and aristocrat of the old paternalistic school, with whom one could have a friendly and rational discussion. He listened carefully when I put ideas to him, and even welcomed me as 'the conscience of the national parks' in a speech to a national park conference. Unfortunately within weeks of his election he resigned the chair on the grounds of ill health, and the Tory caucus sprang on us their decision to replace him by Major Thomas Trollope-Bellew, popularly known as 'Hullaballoo'. He was a big hereditary landowner but he lacked Wyndham's good sense, tact and political skill. He seemed to have too many other commitments to give the national park the time it needed, and he let his vice-chairman Ben Halliday (another landowner) do most of the work in an intimate association with General Wilson. The fourth member of the quadumvirate that steered the park committee into a headlong collision with the Countryside Commission and the government was another government appointee, Squadron Leader Whinney, a retired diplomat and gentleman farmer who later succeeded Halliday as vice-chairman.

The 'Mafia' – and the 'Communist' Outsider

When Guy Somerset, who succeeded Juckes as Chairman of the Exmoor Society, publicly called the ruling group 'the Somerset Mafia' he was, of course, exaggerating. He saw the Somerset

County Council 'Mafia' not as a criminal outfit but as a group of people whose overriding loyalties (as in real Mafias) seemed to be to one another, and whose overriding purpose seemed to be to maintain their power – in their case the right of landowners to do as they pleased with their own land, even in a national park. However, if I saw the Tory landowning 'Mafia' as the real problem, they saw me – as they often told me – as a 'bloody nuisance', 'a stirrer-upper', an 'alien', an 'outsider', a 'foreigner', a 'fanatic', a 'communist' and the cause of all the trouble. The language betrayed both their sense of outrage at the intervention of an 'outsider' in their cosy party and an accurate perception that I had nothing to fear from them precisely because I had no roots in the local community. Douglas Juckes, on the other hand, told me that as a local head teacher he felt obliged, if forced to choose, to side with the farmers and landowners, for Matthew Waley-Cohen, the Chairman of Juckes's School Management Committee, was also a member of one of Exmoor's best-known landowning families and one of the most belligerent enemies of the conservationists on the park committee.

Within five weeks of the new committee's first meeting Ben Halliday came to tea at my invitation and gave me, to quote his words, a friendly but blunt warning not to spoil good ideas, either by going too fast or by putting them forward myself. The next day Squadron Leader Whinney told me, when I went to see him at his farm, that he was being rung up by people asking 'Do you know we've got a communist on the national park committee?' I got the message that my ideas were unlikely to be popular, but I did not realise how obsessed Whinney and his friends were about the 'Red menace'. Three years later he told the Porchester inquiry, in all seriousness and in writing, that Exmoor was threatened 'by the Marxist wing of the Labour Party working through the Council for the Protection of Rural England'. This greatly amused Lord Henley, the Liberal peer who chaired the Council for the Protection of Rural England (CPRE), and I told the park committee that if I was going to raise the red flag of revolution I would not start from Dunkery Beacon.

Matthew Waley-Cohen was by far the noisiest, most disruptive and eccentric member of the park committee. His brother, Sir Bernard Waley-Cohen, was a powerful figure in the City (having been Lord Mayor of London) as well as a big landowner and keen stag-hunter in Exmoor. Matthew, who died in 1989, called himself a 'retired farmer', although I doubt if many farmers would have recognised the description. He had a business career with Shell and represented the Exmoor heartland on Somerset County Council. Although he instinctively took the landowners' side he was an effective local member and obstinately refused to toe the official Tory line unless it suited him.

Matthew's main characteristic was an ungovernable temper. He would try to get his way by shouting down any opposition (including the committee chairman) in a voice like thunder, bawling 'utter rubbish' and other equally abusive phrases which the *West Somerset Free Press* called 'characteristically incendiary language'. Officials, who would not dare to answer back, got the same treatment as members. Trollope-Bellew, to whom I formally complained after some three years of the treatment, made not the slightest attempt to control him, although Matthew was constantly in breach of the standing orders on procedure. I made a list of the words that would trigger a Waley-Cohen explosion, among them 'planners', 'architects', 'the Exmoor Society', 'officials', 'the Standing Committee for National Parks', 'the Council for the Protection of Rural England', even 'the National Farmers' Union' and, before long, 'Malcolm MacEwen'. Matthew had no time for what he called 'do-gooders' or conservationists or outsiders – although the Waley-Cohens were themselves outsiders who had bought their way into Exmoor, and he was a firm believer in the 'Red menace', even detecting the 'odious Marxist philosophy' in a mild sentence in the draft National Park Plan that seemed to him to denigrate the profit motive.

Why So Much Fuss About Moorland?

The personalities are central to an understanding of the Exmoor set-up, but they make no sense without some understanding of what the rows were all about – the future of the moorland. It had been government policy since the war to subsidise hill farmers to carry many more sheep or cattle by paying half or more of the cost of converting open moorland to enclosed farmland, plus a subsidy on every sheep or cow. Coniferous plantations were also heavily subsidised through grants and tax concessions. Farmers and conservationists had been on a collision course in Exmoor since the early 1960s, for Exmoor with its mild climate, low altitude and better soils was the most favoured of what were called the agriculturally 'Less Favoured Areas', and farmers took advantage of the government's subsidies to plough up more and more moorland. It is also one of only two extensive areas of open, more or less wild, moorland in Southern England, Dartmoor being the other. Its 40,000 acres of moorland are a rare and precious resource for their beauty, their wildlife and the freedom that open country alone can provide. It was the moorland above all that justified Exmoor's national park designation in 1954.

Intensified exploitation of the land reduces the area of wild, open country and impedes access to what remains. It replaces heather and native vegetation or ancient broadleaved woodlands with enclosed fields or coniferous plantations. It also undermines the social structure of the upland communities by concentrating hill farming into an ever-shrinking number of larger farms, employing fewer and fewer people. In the 20 years between 1952 and 1972 the farm workforce in Exmoor had fallen by more than half, and the extra beef or lamb produced in this way is only profitable because it is so highly subsidised.

The Exmoor Society's success in stopping the afforestation of The Chains in 1959 was followed by a wave of moorland reclamation in the 1960s, subsidised by the Ministry of Agriculture. The landlords and farmers denied that reclamation was taking place on any appreciable scale; alternatively they argued that the ploughing did not threaten the integrity of the moorland, but in 1966 the Exmoor Society published 'Can Exmoor Survive?', an authoritative survey by Geoffrey Sinclair which proved that Exmoor's already fragmented and fragile moorland was disappearing at the rate of 700 acres (300 hectares) a year, and that nearly a sixth of it had been converted to farmland or afforested since the national park had been designated to protect it in 1954.

The response of the Country Landowners' Association and the National Farmers' Union was to assert that agriculture must be accorded 'first place in the order of priorities'. It was, they said, 'the right and duty' of farmers 'to expand their enterprises and to improve their productive capacity to the maximum', albeit at the taxpayers' expense. In 1969 they negotiated what they called 'a gentleman's agreement' by which farmers voluntarily notified the national park committee of any proposals to reclaim moorland that was 'critical to amenity'. Yet by the time the new national park committee took over in 1974 not one agreement to conserve the moorland had been negotiated with the farmers.

From 1973 a slump in farming led to a lull in reclamation, and no proposals to reclaim moorland were notified to the new park committee in its first year. The overriding need was obviously to clarify the committee's policy, and to persuade government to give it the powers and the money it needed to conserve the moorland, so we would be able to deal with the next wave of reclamation when it came. The committee decided at my suggestion to appoint Geoffrey Sinclair, the Exmoor Society's moorland management adviser, as a consultant and to set up a working group to revise the map of moorland that was 'critical to amenity', but General Wilson neither informed Geoffrey of his appointment nor answered letters from him seeking some elucidation. He never convened the working group, and after a year the committee accepted Wilson's recommendation to disband it. When the lull broke in 1976 the park committee had neither a revised map nor a policy for moorland conservation.

From 'Dear Malcolm' to 'Dear Mr MacEwen'

Farming policy was so obviously the key both to the conservation of the Exmoor landscape and the survival of the farming community that I had to learn as much as I could as quickly as possible about farming and its place in ecological and social systems. In 1974 the Countryside Commission published a report on *New Agricultural Landscapes*, which suggested that modern farming could create new landscapes as good as those they replaced. This gave Leonie Cohn and me the idea for some Radio 3 programmes that challenged this proposition by asking the question 'Is modern farming out of control?'. To find answers to this question I had to get to know farmers and experts in land management in many parts of the country. Several of them also contributed to 'Future Landscapes', a symposium which I compiled and edited for the CPRE's jubilee in 1976, and took part in another series of radio programmes on the national parks which went out that summer. In this way I became familiar with all the national parks.

At the outset both the Exmoor Society and I tried to establish good personal relationships with Ben Halliday and General Wilson. In 1975 Geoffrey Sinclair took members of the society and Halliday on an instructive trip round the critical parts of the moorland, as a result of which I drafted two papers on short-term and long-term moorland policy which I submitted to General Wilson. The General, however, did not submit them to the committee.

Wilson obviously found me as difficult as I found him, but he was not loved even by the landowners who had appointed him. They sabotaged his very sensible proposal to prepare a map of landownership that would have violated the secrecy to which landowners are obsessively attached. His clumsiness in personal relations was very well illustrated by the row in the spring of 1975 that terminated what I might call our 'honeymoon'. I had taken up with his information officer the grievance of a member of his staff whose pay had been severely cut as a result of the reorganisation of 1974. The General rebuked me for talking to his subordinate, and the committee, acting on his advice, ticked me off for concerning myself with 'staff matters'. I told the story to Chris Hall, the Director of the CPRE, who told it to *The Guardian*. They rang up the General who had to run around in circles to keep the story out of the press. The threat of publicity won for the officer the money that private representations had failed to secure, and he thanked me warmly for my help. However, Wilson signalled the end of our intimacy by reducing me to the ranks: 'Dear Mr MacEwen' replaced 'Dear Malcolm' in his letters.

I greatly irritated the General by repeatedly writing letters seeking what I regarded as essential information. He responded by seeking 'guidance' from the county council solicitor on whether he was 'obliged to serve individual members'. Not only did he try to block my access to information but he ordered his staff not to speak on their own subjects to committee members. One of his senior officers, who rang me up at the height of the moorland crisis in 1977 to congratulate me on the stand I was taking, said 'I can feel the Elastoplast over my mouth.' By failing to delegate and by insisting that members must never take up issues directly with any officers on his staff, the General turned himself into a one-man bottleneck.

My row with the General kept breaking out over specific issues because beneath these disagreements there lay a profound difference of opinion about the way in which democratic local government should operate. Halliday shared Wilson's objection to what they both called my 'interference in detail' with the park's administration. In Halliday's view, as he told me, it would be 'disastrous if we, the members, were to get onto the field ourselves and play the game ... The only way to get things done is to appoint the right man as National Park Officer and work through him.' I too wanted to work through 'the right man' (or woman) but we had appointed the wrong one. I also believed that, in a democracy, members (and the public for that matter) had an unqualified right to information to enable them to make the right policy decisions and monitor their implementation.

Secrecy ...

So much combustible material had collected by the summer of 1976 that it was only a question of time before somebody ignited the inevitable explosion. When it happened I was taken by surprise. In January and again in March 1976, when it was clear that the lull in moorland reclamation was already coming to an end, I wrote to Wilson expressing my frustration at the failure of the committee to have had a single well-prepared discussion of moorland policy in the first two years of its existence. His immediate response was to advise the park committee that papers from the Exmoor Society should not be circulated to members, advice which the committee accepted, but eventually the General agreed to place a summary of the Exmoor Society's policy papers on the agenda of the National Park Plan Steering Group on 17 March 1976. As I expected, both the General and Halliday weighed in strongly to secure the defeat of my arguments for a firm moorland conservation policy. Wilson then submitted his draft 'National Park Plan', which contained none of the key policy commitments urged by the Exmoor Society, to the park committee. When the committee met on 23 June to discuss the plan in a secret session it rejected my motion to discuss it in public by eleven votes to three, and the plan was then steam-rollered through.

The Tory Mafia's obsessive secrecy was contrary to both the spirit and the letter of the law. The Public Admission to Meetings Act of 1960 had opened all county council committee meetings to the public unless to do so would be 'prejudicial to the public interest', yet all proposals by farmers to plough up moorland were automatically taken in secret. After the committee had rejected my motion to discuss the plan in public, Major Trollope-Bellew ordered the press and the public to leave. Guy Somerset, the Chairman of the Exmoor Society, rose from the public bench to protest that the decision was illegal, and to ask that the chairman should give the reason for closing the meeting, as the law required. Trollope-Bellew's response was to order Guy from the room and to despatch General Wilson to fetch the police. This comedy-drama was quite unnecessary as Guy had no intention of defying the chair once he had made his protest, but his intervention proved to be a master-stroke because it led Trollope-Bellew and his friends to make the first of what proved to be a series of monumental blunders. The splash headlines on the front page of that week's *West Somerset Free Press* were predictable:

General Steps Out to Call Police
Press Gag Foray Shocks National Park Meeting

Chris Hall issued what the local press called 'a stinging attack' on the committee's habit of secrecy in the first of a number of initiatives by the CPRE that pushed the issue into the national press. From that moment onward the press found endless copy in the unfolding of the Exmoor saga.

... and Suppression

In July 1976 I discovered by chance that when General Wilson had spoken so strongly at the plan steering group in March against including a firm moorland conservation policy in the national park plan a consultant's report calling for precisely such a policy had been lying on his desk for a week. On Wilson's advice the committee had decided in December 1975 to seek advice on heather management from John Phillips, a Scottish expert, but his advice, when it arrived at the beginning of March 1976, was most unwelcome to Wilson and Halliday, for the report concluded that unless the committee spent 'every penny' it could on a firm conservation policy 'Exmoor as it is today will go on being eroded until one day people will wake up to the fact that it has disappeared except as a name on the map'. When asked to explain why this report had been withheld from members throughout the discussion of the draft 'National Park Plan' the General wrote to me explaining that he had done so because it might 'unduly influence members'! I took the opposite view, that members had a right to decide for themselves whether to accept the advice of expert consultants. I revealed the report's conclusions and the fact of its suppression to the Exmoor Society and to the press, which burst into flames once more. I put down a motion mildly censuring the General, and requiring consultants' reports to be made available to members in future.

The committee heard me in a chilly silence and I was accused of the cardinal sin of 'leaking' a 'confidential' document. My motion would have been rejected almost unanimously had it not been for a statement by the chief executive of the county council, John Whittaker, who had clearly had enough of the goings-on in the Exmoor National Park Committee. He told the committee that in his opinion, and with the benefit of hindsight, the report should not have been withheld from members. I withdrew my motion and the minutes record the committee's view that in future consultants' reports should be made available to members as soon as possible. In fact no decision was taken, and nobody except Whittaker and I had expressed such an opinion, but it's what the minute says, not what the committee decides, that matters, and Whittaker had the crucial power to dictate the minute.

I did not know that arrangements had already been made for me to be tried in secret by the committee in what I called a 'Kangaroo Court'. No sooner had my motion been withdrawn than the committee went into secret session to discuss some allegedly 'confidential' business. Once this was out of the way Halliday launched a vehement attack on me for 'leaking' the Phillips report and other 'confidential' information to the press. He demanded an assurance (which I refused to give) that I would abide by a standing order which placed a cloak of secrecy round virtually all committee proceedings and papers. I

was so taken aback that it was not until I got home that I realised how grossly this ambush broke both the law on the secrecy
of meetings and the convention by which notice must be given
of any personal attack on the conduct of a member. When I
studied the standing order I discovered that Somerset County
Council had never revised it to take account of the law passed
16 years earlier opening local authority committee meetings to
the public. There were red faces all round when the county
solicitor had to redraft the standing order to conform to the
law and reported, to the visible chagrin of the 'Mafia', that
there was no way in which I could be disciplined.

Halliday's initial assault was only the start of a concerted
attempt to force my resignation or, if this failed, to put pressure
on Peter Shore, the Secretary of State for the Environment in
the Labour government, to sack me. Halliday and Whinney
wrote to him threatening to resign and 'Penny' Phillips wrote
to Shore (copy to me) to tell him how much bitterness my
'leaks' were causing, and how much she would miss Halliday
and Whinney. However, it was Halliday who resigned in
December in protest against what he called 'the innuendoes,
unauthorised releases of information and unnecessary contro-
versy' emanating from one (unnamed) member that were
'making life impossible for the committee and the staff'.

The suppression of the report and the 'Kangaroo Court'
became a public scandal. The government, having recently
reappointed me, had no wish to sack me, and no power to do
so for another two and a half years. Dennis Howell, a professional football referee who was responsible for national parks as
the Minister of State for Sport and the Countryside, told Anni
and me afterwards that the demands for my removal convinced
him that I must be a good man to have on the committee. One
of the last things he did before the Labour government fell in
1979 was to reappoint me despite renewed demands from Tory
members for my removal. I was relieved that I had survived the
ambush, but the 'Mafia' had by no means shot its bolt.

22

'Who Is This Scottish Popinjay?'

The focus of the conflict shifted dramatically in the autumn of 1976 when a three-year lull in moorland reclamation was broken by the biggest wave of reclamation proposals that the Exmoor National Park had ever seen. Ironically it was initiated in August 1976 by the park authority's vice-chairman, Ben Halliday, who notified his intention to plough up most of the 350 acres of heather moor on his Glenthorne Estate. Initially I had some sympathy with Halliday, for he personified the dilemma facing Exmoor farmers who were simultaneously asked to conserve their moorland and woodland and offered enormous subsidies to plough up the moor or to plant conifers. His estate, which straddles the Devon–Somerset border on the north shore of the Bristol Channel, is spectacularly beautiful. His moors were among the most precious remnants of the coastal heaths sweeping down to the sea that are one of the glories of Exmoor. But Glenthorne is difficult and costly to manage, and it seemed to me that it should have been acquired by the National Trust (which had already acquired other parts of the estate) and managed for the primary purposes of nature and landscape conservation and public enjoyment.

Halliday was opposed in principle to a rigorous policy of moorland conservation, being 'loath to sterilize good land for seasonal amenity' and argued that his farm must convert moorland to level pasture if it was to survive. He told me recently that he was fighting for the survival of the Exmoor farmer, whose future is indeed menaced. Halliday had a genuinely innovative idea (even a 'green' one), that the park committee should enter into a 'management agreement' that would make conservation an integral part of estate policy, and provide national park money for conservation, rhododendron clearance and footpath improvements. However, this idea was vitiated by

263

his overriding priority to make his estate 'cost-effective' by converting moorland to enclosed farmland. I told the park committee that if it agreed to the conversion of moorland on the coastal ridge it would be stripped of whatever reputation it had.

Almost at the same time, in the summer of 1976, 375 acres of moorland at Stowey Allotment came on the market. It adjoins Glenthorne and links the coastal heaths to the heart of the open moor. The committee realised that if Stowey Allotment was sold to the highest bidder at a price reflecting its suitability for conversion to farmland the purchaser would plough it up and thereby set a precedent for the loss of the remaining privately-owned moorland in Exmoor. The committee decided unanimously to bid for it, but the County Valuer put an unrealistically low limit of £26,000 on its bid. The land was knocked down to Halliday's neighbour Brian Woollacott for £34,000 and, in accordance with the 'gentleman's agreement' between the National Farmers' Union and the park committee, his agent gave the committee six months' written notice on 13 September of his intention to plough up Stowey Allotment.

The committee had until 13 March 1977 to negotiate an agreement but it took General Wilson seven weeks to inform the committee of Woollacott's intentions and three months before he put Stowey Allotment on the park committee's agenda for 13 December. It was then referred to a working party (of which I was not a member) that was already considering Glenthorne. When this became public knowledge Chris Hall organised a press conference on 26 January 1977 at which the CPRE and the Exmoor Society, supported by the Ramblers' Association, the Youth Hostels Association and the Commons, Open Spaces and Footpaths Society launched a national campaign to stop the Ministry of Agriculture's ploughing grants and to save the moorlands of all the national parks. Geoffrey Sinclair, Guy Somerset and I made it clear at the press conference that nothing less than the future of the Exmoor National Park was at stake. The CPRE's President, Lord Henley, condemned the pending reclamations on Exmoor as 'the biggest carve up since Carver Doone' and the national press took up the issue, its appetite having been whetted by earlier scandals.

Howell Blows the Whistle: Cripps is Gagged

On the day of the press conference Dennis Howell, the Minister of State, blew the whistle. He issued a statement expressing the government's concern, spelling out the significance of moorland reclamation for the national park and drawing attention to the implications for the Countryside Commission, which had refused to intervene. Despite Howell's statement the park committee made no serious effort to save either the Glenthorne or Stowey Allotment moorlands.

The first serious meeting of the Glenthorne/Stowey Allotment working party on the morning of 4 March was farcical. The only paper before the working party was a sheet written by Whinney, its chairman, giving nine reasons why Stowey Allotment should be ploughed up and none why it should not. This was too much even for the working party (all but one of them landowners) and it was unable to agree on any recommendations. When the full committee met that afternoon it had no papers whatever – no factual information, no assessment of the implications for wildlife, landscape or farming and no recommendations, five and a half months after the proposal to plough Stowey Allotment had been notified. That was not all. The committee was not even told that Sir John Cripps had written on 18 February asking that decisions be deferred until there had been a joint site inspection with members of the Countryside Commission. In ignorance of Cripps's request the committee voted by a majority (against my opposition) to agree in principle to some moorland reclamation as part of the Glenthorne deal. The committee then went into secret session (despite my usual protest) and decided (despite an undertaking by the chairman that no decisions in principle would be made) by a large majority to raise no objections to the ploughing of one-third of Stowey Allotment if Woollacott would sell the remainder to the national park and lease it back. Nothing came of this proposal because Woollacott, egged on by the National Farmers' Union, was demanding a sum in compensation which, the County Valuer advised the committee, was 'daylight robbery'.

The entire conservation movement was outraged by the park committee's suppression of Cripps's letter and by its decision to approve the destruction of Stowey Allotment without even giving the Countryside Commission a chance to offer some advice or financial help. Chris Hall issued a strongly-worded CPRE press statement giving my name to ring for further information, which seemed to act as the proverbial red rag to the Exmoor bulls. They proceeded to charge at Cripps and me with their heads down, their eyes shut and their minds closed.

When Cripps, Reg Hookway and members of the Countryside Commission visited Stowey Allotment and Glenthorne on 25 March for a 'joint site meeting' fewer than half the members of the park committee turned up, for General Wilson's notice told them there was no need to attend! Cripps asked the committee to defer any decision for a week so he could report to the Countryside Commission, but the committee voted by a large majority to raise no further objection to the reclamation of the whole of Stowey Allotment.

Another 'Kangaroo Court'

There was, however, another matter on the committee's agenda, to which it now proceeded – the CPRE press statement on the suppression of the Cripps letter. Once again I was given no notice of the real purpose of the meeting – a motion by Mrs Phillips to censure me for my 'journalistic activities' which were supposedly 'obstructing the activities of the national park'. When I asked her which of my articles or radio programmes she took exception to she was unable to name one. She had to withdraw her motion, and substituted a mild request that I would be 'supportive' of the national park in future. Trollope-Bellew, the supposedly impartial chairman, then read a carefully-prepared speech accusing me of being 'anti-farmer' – the code-word for anybody who criticised agricultural subsidies. Squadron Leader Whinney, the vice-chairman, called me 'a professional rabble-rouser' and asked rhetorically 'Who is this Scottish popinjay who comes in here and tells us what we can and cannot do?' before calling on me to 'cease my activities forthwith' or resign, but not a single member supported the three prosecutors, three spoke in my defence, and no vote was taken. The 'Mafia' was losing its grip.

When all this and much more was reported fully in the press Trollope-Bellew summoned Ian Cummins, the reporter who covered the national park for the *West Somerset Daily Press*, to

Exmoor House. Ian rang me up afterwards to tell me that he had been 'court-martialled', for he found himself confronted by Major Trollope-Bellew, Major-General Wilson and Squadron Leader Whinney, all of whom objected to being given what they called 'a bad press'. They took particular exception to the splash headline in the *Free Press*:

Member told 'resign or cease'
Popinjay jibe at Exmoor park discussions

Ian told the 'court martial' that what they were complaining about was accurate reporting, and suggested that if they wanted a 'good press' they should provide less sensational and more positive copy.

The 'Kangaroo Court' boomeranged (to mix some Australian metaphors), as might have been expected. The carpeting of Ian Cummins only strengthened the determination of the press to cover the Exmoor drama. *The Guardian* wrote a leading article, and Tim Burton taught the 'Mafia' the use of ridicule and wit by writing a letter to the *Free Press* in which he called on the park committee to carry out its statutory duty to protect that rare ornithological specimen the *Scottish Popinjay*, which had been spotted on Exmoor.

The Exmoor 'Watergate' Tapes

Although they had left the meeting on 25 March (as Hookway told me) 'hopping mad', Cripps and Hookway returned politely on 4 April with an offer by the Countryside Commission to pay half the cost of a management agreement for Stowey Allotment for one year on Woollacott's terms. This would have given all concerned time to find a solution, but my motion to accept the Commission's offer was defeated by eleven votes to six and the committee went on to decide by a large majority to adhere to its earlier decision to raise no objection to the ploughing of the whole of Stowey Allotment. Ploughing began a few days later, and, had this not forced the government to act, would have marked the beginning of the end of Exmoor as a national park.

The good thing to come out of the meeting was that Cripps and Hookway experienced for themselves what the Exmoor National Park Committee was really like. At the beginning of the meeting they had to sit through half an hour of wrangling while I tried to correct the inaccurate minutes of the previous meeting. Hookway told me later that this experience was an eye-opener. The incompetence and studied discourtesy of the park committee, together with a detailed dossier that I sent to Hookway, persuaded the Countryside Commission to report the committee's maladministration to the Secretary of State and led the government to set up the Porchester inquiry into Exmoor.

Minutes are unbelievably boring, and people who raise endless points about the accuracy of minutes can be an unmitigated nuisance, but it is not mere pedantry to ask for accurate minutes because the minutes of a local authority must be accepted without question in a court of law as a true record. The minute of the Kangaroo Court was almost pure fiction. If it was to be believed, I had remained dumb throughout and the committee had made a 'clear decision' that my press activities were destroying good relations with the 'farming and land-owning community'. When I discovered that General Wilson had taped the proceedings I asked for and was given a copy of the tape and a transcript. They proved that the minute had been cooked. Although the county council solicitor dismissed my complaint as 'verbiage' it took me only half an hour to agree an accurate minute with the minute clerk.

The committee, when confronted with the transcript of the tapes and the accurate minute, agreed unanimously to delete the fictitious decision about my journalistic activities, but my motion to insert the correct minute stuck in the gullets both of the 'Mafia' and of those who thought I was becoming a bloody nuisance. Four members voted for my motion and four against, while eleven looked fixedly at the floor or the ceiling and abstained. The motion was defeated by Trollope-Bellew's casting vote.

The Porchester Inquiry

By this time the Tory caucus was beginning to worry about the appalling publicity it was getting, both locally and nationally. Mrs Phillips led a deputation from the county council to Howell and asked the government to hold an inquiry, a suggestion that had been ignored when I had first made it six months earlier. The Department of the Environment and the Ministry of Agriculture, which had never collaborated on a conservation issue before, jointly asked Lord Porchester to undertake an inquiry into 'land use in Exmoor'. My first reaction was one of alarm. Why on earth had Howell invited a Tory landowner, the heir of the Earl of Carnarvon, a former Chairman of Hampshire County Council and the Queen's racing manager, to adjudicate on Exmoor? In fact the appointment of Porchester proved to be a stroke of genius, for he had no sympathy with the Somerset County Council dinosaurs, and his credentials made it impossible for the Tories to attack him. The inquiry was held in Taunton in June and July 1977.

The mere fact of having to give evidence and face up to cross-examination had a sobering effect on some of the combatants, notably the Country Landowners' Association and the National Farmers' Union. They played down their traditional rhetoric and emerged as believers in voluntary conservation, provided farmers were handsomely compensated for profits forgone. The Ministry of Agriculture, acutely embarrassed by the exposure of its policy of secrecy and non-co-operation with the park committee, produced statistical evidence that fully confirmed Geoffrey Sinclair's figures (long disputed by the CLA and NFU) on the rate of moorland loss.

The Nature Conservancy Council (NCC) appeared on the scene for the first time to demand the conservation of the entire moorland ecosystem. The Countryside Commission presented detailed arguments, which it should have produced years earlier, for the conservation of the Exmoor landscape. Geoffrey Sinclair took Porchester on a tour to show him all the more critical parts of the moor. The majority of the park committee presented a paper damning the Countryside Commission's recommendation that the Exmoor National Park Authority should have powers of compulsory land purchase, but the 'Mafia' was so demoralised that neither the park committee nor its national park officer presented written evidence on the main policy issues. I presented a case for the conservation of the moorland signed by five of the seven government appointees.

The Porchester report, which was published in November 1977, was a complete vindication of the position consistently taken by the Exmoor Society. It established the facts about reclamation and the threat it posed to the fragmented and highly vulnerable moorlands in the Exmoor National Park. Lord Porchester was forthright about the feebleness of the park committee, doubting whether it would use any powers to control moorland even if it had them. He pinned the main responsibility on the Ministry of Agriculture for its secrecy and its policy of subsidising the destruction of moorland. He sympathised with farmers who were paid by one government department to plough up the moorland and then blamed by another for doing so. He criticised the lack of any effective powers of control or compulsory purchase. He argued for a radical change in agricultural policy, and recommended that the park committee should be given the power to make Moorland Conservation Orders and to buy land compulsorily for conservation purposes at normal compensation rates.

The Porchester report proved to be a landmark in the history of nature and landscape conservation. It forced the Exmoor National Park Committee to execute a complete about-turn. When the park committee met in December 1977 it accepted the Porchester report, with a reservation on the terms of compensation, by 19 votes to none, although the committee revealed how much its decision went against the grain by approving the Glenthorne management agreement, under which Halliday ploughed up 100 acres of coastal heath that Porchester had included in the areas to be most rigorously protected. General Wilson resigned at the end of 1977 and was replaced by Dr Len Curtis, a Bristol University soil scientist with an international reputation, who knew Exmoor intimately and had long been a member of the Exmoor Society. The Tory caucus replaced Trollope-Bellew as chairman by Air Vice-Marshal Harold Leonard-Williams, the chairman of the county council. In the course of the next year the committee prepared maps defining the area (more than 80 per cent of the moorland) that would be protected under an unambiguous conservation policy, which it adopted unanimously.

Enter the Tory Government

The Labour government of 1974–9 had neither any understanding of conservation nor any real commitment to it. Dennis Howell's intervention, which was decisive, had been motivated primarily by the need to attract conservationist or Liberal votes at a time when Labour had a wafer-thin majority. His Wildlife and Countryside Bill, which would have given the park committee the power to make Moorland Conservation Orders (to which the Tory Party was opposed) fell along with the Labour government in May 1979, but there could be no going back to the pre-Porchester situation. The 90 per cent grant for moorland conservation in Exmoor which Labour introduced in 1978 survived. Even the Ministry of Agriculture began to change slowly, if reluctantly. Before Porchester it had never refused an agricultural grant on environmental grounds. After Porchester the Ministry lifted the veil of secrecy with which it had shrouded farmers' grant applications, and submitted agricultural evaluations to the park committee. From 1980 the ministry required farmers to clear their proposals for grant-aided operations with national park authorities and the Nature Conservancy Council. In 1985 it finally withdrew the grants for moorland reclamation.

The Tory government refused, however, to give the park committee the powers it needed. An amendment to its Wildlife and Countryside Bill, backed by the Exmoor National Park Committee, that would have given national park authorities power to control moorland reclamation, was defeated in the House of Lords by six votes. Michael Heseltine, the Secretary of State for the Environment, preferred to rely on voluntary agreements on terms that were attractive to farmers and landowners. In 1981 the Exmoor National Park Committee, the CLA and the NFU agreed guidelines for management agreements by which farmers who agreed not to convert moorland were compensated by annual payments for loss of grant and profit. These guidelines became the prototype for the government's guidelines on the management agreements that all national park authorities are required to offer to farmers under the Wildlife and Countryside Act of 1981.

This approach has worked for the time being in Exmoor, for reasons that are peculiar to Exmoor – notably the 90 per cent grant for moorland conservation that is available nowhere else, and the warnings given by Tory ministers that the voluntary system must be made to work in Exmoor if compulsion was to be avoided. Moorland reclamation in Exmoor virtually ceased after the Porchester report, but the 'pay-through-the-

nose' voluntary approach to conservation is entirely negative.
It can be a rip-off as it encourages bogus reclamation proposals
whose real purpose is to get the compensation. It does not
tackle the root causes of moorland destruction or degradation.
The absurdity by which one government department degrades
the natural environment (for example by subsidising farmers
to overgraze moorland) while another subsidises management
agreements to stop the degradation continues to this day.

National Parks: Conservation or Cosmetics?

The scandals that provoked the Porchester inquiry taught me a
lot about the realities of countryside conflicts. Although the
landlords and big farmers behaved as any Marxist textbook
would have predicted, I was surprised by the lengths to which
the coterie in power would go to protect what it conceived to
be its interests – illegal secret sessions, the suppression and
manipulation of information, 'cooked' minutes, arm-twisting
and attempts to have me sacked or to force me to resign. The
ruling clique, although playing Tory politics, claimed to be
'non-political', whereas those (like me) who took what would
now be called a 'green' line were alleged to be bringing 'politics'
into the national park. The conflict was, of course, highly political and released the long-suppressed political activist in me. It
also gave an ever-stronger 'green' tinge to my socialist beliefs.
Hard experience also taught me that, however good the 'green'
case, entrenched interests could only be defeated by keeping
cool whatever the provocation, making that case heard in the
media, winning allies, making some compromises where necessary and bringing political pressure to bear at every level of
government.

At the height of the Exmoor crisis in 1977 my sense of
outrage at the way the national park system was being abused
gave me the idea of writing a book on the subject. My first
thought was to write a lively polemic about Exmoor, but Anni
persuaded me that what was wanted was a serious study of the
national park system, that treated national parks as one
element in the arrangements for protecting landscape, wildlife
and natural resources. She suggested that we should write the
book on national parks together, combining my skill as a
writer, my firsthand experience of the system and my tendency

to jump impulsively to conclusions with her skill and experience as a planner, and her slower but more systematic and thorough method of analysing problems before forming opinions.

Anni resigned her job as a senior lecturer at the School for Advanced Urban Studies in Bristol University in the summer of 1977 and we set about raising the £15,000 we needed to meet the costs of a three-year (unpaid) study of national parks. The Nuffield Foundation put up the bulk of the money and we began work at the Bartlett School of Architecture at University College London (UCL) at the end of 1977. We delivered the text of our first book, *National Parks: Conservation or Cosmetics?* on the day that I retired (at my own request, on the ground that I was in my seventieth year) from the Exmoor National Park Committee on 31 March 1981. It was a much better book than I could have written by myself. It also proves that oil and water *do* sometimes mix, and that hares and tortoises, if harnessed together, can form a creative team.

23

Conservation or Cosmetics?

The ploughing up of Exmoor is a petty and parochial issue compared to the dangers that threaten the very basis of life on earth – the thinning of the ozone layer, the warming of the earth's surface through the burning of fossil fuels, acid rain, the destruction of the tropical forests, soil erosion, pollution of air, soil and water, the gulfs between rich and poor and between the First and the Third Worlds, the devastation caused by civil nuclear disasters or 'conventional' war or the nuclear winter that could be caused by nuclear war. In our defence of Exmoor we could be accused of falling victims to the 'NIMBY' syndrome – 'Not In My Backyard' – but our interest in conservation was not parochial. The row over Exmoor led Anni and me into a new academic life that added new dimensions to our understanding of conservation.

I cannot imagine a better way of spending one's 'retirement' than as we did, working flat-out in a university as unpaid, honorary research fellows on utterly absorbing programmes. It proved to be a continuation of the process that began when I first questioned the insane waste and destruction caused by the private car in 'Motropolis' in 1959. I also discovered what Anni knew already: that our research involved an enormous amount of systematic desk work, reading an immense number of books and reports, mastering the complexity of local government finance, learning how *not* to misuse statistics and analysing responses to interviews and questionnaires. Tedious as much of this was the discovery of conservation in the fullest sense of the word was as exciting as discovering Marxism 30 years before.

University College London was at the centre of a conservationist spider's web, and in the forefront of conservationist thinking. People half our age or less blew the cobwebs out of our minds and opened them to new ideas. For our first book on national parks three young consultants – Carys Swanwick, Rachel Berger and Geoffrey Sinclair – supplied expertise that we lacked. We got to know the most beautiful parts of England and Wales in the company of farmers, landowners, national park officials, councillors, conservationists and many other kinds of people. We made many friends, and even those who disagreed with our approach were helpful. We visited national parks, nature parks and regional parks in France, Germany, Canada and the US and learned to see my old haunts in the Scottish Highlands in a new light. We took advantage of a trip to see Anni's daughter Janet in Western Australia to study the destruction of the state-owned forests whose superb Karri trees (which grow to nearly 300 feet) are being cut down to supply Japan (which protects its own forests) with cheap packaging.

The Meaning of Conservation

Our first book *National Parks: Conservation or Cosmetics?* became the standard work on the national park system of England and Wales, but it was also a reassessment of national policies for the conservation of the countryside and the social and economic life of rural areas. Any such assessment has to start from the fact that the UK is almost unique in splitting the conservation of 'nature' away from the conservation of 'landscape', with separate government agencies – the Nature Conservancy Council and the Countryside Commissions for England and Wales and for Scotland.* In the real world nature and landscape are inseparable, and we formed the view that the division sprang from the restrictive view of successive British governments that nature conservation is primarily concerned with the protection of rare species and special sites – such as National Nature Reserves or Sites of Special Scientific Interest – and not with the good health of the countryside or, to put it another way, with entire ecosystems or the national 'habitat' that human beings share with wildlife.

Another British peculiarity is the fact that the national parks of England and Wales do not conform to the definition

---

* In 1989 the government announced the merger of the two agencies in Scotland and Wales but kept them separate in England, thereby weakening nature conservation without securing the benefits of a unified agency on a UK-wide scale.

adopted by the International Union for the Conservation of Nature and Natural Resources (IUCN) in 1969. The internationally-recognized national parks are supposed to be relatively large areas whose ecosystems have not been materially altered by human exploitation and occupation, and which are owned or managed by the state for the overriding purposes of nature conservation. National parks in England and Wales are areas of great 'natural beauty' which *have* been 'materially altered by human exploitation and occupation' for thousands of years, and are currently changing faster than ever. They are farmed, afforested, criss-crossed by roads and power lines, worked for their water and minerals, studded by hamlets, villages and small towns and thronged at busy times with millions of tourists with their vehicles.

The unusual character of the English and Welsh national parks (the landowners, forestry interests and the pressure for development in the Highlands ensured that none were established in Scotland after 1945) actually enhances their international significance. For they are a pioneering attempt to protect nature and landscape in areas that are to a high degree exploited and 'man-managed' and are mainly in private ownership. To protect the nature and landscape of such areas is a far more difficult task than conserving nature in a state-owned 'wilderness' from which all human occupation or exploitation has been excluded or removed. It also avoids the mistake (or crime) committed in too many national parks (for example in the US and Brazil) of driving indigenous people out of their forest habitats or off their traditional pastures, hunting grounds or sacred sites. Management techniques for the conservation of wilderness have a limited application outside wilderness areas, but techniques that attempt to reconcile the conservation of natural resources with human occupation have lessons for land management throughout the inhabited world. Important as it is to save the remaining wilderness areas, the outcome of the struggle for human survival depends on curbing the abuse of natural resources in areas where life and development go on.

The system we examined was essentially cosmetic. Government policies were on a collision course both with the conservation of natural resources and with the social and economic well-being of the working population on the land. National park authorities rely primarily on goodwill laced with bribery to control farming, forestry and other activities that are incompatible with national park policies. Most of the hill farmers we interviewed or talked with had split personalities. They loved the countryside, but they saw their farms (in 1977–81) solely as food production enterprises. They prided themselves on their right to do as they pleased with their land but were hooked on the subsidies that pushed them – often against their own better judgment – to maximise production, to shed workers and to squeeze out the smaller farmers. We saw the immense potential in national parks for making the conservation of natural resources an integral part of every farm plan and of every land management decision, but the national parks could not achieve their potential unless the underlying economic and financial causes of the problems we had identified were diagnosed and treated.

Iniquitous – and Inequitable – Subsidies

National Parks: Conservation or Cosmetics? was much stronger in diagnosing the causes of the conflict between conservation and farming and forestry (the two main land uses in the countryside) than it was in suggesting alternatives. To make good this defect I initiated a research project with Geoffrey Sinclair at University College London into hill farming. Our report, *New Life for the Hills*, incorporated striking new evidence that Geoffrey had acquired (in the course of a study of the uplands for the Countryside Commission) on the iniquity and inequity of the Ministry of Agriculture's livestock headage subsidies. On average each of the 760 largest hill farmers in England and Wales was paid £13,000 in 1981–2 while each of the 15,300 smallest got £990. Most help went to those on the best land and the least to those on the worst. The system encouraged farmers to overstock their land and deprived them of the labour to maintain hedges, woodlands and natural features. Geoffrey and I proposed a scheme for recasting the livestock subsidies in two ways: to discriminate in favour of the smaller farmers on the worst land, and to encourage all farmers to optimise (not to maximise) food and timber production, to conserve nature, wildlife and landscape, to bring back wild country and native woodlands and to provide recreational opportunities – all of which would create jobs and keep more people on the land.

This report, when published by the Council for National Parks in 1983, aroused considerable interest but fell on deaf ears in government and in the landowning and farming lobbies. The iniquity and inequity of flat-rate or percentage subsidies remains unchanged today.

By 1985, however, the crisis in the European Economic Community (EEC) over food surpluses and the huge cost of farm subsidies led to the imposition of milk quotas. It was widely seen as the beginning of the end of highly-subsidised intensive farming and it produced some new thinking about conservation. The National Farmers' Union, whose president had recently denounced conservationists as 'braying do-gooders', suddenly discovered that 'organic' farming and conservation might yield farmers new incomes. By the time our second book on the national park system, *Greenprints for the Countryside?*, appeared in 1987 we had become more sympathetic to farmers, and more farmers and landowners had become interested in conservation – mainly as a potential source of income to replace lost production subsidies. In 1982 the NFU boycotted an Exmoor Society conference that discussed the new approach to hill farming that Geoffrey Sinclair and I were to advocate in *New Life for the Hills*. By 1987, however, farmers packed the hall at the society's conference on farming and conservation with speakers from as far afield as Brussels, and Ben Halliday and I found ourselves, if not in total agreement, more or less on the same side.

Greenprints for the Countryside?

The reasons why we called the national park system 'cosmetic' have not changed fundamentally, but by the mid-1980s new rules requiring farmers who want to claim farm improvement grants to consult the national park authorities, the switch of farm grants towards conservation, and small additions to national park budgets had created a healthier relationship between farmers and the national parks. More farmers began to see the national park as a potential help rather than as a hindrance. By offering money under management agreements, by acquiring land and initiating experiments in conservation-biased farm plans, the park authorities began to encourage more benign, low-input farming systems, albeit in relatively small areas. We called our second book *Greenprints for the Countryside?* because prototypes (or 'greenprints', as we called them) for low-input farming could be found in the national parks, although in imperfect forms. We rejected the government's view that the limited resources it made available for conservation should be concentrated almost entirely in 'sensitive areas' such as national parks. We saw national parks as *redoubts* to be held at all costs against the day when the whole countryside would be managed on the basis of conservation principles; as *laboratories* for research and development into the techniques of integrated land management of which conservation is a central part, and as *bridgeheads* from which conservation could advance into wider territory.

The government could have solved the problem of costly food surpluses in two different ways. One was 'de-intensification', an unlovely word that means encouraging less intensive, lower input, more environmentally benign technologies over the whole farm while employing more people. The other way, which it took in the package of agricultural measures introduced in 1986–8, was to support environmentally benign farming in a few 'Environmentally Sensitive Areas', to take 'surplus' land out of production while intensifying production on the rest, to subsidise certain conservation operations and to encourage farmers to 'diversify'. This meant replacing the income they were losing through random afforestation by converting farm buildings to other uses and by developing new enterprises, such as fish farming or tourist or 'leisure' activities that would turn the countryside into a Yuppies' playground for those who have benefited from the Thatcherite 'boom'.

The financial limits imposed by the Treasury have severely restricted the number of Environmentally Sensitive Areas (ESAs), and the terms set by the Ministry of Agriculture have ensured that ESAs are only partially effective and open to abuse. Over the greater part of the countryside intensive farming and all that flows from it – soil erosion, water pollution, loss of beauty and wildlife – continues, and falling farm incomes push many farmers still further into over-exploitation of the land. The government's overriding motive in cutting farm support was less to promote benign technologies than to introduce free-market economics in so far as that could be done within the constraints of the EEC's Common Agricultural

Policy. John Macgregor, when Minister of Agriculture, proclaimed his belief that small farms are uneconomic. If what is happening in Exmoor is typical (and the annual report of the Dartmoor National Park Authority for 1988–9 confirms that Exmoor is not unique) only those with capital benefit from the new regime which is accelerating the break-up of farms, concentrating farming in fewer but larger units and barring entry to farming to all but the rich.

The World Conservation Strategy

Mrs Thatcher's announcement in September 1988 that the ozone layer, acid rain and the 'greenhouse effect' were among 'the great challenges of the late twentieth century' was a transparently opportunist attempt to hijack conservation for the Tory Party and to find a respectable justification for the nuclear power programme so dear to her heart. The inconsistencies in her position were cruelly exposed when her government had to withdraw nuclear power from privatisation in November 1989, only a day after she had told the United Nations that 'nuclear power is the most environmentally safe form of energy' and the best way to reduce the 'greenhouse effect'. Until 1988 she had shown no interest in the threats to the global environment, although danger signals had been hoisted as early as 1972 at the Stockholm world conference that launched the United Nations Environment Programme (UNEP). The publication in 1980 of the 'World Conservation Strategy' (WCS), as we were writing *National Parks: Conservation or Cosmetics?*, helped us to put the conservation of national parks in a global context. For the basic message of the WCS is that

> human beings, in their quest for economic development and enjoyment of the riches of nature, must come to terms with the reality of resource limitation and the carrying capacity of ecosystems, and must take account of the needs of future generations.

Two features, it said, characterise our time:

> The first is the almost limitless capacity of human beings for building and creation, matched by equally great powers of destruction and annihilation. The escalating needs of soaring numbers

have often driven people to take a short-sighted approach when exploiting natural resources. The toll of this approach has now become glaringly apparent: a long list of hazards and disasters, including soil erosion, desertification, loss of cropland, pollution, deforestation, ecosystem degradation and destruction, and extinction of species and varieties.

The second is the global interrelatedness of actions, with its corollary of global responsibility.

The objectives of the WCS – the maintenance of essential ecological processes and life-support systems, the preservation of genetic diversity, and the sustainable utilization of species and ecosystems – and its list of priorities for national and international action could have laid the basis for a concerted attack on the problems it identified. It asked for more rapid progress on disarmament to reduce the military expenditure of $400 billion, and called for some shift of resources from the affluent to the poor and from the richer to the poorer nations.

It is not difficult to fault the WCS, for it had nothing to say about the threats to the living environment posed by nuclear weapons or nuclear power. It glossed over the enormous waste of energy and resources in the developed world, and it implied that the rape of the world is caused by an attempt to satisfy real needs rather than by the waste and greed of affluent societies and individuals. Nevertheless the WCS was a landmark in the growth of understanding of the threats to human survival. It also provided us with an invaluable peg on which to hang our argument that the conservation of resources should be seen neither as a desirable extra to be bought with spare cash nor as a device to protect a few 'sensitive areas' – the concept of national parks as islands of conservation in a sea of laissez-faire – but as an integral element in every decision affecting natural resources.

The Livable City

In 1983 the government's reluctance to invest time or money in responding to the WCS led to the preparation of an unofficial response, the *Conservation and Development Programme for the UK*, by a consortium of three voluntary bodies, led by the World Wildlife Fund (now the Worldwide Fund for Nature), and three government agencies, the Countryside Commissions for England and Wales and for Scotland and the Nature Conservancy Council. Their report concluded that implementing the WCS to meet UK conditions required:

> a) integrating conservation of both living and non-living resources with development; b) developing a sustainable society in which both physical and psychological needs are fully met, and c) developing a sustainable economy through the practices of resource conservation in all spheres of activity.

The job of writing a report to apply these principles to British urban society was entrusted to two women – Joan Davidson, a geographer with a degree in conservation, and Anni, an urban planner. Their work was based in the Bartlett School at University College London (where Anni and I were working) and it proved to be an intensive, frustrating but ultimately rewarding study that attempted to make good the starkest defect in the WCS – its failure to comment either on the waste of resources in urban areas or on nuclear energy. As our hill farming study was taking place at the same time, Geoffrey Sinclair and I used to discuss our ideas with Anni, and she discussed with me the enormous problems involved in devising new conservation objectives and techniques for city planning, design, construction and management. These dialogues and discussions with other people involved in the WCS – above all with Joan Davidson and Professor Tim O'Riordan, who wrote the report on countryside conservation – had a mutually beneficial spin-off. Joan's and Anni's report, *The Livable City*, was published as part of the 'Conservation and Development Programme for the UK', and in 1984 by the RIBA.

The government ignored the 'Conservation and Development Progamme for the UK', and *The Livable City* seems to have been particularly unwelcome. One senior civil servant put it in Thatcherite terms: it was 'wringing wet'. Its diagnosis and remedies did indeed flatly contradict the government's thinking and policies at that time. Its starting point was the enormous scope in cities for saving energy and other resources. The essence of its message was the need for urban societies to become 'leaner on resources' and 'richer in the skills of doing more with less'. Far from implying an era of austerity,

Joan and Anni argued that this could produce many benefits: more jobs; greener, less polluted environments; buildings that are cheaper to heat and maintain; more efficient and more equitable transport systems, and scope for rekindling skills and community participation. A commitment to resource conservation would mean saving energy; being more thrifty with land; ceasing to regard buildings as disposable containers; using wastes to increase resources; reducing air and water pollution, and increasing green and growing-space in cities.

What must have stuck in Thatcherite gullets was *The Livable City's* firm conclusion that livable and less wasteful cities could not be created unless large sums of public money were invested in the repair and modernisation of housing, water mains and sewers and the development of low energy, non-polluting transport systems to displace much of the car traffic. The market had a role to play, but it could not solve these basic pro blems. *The Livable City's* conclusions about nuclear power are highly relevant today when the privatised electricity industry has refused to pay the horrendous and unknown bills for building, running and dismantling nuclear reactors. John Wakeham the Energy Minister claimed, when announcing the abandonment of privatised nuclear power in November 1989, that he had only discovered the truth about its costs in the previous month. Yet *The Livable City* argued not only that the transport and disposal of high level radioactive wastes, the export of nuclear technologies and the further production of plutonium from Fast Breeder Reactors (FBRs) threatened living systems on a global scale, but also that these risks were not reflected in the accounting procedures by which the CEGB claimed a cost advantage for nuclear generation. The report also questioned whether the problems of the (now abandoned) FBR programme, on which nuclear fission depends in the long term, were likely to be solved quickly. It concluded on balance that there were 'sufficient uncertainties to argue against investing now in new nuclear capacity'.

It took Mrs Thatcher's government six years to produce the urgent response which the International Union for the Conservation of Nature and Natural Resources had asked for. The response, when it came in 1986, was 'Conservation and Development – the British Approach' – a slim, smug, free, glossy public relations brochure, with a picture of Mrs Thatcher crowned with what looks like a halo, which awarded the government full marks for conservation despite its lamentable record. It was not until 1988 that the British Government announced that it favoured the reinforcement and extension of the United Nations Environmental Programme's role, raising its grant from £1 million to a still beggarly £1.25 million a year. The governments in the UN spend more on military budgets in six hours than they give to UNEP in ten years. There is still no sign that the British or any other government understands the nature or the scale of the economic, social and cultural revolution that will be needed to put the world's economy on a sustainable basis.

24

Red *and* Green

When I became a Marxist in 1935 I saw the earth much as it was seen by the Victorian capitalists and by Marx and Engels: as a cornucopia, a source of endless wealth waiting to be developed by human labour using science and technology. In the 1930s the capitalist system looked bankrupt. Whole industries closed down, whole regions were unemployed, crops were destroyed and land was taken out of production while people starved. In sharp contrast, the Soviet Union's Five Year Plans were industrialising the most backward of the big states at an unheard-of speed, and seemed to offer the prospect of full employment and a steadily rising standard of living.

Socialists and communists believed that a planned socialist economy, producing not for profit but to satisfy everybody's reasonable needs, would eliminate waste and use the world's resources to create a new kind of society. The techniques of mass production would produce a superabundance. In time, work would become a pleasure as the manual worker was encouraged to use his brains and the intellectual worker learned to use his hands. People who were guaranteed *enough* would lose the mania for acquiring *too much*. Neighbourly, caring, unselfish, co-operative ways would displace envy and greed and eliminate the basic causes of war and civil strife. A socialist society would liberate humanity – politically, culturally, sexually and in every other way.

In 'The Communist Manifesto' of 1848 Marx and Engels called for the overthrow of the capitalist class, the bourgeoisie, by the working class; but, much as they detested the brutality of capitalist exploitation, and the human and material waste caused by alternating booms and slumps, they had unbounded admiration for the way in which, in barely a century, capitalism had created more colossal productive forces than all

285

preceding generations. 'What earlier century,' the Manifesto asked, 'had even a presentiment that such productive forces slumbered in the lap of social labour?'

The Myths of Inexhaustibility

The irony of today's situation is that the Soviet, supposedly Marxist, system has failed to deliver the abundance it promised while the success of the capitalist system in material production is heading for an ecological and social catastrophe. Marx and Engels might have anticipated this possibility had they heard of the one man who could have turned their thoughts in that direction. Twenty years before Marx died, George Perkins Marsh demolished the American myth of the inexhaustibility of the earth's resources. Marsh's travels in the US and in the Mediterranean, where he had been the US Minister to Turkey, had led him to observe that the same process of deforestation, erosion and land abandonment that had caused the physical decay of the Roman Empire was at work on the sheep farms of Vermont and the tobacco farms of the American South. Marsh's words in *Man and Nature*, published in the US in 1864, were prophetic. Marsh argued that 'through wanton destruction and profligate waste' the earth was 'fast becoming an unfit home for its noblest inhabitant' (man), and he warned that 'another era of equal human crime and human improvidence would reduce it to such a condition of impoverished productiveness, of shattered surface, of climatic excess, as to threaten the depravation, barbarism and perhaps even extinction of the species'.

Engels came near to anticipating this possibility in his *Dialectics of Nature*, in which he warned that unforseen effects tended to cancel out mankind's immediate benefits from the conquest of nature. Deforestation, for example, had laid the basis for the devastation of Greece, Asia Minor and other countries. In his Introduction, which was not published until 1925, Engels said that 'only the conscious organization of social production can elevate mankind above the rest of the animal world.' This was becoming daily more indispensable and more possible, and would inaugurate a new epoch, in which 'mankind itself, and all branches of activity, and especially natural science, will experience an advance before which everything preceding it will pale into insignificance.'

Marx and Engels exposed the wastefulness of capitalist production but the conclusion they drew was that socialism plus science and technology could create abundance and distribute it fairly. The Communist Party of the Soviet Union set out not to work with nature but to conquer it, and it recognised no limits to what man could do to natural systems. The achievements of the first Five Year Plans, such as the Turk-Sib railway (the subject of an epic film) and the Dnieper dam, inspired a generation of socialists. But nobody who had read Marsh (or Engels) on the ecological consequences of deforestation or the diversion of rivers could have approved the megalomaniac Soviet schemes for harnessing natural resources that are now reaping such bitter harvests as the drying up of the Aral Sea, or the crude industrialisation that has turned Magnitogorsk, or Nova Huta in Poland, into hells on earth. Marsh's dire warnings expose a flaw in Marx's thinking and give a new meaning to the prediction made in 'The Communist Manifesto' that the class struggle could end in the mutual ruin of the contending parties.

Conventional politicians, economists, financiers, businessmen and trade unionists, in both the capitalist and Soviet blocs, whether Labour, Liberal, Tory, Christian or Communist, agree that prosperity depends upon continuous economic growth. 'Growth' is measured in money. The success or failure of capitalist enterprises is measured by their profits and the growth of their capital assets (hence the mania for take-overs and mergers) and that of capitalist economies by the Gross National Product (GNP) per head of the population. For growth to fall to zero is a crisis, and negative growth is a disaster that no government can survive unless it can put the economy back on the upward growth curve. This makes sense if the object of production is to make ever more money, but if the object is to improve the health and happiness of the present population and to conserve resources for the future, entirely different indicators of prosperity are needed. The GNP makes no distinction between the useful and the useless or between the benign and the malign. More armaments, alcohol, motor cars, accidents, drugs and wastes all add to the GNP and 'growth'. So does the consumption of imported cash crops or materials whose production in the Third World reduces the land area for food production for local consumption or devastates the environment. The greater the waste and the worse the damage the higher the GNP.

In 1972 Lewis Mumford attributed the mistaken belief that growth has no limits, to the failure to understand the world as an organic system, and to the fact that capitalism, unlike earlier civilisations, is driven by the pecuniary motive. He pointed out that money has the peculiar capability, true of nothing else in the physical world, that it can be made to increase indefinitely. Credit can be created out of nothing, as recent credit booms testify. All organic forms, on the other hand, have a limited capacity for growth, and there comes a point when the organism dies from overgrowth. Indiscriminate economic growth measured by the GNP is a cancer that will end up killing the host on which it feeds. 'Going for growth' is as meaningless a slogan as 'no growth' which is favoured by some Greens, but far more dangerous. The way forward for an increasing world population, if it can be found, is to encourage ecologically and socially benign growth, to stop malignant growth, and to place the entire world economy on an infinitely sustainable, stable basis by reducing humanity's demands on nature.

The Crisis of Socialism

The political pundits told us at the end of 1989, in the aftermath of the wave of revolutions that shook the entire Soviet bloc to its foundations, that socialism was finished. We were told that 'economic liberalism' (the latest euphemism for capitalism) had finally triumphed. The euphoria of the anti-socialists was understandable, but judgments made at moments of revolutionary tension are highly suspect. Every revolution, even one that has long been predicted, comes as a shock, and it releases tidal waves of emotion and repressed ideas with unpredictable consequences. The destruction of Stalinism took eight years in Poland, a year in Hungary, a month in East Germany, a fortnight in Czechoslovakia and seven bloody days in Romania. Simultaneously, *perestroika* and *glasnost* set in motion nationalist and other tendencies that could reconstruct or destabilise the entire Soviet Union. I was exhilarated by these events, although astonished by the speed with which apparently strong regimes collapsed like a house of cards. I thought I had seen through Stalinism more than 30 years ago, but even so I was appalled by the extent to which communist ideals had been corrupted.

In fact neither socialism nor Marxism has failed, although there are elements in Marxist ideology (above all, the conviction of too many Marxists, like me in my time, that they know all the answers and have a duty to impose them on others) that contributed to its corruption. Stalinism is the antithesis of the democratic, self-governing, decentralised workers' co-operative of which Marx perceived the embryo in the Paris Commune of 1871 and which inspired the Soviets in the Russian revolutions. The very word 'soviet', a 'council' of workers' and soldiers' deputies, tells us that the original soviets were organs of grass-root democracy. By the 'dictatorship of the proletariat' Marx and Engels meant nothing like Stalin's or Ceausescu's blood-thirsty tyrannies. They saw the working class taking power not for itself alone but for society, and establishing the socialist state from which the free, classless communist society would evolve as the state's coercive powers withered away.

Soviet leaders were understandably obsessed with military threats to their security, and failed to use technology either to lighten the burden of work or (to quote André Gorz) to put the economy at the service of man's real, non-economic priorities – 'social, cultural, ethical, ecological, religious or the free unfolding of individualities'. Plans were imposed from above, not created by the people from below to satisfy their needs and aspirations. Nevertheless Marxism continues to inspire and to inform many of the world's poor and exploited and many of its best thinkers because it explains the exploitation of the working people, the gulf between rich and poor, the cycle of boom and slump and the process of capital accumulation. When people revolt against the cruelty and self-destructive nature of the capitalist economy and look for another way they will discover the range and variety of forms that socialist societies could take. The collapse of Stalinism no more proves that 'socialism is finished' than organised Christianity's identification over centuries with holy wars, repressive regimes and torture signalled the rejection of Christ's egalitarian and compassionate message.

It is not surprising, after their experience of an inefficient and repressive system, that many people in Eastern Europe imagined that free elections, a free press and the free market would solve all their problems. Those who flocked through the Berlin Wall from the German Democratic Republic often seemed unaware that choosing the uncontrolled free market might also mean choosing endemic unemployment (17 million in the EEC in 1989), widespread homelessness and destitution, and the destruction of the human habitat. Their disgust with the distorted version of socialism that they knew prevented many from appreciating that without the ethic and practice of socialism, which puts the common human interest first, the world cannot hope to survive.

Poverty in the Midst of Plenty

It would be foolish to deny that the collapse of Stalinism has created a profound crisis for the Soviet bloc, and unwise to predict what the consequences are going to be. Whereas the initiative for reforming socialism came from within the Soviet system, the apologists for capitalism are blind to the instability of the capitalist system and the unbearable, increasing social tensions it generates. In a world that is awash with money and consumer goods the Worldwatch Institute in Washington has documented what it calls 'the explosion of destitution' in the 1980s, including an increase of poverty in some Western countries – particularly Britain and the US – and in the Soviet Union.

Its report 'Poverty and the Environment' (1989) shows that almost a quarter of humanity, 1.2 billion people, do not earn enough to meet the most basic biological needs of food, clothing and shelter. Poor countries (the so-called 'Third World', or 'The South') have to pay high prices for manufactured imports, but the prices they get for their food are undercut by the dumping of surplus food from the EEC and the US, a process that puts indigenous farmers out of business. The aid they get has fallen, and most of their exports go to pay high rates of interest on the trillion dollar debts owed to the banks and institutions of the rich nations. In 1988 the poor countries paid the rich countries over £30 billion more than they received, thereby impoverishing their own peoples and subsidising the extravagant consumption, the arms expenditures and the waste of natural resources by the Western societies. The inability of the Third World to pay the interest or to repay the capital on their debts presents a continuous threat to the stability of the world's financial system.

The World Health Organisation has predicted a catastrophe as world population, set to double in 25–40 years, outstrips food supplies. These in turn are threatened by soil erosion, pollution, deforestation, desertification, by the hole in the ozone layer and by the greenhouse effect. Famines are endemic in Africa and parts of Asia. Incomes per head in sub-Saharan Africa have been falling from already desperately low levels, and long-term debts to the big capitalist nations increased 19-fold from the 1970s. Such disasters as the destruction of the tropical rainforests are no longer due to ignorance, for which there is now no excuse. Nor are they to be prevented by putting a ring round a relatively small area as a national park and excluding the indigenous inhabitants who have lived there in harmony with nature for millennia. It seems wildly improbable that (as some economists have suggested) the rich nations will place a value on the forests and meet the cost of sustaining them, and even less likely that such payments, if made, will reach the disadvantaged people. These disasters are caused either by poverty, which drives the poorest into destructive practices to survive, or by ruthless entrepreneurs, some of them multinational companies, subsidised by their governments and frequently financed by the World Bank or Western governments. Their purpose is to extract the maximum profit by supplying goods to the affluent, because all most of them care for is money and power.

Nor does one have to go to the 'Third World' to see massive destitution. Britain now has a two-thirds/one-third society in which some 15 million people live at or below the 'decency' level and are excluded from the benefits of the affluent society. The politicians of the rich nations (the Greens apart) still believe that the problems of the affluent society can be solved by marginal adjustments which seem to offer consumers ever-rising consumption in a cleaner, healthier environment. If the people of the 'Third World' and the depressed segments of society in the rich nations are to be denied a tolerable living while others luxuriate in a surfeit of goods it can only be a matter of time before the tensions explode. In fact the gap is widening and the economies of the whole world are heading towards social and ecological disaster, as an unregulated market economy fosters accelerated ecological degradation and resource depletion and makes the poor bear a disproportionate share of the cost and the sacrifices. The scene is being set for class, national and ethnic conflicts. There has to be a better way.

The Green Revolution

I keep coming back to Mumford's view that no lasting solution to the problems of war, social disorder and environmental degradation can be found without abandoning the high-energy, high-mobility, intensely individual style of life developed by the advanced industrial nations. This is as revolutionary a concept as that of Marxism was in its time. Marx and Engels clearly described in *Capital* the tendency of capitalist agriculture to rob not only the labourer, but also to rob the soil of its fertility. Were they alive today they would have no difficulty in incorporating a new ecological dimension into their thinking. The ecological crisis demands, above all, the satisfaction of collective needs rather than individual desires that only green socialism can provide. But history has no precedent for carrying through such a profound change, one that challenges so many established and selfish habits and interests, in a short time and in a global economy. Can habits and attitudes generated in a culture of greed, selfishness, ignorance and indifference be changed quickly enough? Can politicians, economists, financiers, industrialists and trade unionists change their aims and values? Will individuals give up some of their most cherished possessions, habits and ambitions? Will society learn quickly enough to do more with less? Will it be possible to carry through a redistribution of power and wealth?

All this is easier said than done. It may be easier to convince some capitalists of the need for change, and of the opportunities for profit in benign technologies, than it will be to persuade trade unions to accept redundancies in the armaments, nuclear, motor vehicle and other major industries that will have to be drastically cut down. The cry for jobs, for *any* job (because a job in capitalist society is the ticket to a livelihood), without a new approach to work and incomes, can be as destructive as the drive for profits. People will only go along with the changes if their consent is won by securing their participation and treating them fairly. The changes will have to begin within the present political and economic framework, but they can hardly be completed without a radical redistribution of wealth and power. The question is whether an orderly transition to a sustainable economy can be made before ecological catastrophes bring about forced change, in conditions of chaos and violence, with all the suffering and inequity that would ensue, or before nuclear war (whether intentional or accidental) signals the end of the human story. Can the peaceful green revolution be carried through in time?

The New Personality

Václav Havel, the modest, banned playwright catapulted almost from jail into the presidency of the Czechoslovak Republic, seems to me to personify the new people with courage, integrity and fresh ideas (or old ones recycled) that give us grounds for hope. His political philosophy goes far beyond the right to vote in free elections and basic civil liberties. He speaks for an East European generation that has been inoculated against 'ideological platitudes, clichés, slogans, intellectual stereotypes, insidious appeals to our emotions ... and all hypnotic enticements, even of the traditionally persuasive national or nationalistic variety'. He objects to people being lumped together in homogeneous masses – as 'classes', 'nations' or 'political forces' – to be extolled, denounced, loved or hated, maligned or glorified. Although a believer in the 'free-market' he distrusts both the communist and the capitalist systems for, echoing Mumford, he sees the greatest threat to the world in 'self-propelling mega-machines, large-scale enterprises, faceless governments and other juggernauts of impersonal power' which treat people as mere objects. The totalitarian impulse to overcome all opposition derives, he believes, from man's arrogant presumption that he is 'the lord of creation', which he sees as the root cause of the nuclear, ecological and social catastrophe threatening humanity.

The revolution he worked for was not a mere transfer of power from one set of dogmatists to another but a cultural, people's revolution from below, 'growing from the heart, not from a thesis'. Unlike the Labour Party, which discarded its principles and used market research to find 'electable' policies, Havel emphasises 'the inexhaustible strength which flows from sticking to principles'.

The problem is how to translate this philosophy into action

in the actual political, economic and social situation that exists in our own country, in the EEC and in the world. Most people who feel strongly about politics (and I include myself) tend to be dogmatists, if only because it is impossible to act decisively without some confidence that what one is doing is 'right'. Most politicians, moreover, are men with a masculine outlook, and it is highly ironical that the best-known woman politician of our time should scorn caring, compassionate, feminine values. The 'conviction' politician who tries to impose her or his dogmas on society is bound to make bad decisions, but the man or woman who is eternally beset by doubts will either fail to make decisions or will, as often as not, make the wrong ones. It is much easier to stick to principles when in opposition than when in government, and governments of all political persuasions are notoriously reluctant to introduce the checks and balances necessary to prevent power corrupting those who exercise it.

Nevertheless I now regard people like Havel, whom I would have dismissed not long ago as woolly-minded idealists, as the true realists, because they confront the real problems. They do not pretend to have all the answers but at least they are asking the right questions and trying to form broad alliances reflecting the common human interest in survival, unlike the ideologues of Western Europe who are leading us into the Single European Market. All the Western businessmen could think about, as they hovered like vultures over the 'corpse' of 'socialism', was how to lay their greedy hands on Eastern Europe, frankly regarded as the 'new Korea' in which cheap skilled labour offers capital an exceptional rate of profit. 'Freedom' was on everybody's lips, but the freedom that interested the fifty billionaires who control the Western European financial world was freedom to operate in an expanding market. Although parading their 'realism' they either seem oblivious to the nature of the problems they are aggravating, or delude themselves into thinking that they know the answers. However green their disguise, they are creating more space for the cancer of undifferentiated economic growth.

A New Alliance?

No one country can solve gobal problems, but Britain can make a contribution towards the solutions that it is out of all proportion to its population or its geographical size. Despite our decline we are still one of the world's more advanced economies. Despite our chauvinism we still have exceptional opportunities – thanks to our language, our culture, our experience and our world-wide connections – both to give a lead ourselves and to be the first to follow where others have led the way. The question in Britain, particularly for greens and socialists, is how to create the conditions in which new people with fresh ideas can take over from the tired politicians who are almost as irrelevant as the Politburo members who were forced out of office in Eastern Europe. The new people are all around us, but our 'elective dictatorship' (as Lord Hailsham revealingly called it) is very repressive in its seemingly civilised way. It allows a minority to impose its dogmas on the majority and to whittle away the democracy won by the people in the past.

The so-called 'British Constitution' guarantees no civil rights or liberties. If we are to establish a sustainable economy we need to democratise government at every level, and to replace the obsessive secrecy of British society with *glasnost*, or openness. Without the fullest access to information the people cannot make democracy work or take well-informed decisions. We need to become citizens, with statutory civil rights, not subjects of the Crown whose imagined rights can be whittled down by the Executive using the Royal Prerogative, or by judges making new law. The House of Commons should be reformed so that it genuinely represents the people, and it should control the Prime Minister, not the other way round. There is no place in a democratic constitution for a non-elected House of Lords. We should follow the lead of the Eastern European countries that have abolished the leading role of one political party. For although the Conservative Party's leading role is not enshrined in a written constitution it is none the less entrenched for all that. Whatever party is in office Conservative interests remain dominant in the media, business, finance, the judiciary, and the civil and armed services. The need for the majority of the people to have real power is almost as pressing as it was in Prague or Budapest. The election of a Labour government on its revised programme would not change this situation – or would only do so temporarily – unless it was committed to electoral and other radical reforms.

There is a weird lack of realism in the attitudes of the opposition parties, each of which – even the Greens – make the absurd pretence that they, and they alone, provide a realistic alternative to Thatcherism. The reality is that no lasting, far-reaching changes can be made in the British political and economic situation within the straightjacket of the party political system inherited from the past. The first priority is to break the grip of Thatcherism by reforming the British electoral system that keeps the Thatcherite minority in power, and splits the opposition by forcing people to choose between the different parties and to waste their energies on fighting or denouncing each other. The way forward, in the new situation arising from the ending of the Cold War, the recognition of the ecological dangers and the disillusionment with Thatcherism, lies in combining elements in all parties, and fusing them with other reforming trends in British society – such as the 'Charter 88' movement for constitutional reform, the Campaign for Nuclear Disarmament (which has now adopted 'green' objectives) and the movements for real gender and racial equality. We do not have the time to indulge in the luxury of old-fashioned party politics.

As a green Marxist I see the best and perhaps the only hope of breaking the grip of the elective dictatorship and carrying through serious reforms, and ultimately a peaceful green revolution, lies in forging a broad alliance at the heart of which lie the Labour Party and the Green, anti-nuclear and women's movements. The Green Party has introduced a new dynamism and new thinking into British politics. Without it none of the others would have moved as far or as fast as they have done to adopt green policies or postures. Some of the Green Party's policies reflect their inexperience, their tendency to equate socialism with Stalinism or Labourism and their reluctance to face the revolutionary implications of their ideas. Their proposal that district councils should decide the scope of central government planning and decision-making takes the sense out of their desire to give local communities a real say in the political and productive processes. They have not thought through the enormous problems (given British membership of the EEC, the European Market and the forces at work in the global economy) of making the transition from a profit-driven market economy to one aiming at human well-being and the conservation of resources. I see no prospect of a Green Party government, but I want the Greens' enthusiasm, youth, self-lessness and fresh ideas, their understanding of the connection between social and ecological problems and their impatience with the status quo to permeate the Labour Party and to strengthen the greens, democrats and socialists within it.

It is not difficult to imagine tragic scenarios for humanity and for planet earth. The world and human society being what they are, the end will never be reached and the way is bound to be painful and messy. Violent revolutions designed to impose dogmatic solutions (in which I once believed) tend to be self-defeating although, as Romania has shown, sometimes unavoidable, but the very instability of today's set-up could generate violence and intolerance on a scale that would wreck the hopes of peaceful change.

Nevertheless, there is more room for hope today than for many years. The world's politics have never been as fluid as they are now. The political time-scale is quickening all the time. In a world of instant communication what happened in Berlin one day turned Prague upside down the next. People in many countries have begun to discover their own power. Is it beyond the bounds of possibility that half a million people might march down Whitehall one day soon demanding the scrapping of British nuclear weapons and the poll tax, the restoration of democratic local government, the replacement of the elective dictatorship of a rich minority by a real democracy – and, of course, a green social revolution? It seems wildly improbable now: but nobody dreamed that the tough East German state would disintegrate within a fortnight, or that Ceausescu would be an unchallenged tyrant one week and a corpse the next. The greatest mistake, now that new movements, new thinking and new people are on the move would be to underestimate the possible.

Index